TO

THEODORE BAKER, PH. D.

THIS BOOK IS GRATEFULLY

INSCRIBED

PREFACE

I.

Musical composition, in its creative aspect, cannot be taught. It is a distinctly subjective expression of the individual; it comes from within, not from without; its **individuality** is what gives it value.

But there is a necessary medium, a **technic** of expression, and this technic can be taught, and must inevitably be acquired. He who would write English poetry must first learn the grammar, and other elements, of English expression. No matter how great the genius, or how overwhelming his thought and emotion, he can no more dispense with technic than he could dispense with a tongue in speech.

A text-book of harmony, and of the elementary technic of musical expression, is, therefore, a necessary and important thing for him who desires to understand what great musical minds have recorded, and who purposes to express himself in the language of tone.

II.

The present volume is a completely re-written and slightly enlarged version of *The Theory and Practice of Tone-relations*, first published in 1892.

The objects of this revision were: To purify and simplify the diction; to clarify the musical illustrations; to increase, considerably, the exercise-material; and to render the latter *as easy as possible of solution* for the student.

Particular emphasis is laid, throughout, upon the element of **melody,** since melody is the soul and life of good music.

In all outward respects this new edition corresponds exactly to the previous ones, the order of chapters and their contents having been retained. Only the numbering of paragraphs and examples has been partly changed.

III.

Those who intend to continue their studies, after completing this elementary course in harmony, may proceed with the larger and more exhaustive text-book, *The Material Used in Musical Composition.* Their preparation will justify them in passing rapidly over the first hundred pages of this book, and this they are advised to do, beginning their thorough work at Part III.

PERCY GOETSCHIUS.

NEW YORK CITY, *October*, 1916.

PREFACE TO 24th ISSUE

The present edition has been enlarged by the addition of a *Reference-Index*, and an *Appendix* containing a solution of one exercise from each important Lesson.

PERCY GOETSCHIUS.

MANCHESTER, N. H., *February*, 1931.

CONTENTS.

DIVISION I. CONCORD HARMONIES.

DIVISION II. DISCORD HARMONIES.

DIVISION III. MODULATION.

THE THEORY AND PRACTICE OF TONE-RELATIONS.

DIVISION ONE.

CONCORD HARMONIES.

CHAPTER I.

TONE AND KEY.

1. A Tone, or musical sound, is distinguished from sound or noise in general, in being *fixed*, instead of undulating; in maintaining a certain location in the realm of sound like the tone of a bell or whistle, in distinction to the ever-varying moan of the wind. This distinction is most apparent in our treatment of the voice in singing and in speaking, respectively; in singing we produce *tones*, by firmly maintaining a certain degree of tension of the vocal cords for each utterance, while in speaking no such tension is sustained, and the voice therefore simply undulates.

2. Like the tones of the voice, so all tones in nature are owing to the intentional or accidental tension of some elastic body, which, on account of this tension, maintains its vibration, when set in motion, at the same (inconceivably high) rate of speed, thus fixing the location or pitch of its tone. This *fixing* of the sound is the very first act in the evolution of musical science. By fixing the sound, as tone, it becomes an object of experiment, observation and association; it enters into perfectly definite relations with other fixed tones, which cluster about it as their centre, and thus it becomes an art-factor.

3. The sound-waves, generated by the vibration of the elastic body from which a tone is to be elicited, are as regular in their velocity as the succession of vibrations, and can therefore be indicated by an arithmetical ratio or *number*.

Hence, a tone, being a fixed quantity, can be designated by a number, and the relation of tone to tone is purely a matter of mathematical ratio.

4. For illustration, the sensation or tone called a^1, and written on the second space of the G-staff, is aroused by sound-waves acting upon the drum of the ear at the even velocity of 435 strokes (870 alternate condensations and rarifications of air) in a second of time. Therefore this tone, a^1, is designated by the number 435. Every pianoforte string or violin string vibrating at exactly this rate of speed will be in perfect Unison with the tone a^1, and the arithmetical ratio of one to the other is 435 to 435, or 1 : 1.

5. Another string of half the length, and vibrating exactly *twice* as fast (870 times a second), will produce sound-waves with which the sound-waves of the first tone obviously agree, stroke for stroke, so that there is no actual conflict of pulsation, and the effect upon the sense is that of consonance (agreement or harmony of sound). But the shorter string adds an intermediate wave to each wave of the longer string, thus altering the *quality* of what is virtually the same tone, so that it impresses the ear more acutely, and sounds (as the parallelism of sensation involuntarily induces us to assume) *higher*. This new tone, designated by the number 870, is then the closest relative of a^1; it is therefore also called *a*, but the distinction in quality, or degree of acuteness, or location, is indicated thus — a^2 — and it is written on the first leger-line above the G-staff.

6. The relationship thus established (435 to 870, or 1 : 2) is called the Octave, and is the same in both directions, self-evidently. That is, a string vibrating 217½ times a second, or *half* as fast as the first one (a^1), will produce the next *lower* octave, *a*, written on the second leger-line below the G-staff.

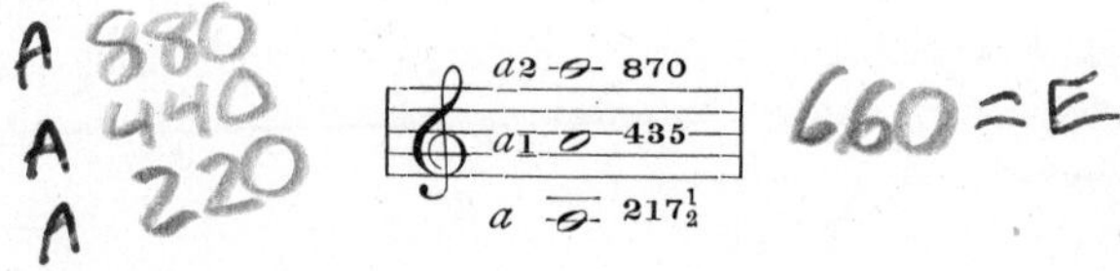

The tone-relation of the octave *does not arise from the association of two different tones*, but merely indicates a *distinction of register*. For this reason the octave is of no other value in active harmony than to effect the *duplication* of tones, or the extension of the harmonic body into higher and lower registers, without adding any new factor.

7. In order to find a **new** tone which, while associating harmoniously with the first, will still furnish a starting point for actual tone-combination, it is equally obvious that the *next simplest* mathematical ratio must be taken; that is, 1 to 3, or 217½ : 652½. The sensation (or tone) produced by the action of 652½ sound-waves in a second upon the ear, is e^2, written on the fourth space of the G-staff, and constituting the interval of a **perfect fifth** with the middle *a* (a^1, representing the ratio 2 : 3 with e^2, while 1 : 3 is the ratio with the *lower a*). Thus:

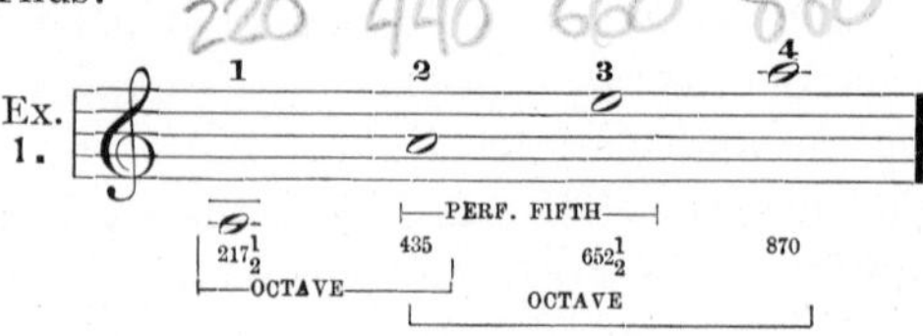

8. From this the facts are deduced, that, while the unison and octave are the simplest and most intimate tone-relations,

> **the perfect fifth is the simplest mathematical ratio and therefore the closest relation that exists between two different tones.**

For this reason the **perfect fifth**, which we will call a **harmonic degree,** must constitute the basis of the whole system of tone-combination, and the **standard of measurement** in harmony.

THE SCALE.

9. From the infinite multitude of possible tones perceptible to the ear, the intuition of man (in civilized countries) has singled out a limited number (at first 7, later 12), which, with their reproduction or duplication in higher and lower registers, by the octave relation, represent the entire absolute tone-material of the art of music. The group of seven tones forms a Key or Scale, and is collected in accordance with the above **standard** (the harmonic degree) in the following manner:

Any tone may be chosen as "keynote" or chief of the group; with this, no other tones will more naturally and reasonably be associated than its perfect 5th *above and below,* as next in order of importance in the group. The next member is the perfect 5th above the upper tone; and in the same manner a new higher perfect 5th is associated with each preceding member, *until a tone is reached which would contradict the lowest one.* Thus, assuming the tone C as keynote:

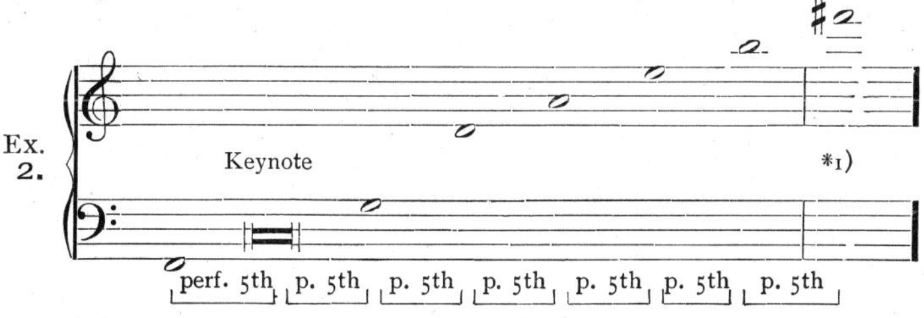

*1) The tone *F-sharp* does not appear in the authentic group, or key, or **family** of C, because it contradicts *F-natural,* the lowermost member. Why the latter, *F-natural,* should be preferred to *F-sharp,* notwithstanding it lies *below* what should properly be the fundamental tone, or basis (C), and how very frequently the *F-sharp* is nevertheless preferred to *F-natural,* and adopted as momentary member of the C-family, will be seen in time.

10. This illustration also accounts for there being no more nor less than just *seven* members in an authentic scale, or **family of tones,** usually called a **key.** There is no question in this case about the six tones, *c, g, d, a, e, b,* all of which lie above the fundamental keynote; and as to F-natural or F-sharp, it is certain that *one or the other* must be admitted into the family of C, and preference is given to the F-natural, because of its direct relation to the keynote.

11. This is the true **natural scale,** composed of equal contiguous intervals. For the sake of convenience, the seven tones are drawn into close proximity by simply transferring certain tones down or up by the octave-relation (whereby, as shown in par. 6, their significations are in no wise altered). In this way the so-called **diatonic scale** is obtained.

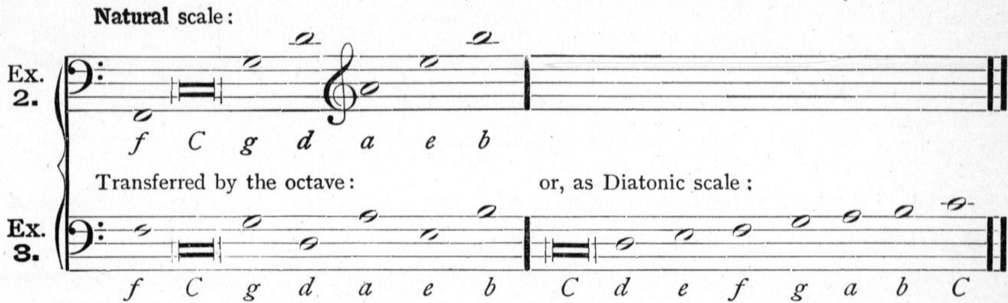

12. This diatonic scale comprises the tones of the **major mode,** so designated for reasons given later. Upon examination it is found that the contiguous intervals of the diatonic scale, unlike those of the natural scale, are *not* uniform, but differ as follows:

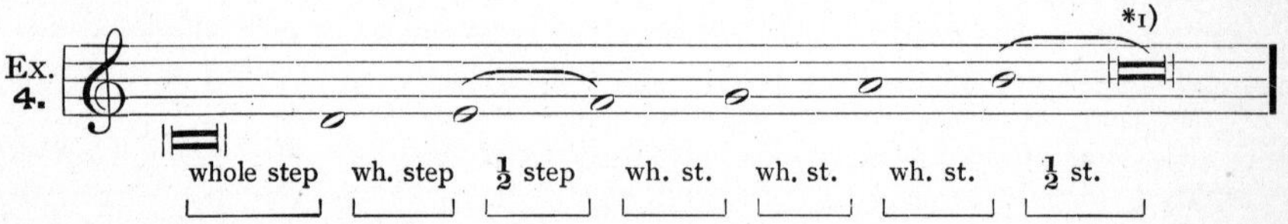

*1) Here the keynote is reproduced in the next higher octave, in order to complete the circuit of tones.

That is, the distance between the *3d and 4th* tones, and also between the *7th and 8th* tones, is only half as great as that between all the other contiguous tones. This has no other importance for us at present than to illustrate the accidental relative location assumed by the seven tones * when transferred from their order in the *natural scale*, to that of the *diatonic scale*. At the same time, it is a convenient external guide to the ready mechanical formation of any diatonic major scale, and should therefore be carefully observed.

*) These tones are called **scale-steps** (or, frequently, degrees of the scale — i.e., *diatonic* scale).

13. The *diatonic* form of the scale is that upon which all practical composition is based. The names given to the seven scale-steps (numbered from the keynote upward), arranged according to their relative importance, are as follows:

First step — Keynote or **tonic;**
5th step (perf. 5th above Tonic) — **dominant** (dominating tone);
4th step (perf. 5th below Tonic) — **subdominant;**
2d step (perf. 5th above Dom.) — **second dominant;** (also known as supertonic);
6th step (midway between Ton. and Subdom.) — **submediant;**
3d step (midway between Ton. and Dom.) — **mediant;**
7th step — leading-tone. Thus:

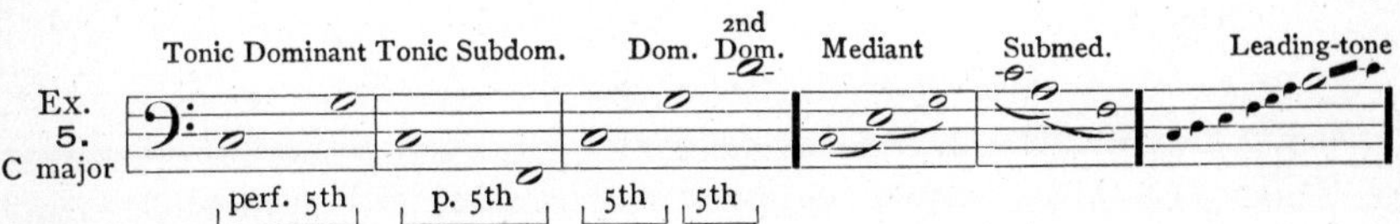

14. Of these seven steps, three are greatly superior to the others and are therefore called **principal** scale-steps.

They are, self-evidently, the tonic and its two perf.-5th relatives, the dominant and subdominant.

The 2d, 6th and 3d steps are called *subordinate.* The Leading-tone has specific melodic qualities.

LESSON I.

A. Write out every major scale, first in its Natural and then in its Diatonic form (Exs. 2 and 4); use no signature, but place the respective *accidental* before each inflected tone.

B. Write out the 7 steps of every major scale in the order of their importance, namely: Tonic, Dom., Subdom., 2d Dom., Submed., Med., Leading-tone.

C. Name, mentally (in response to the teacher's question), the 3 principal tones of every scale.

D. Play the 3 principal tones of every scale on the keyboard in this order: Ton., Subdom., Dom., Tonic.

CHAPTER II.

INTERVALS.

15. The association of any two tones is called an **interval.**

The term interval, meaning a space, refers to the *distance between notes upon the written staff.* But the true musical signification of "interval" is "tone-relation" — the relation established by associating the tones.

Intervals are always counted *upward,*

along the diatonic major scale of the lower tone.

The *number of the step* which is occupied by the upper tone is the numerical name of the interval. For example:

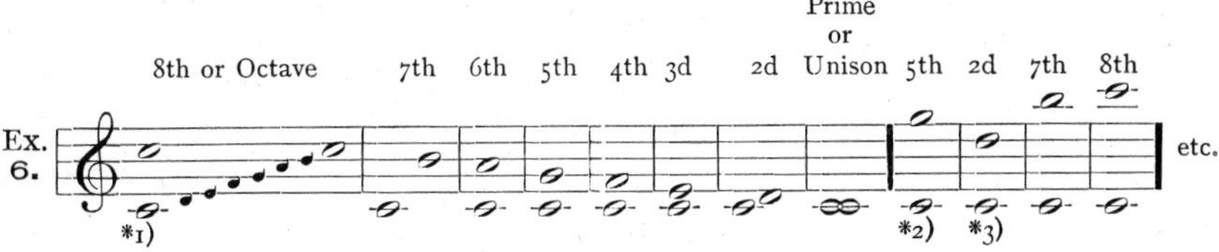

*1) From c^1 to c^2 is an 8th or octave, because, counting upward along the major scale of C, the next *c* is the 8th *step.* C-B is a seventh, as *b* is the seventh step from C, in ascending succession.—*2) Whether within or beyond an octave, the name of the interval invariably corresponds to the *number* of the step of the scale occupied by the upper tone. (Comp. par. 6, last lines.) — *3) The only exception is in the case of the interval next above the 8ve, which in some special cases (see par. 26) is called a ninth, instead of a second.

DIATONIC INTERVALS.

16. All those intervals which agree with the natural major scale (i.e., where the upper tone *corresponds exactly* to the scale-step of the lower tone as tonic), are called natural or **diatonic** intervals. Hence, the intervals in Ex. 6 are all diatonic. They are qualified as *perfect*, or as *major*, as follows:

The diatonic (or scale) unison, fourth, fifth and octave are perfect. The diatonic (or scale) second, third, sixth and seventh are major.

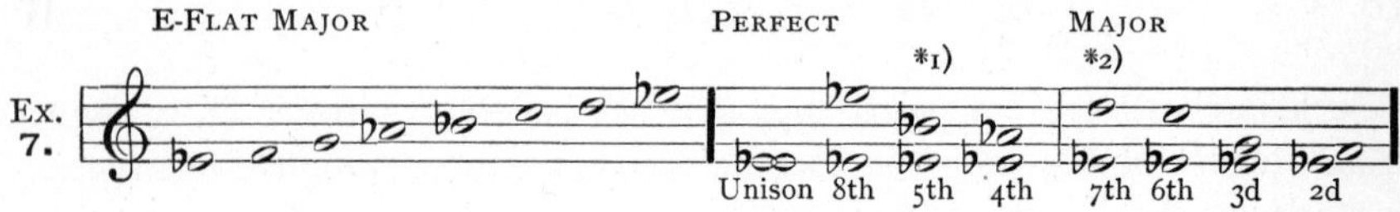

*1) *E-flat – b-flat* is a "perfect 5th"; a "5th," because *b-flat* is the 5th step of the major scale of E-flat; and a "perfect" 5th, because *b-flat* exactly corresponds to the scale of E-flat, and because diatonic 5ths are qualified as "perfect" (not "major"). — *2) *E-flat – d* is a "major 7th" (not "perfect"), for similar reasons.

CHROMATIC INTERVALS.

17. But the upper of two tones does not always agree thus with the major scale of the lower tone; for example:

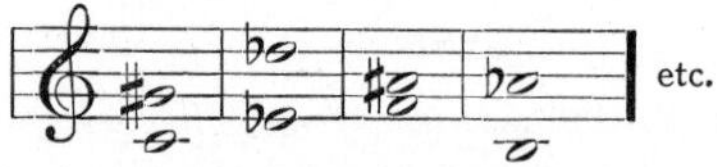

Such tone-relations are termed **chromatic** intervals, and are qualified as follows: Any perfect interval when extended by an *accidental* before the upper tone (the letters remaining the same) becomes *augmented;* when similarly contracted, it becomes *diminished*. Thus:

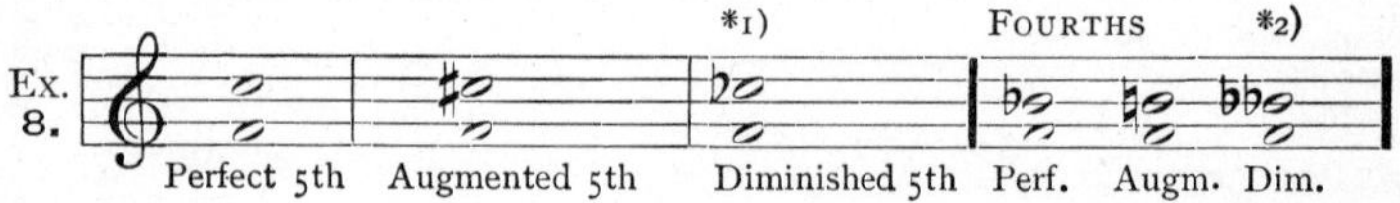

*1) Not *b-natural* instead of *c-flat*. The letter *c* confirms the interval as a "5th" of some kind or other. The letter *b* would be some species of *fourth*. — *2) Not *a* instead of *b-double-flat;* the *letter* must remain unchanged, as it determines the numerical name of the interval.

18. Analogously, any major interval when extended by an accidental becomes *augmented;*

when contracted by an accidental, a major interval becomes minor. One similar contraction of a minor interval, or *two* contractions of the corresponding *major* interval, will result in its diminution. Thus:

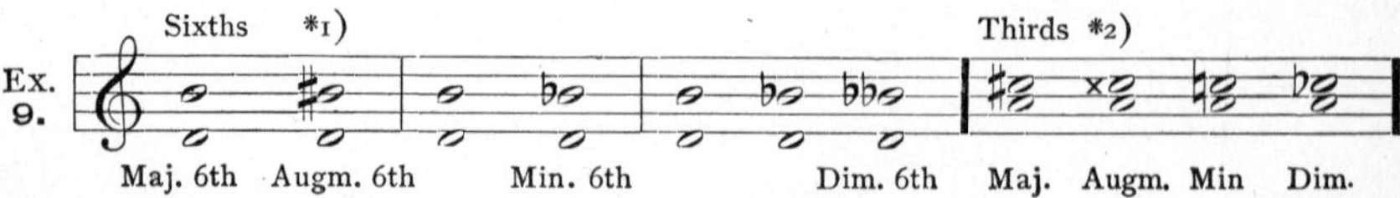

*1) Not *c* for *b-sharp*. — *2) Not *d* for *c-double-sharp*.

19. The application of this rule to certain tones may result in very unusual notation. For example, the augmented 3d of *d-sharp* must be *f-triple-sharp:* the major 3d of *d* is *f-sharp*, and, therefore, the major 3d of *d-sharp* is *f-double-sharp;* this, augmented, becomes *f-triple-sharp*.

Likewise, the diminished 3d of *c-flat* is *e-triple-flat.*

Such intervals are "unusual," but quite as possible as any. They simply lie unusually remote from the tone C, which has been adopted as a centre, or starting point, in music notation.

Further, while it is natural that only the comparatively *related* tones should be associated, it is possible to unite **any** two tones, at least casually and briefly. Thus:

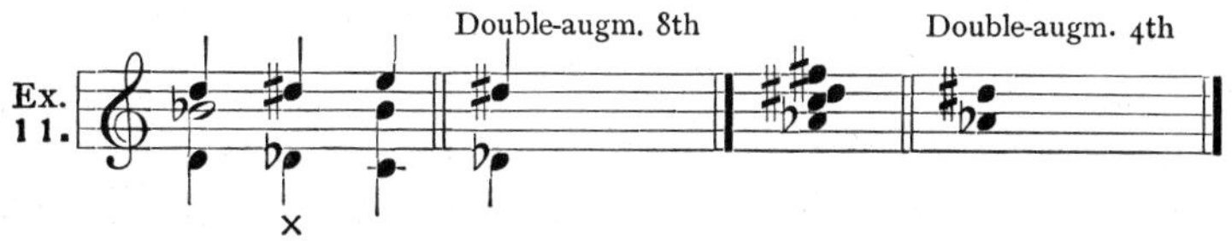

LESSON 2.

A. Write out the perfect 4th and perfect 5th of the following tones: C, G, F, D, B-flat, A, E-flat, E, A-flat, B, D-flat, F-sharp, G-flat, C-sharp, C-flat, G-sharp, D-sharp. — Write out the major 3d and major 6th of the same tones. — Write out the major 2d and major 7th of the same tones, in optional order. — Write out the augm. 2d, 3d, 4th, 5th, 6th, 7th, and 8th of F, B-flat, E-flat, A-flat, D-flat, C, G, D, A, E, B, G-flat, C-flat, F-sharp, C-sharp, D-sharp. — Write out the minor 7th, 6th, 3d and 2d of the same tones. — Write out the dim. 8th, 7th, 6th, 5th, 4th, 3d and 2d of the same tones, in optional order.

B. Name the following given intervals:

*1) The lower tone is to be regarded, in every case, as a tonic. The number of the upper step is the name of the interval; if the upper tone conforms to the scale, the interval is either perfect or major, according to Ex. 7; if not, it is augm., minor, or dim., according to Exs. 8 and 9. — *2) In case the lower tone is an impracticable tonic, as here, *shift the interval bodily* upward or downward, but without changing the letters. Thus:

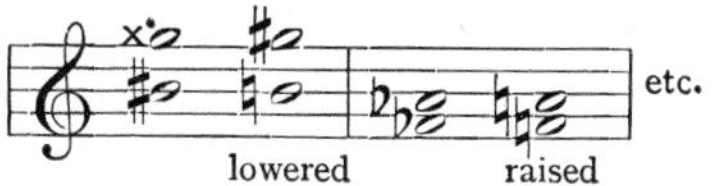

CHAPTER III.

CHORD-CONSTRUCTION.

CONSONANCE AND DISSONANCE.

20. As has been seen, the most intimate intervals are the unison, octave and perfect fifth (par. 8). The other interval-relations are qualified according to the same rule of vibratory ratio, which determines their respective degrees of *consonance or euphony* with mathematical certainty, leaving nothing to the fallible and unreliable ear but to confirm and accept the result, correcting itself, if need be, thereby.

The next simplest arithmetical ratio is 3 : 4; two sets of sound-waves acting upon the organ of hearing in these proportions of velocity produce the double sensation of the *perfect fourth.* This is illustrated in Ex. 1, between the upper two tones, e^2 and a^2. The average ear will perceive that this interval is somewhat less agreeable than the perf. 5th, albeit the tones are the same, and therefore its *harmonic signification* is identical with that of the 5th. The ratio 4 : 5 gives the *major 3d;* 5 : 6 the *minor 3d;* consequently, the former is the better (more consonant) interval of the two. As the ratio becomes more complex, the tones are observed to approach each other, and the *grade of consonance gradually decreases.* Thus:

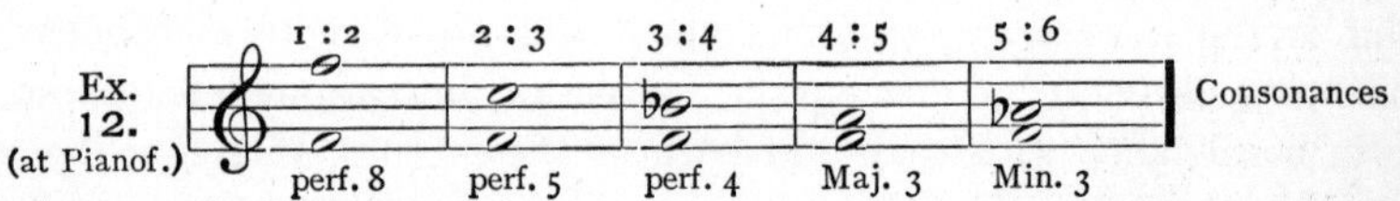

21. The next ratio, 8 : 9, is the *major 2d,* which is palpably no longer consonant, but *dissonant,* because the conflict of tone-waves here reaches an extent which is disagreeable. Hence, *the minor third is the smallest consonant interval.* The ratio 15 : 16 gives the *minor second,* which is still more palpably dissonant.

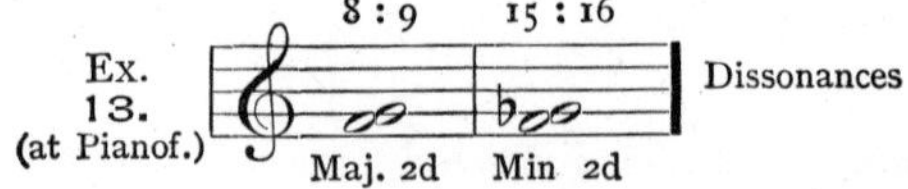

INVERSION.

22. The **inversion** of an interval is obtained by reversing the letters, so that the lower tone becomes the upper.

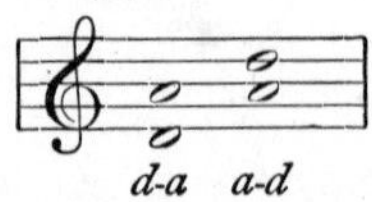

As this merely involves the octave-relation, it is evident from par. 6 that **an interval and its inversion are practically identical.**

23. All consonant intervals remain consonant after inversion, and dissonances remain dissonant. The complete table of consonances and dissonances is therefore as follows:

Consonances		Perfect octaves, and their inversions, perf. unisons;
		Perfect fifths, and their inversions, perf. fourths;
	*1)	Major thirds, and their inversions, minor sixths;
	*1)	Minor thirds, and their inversions, major sixths.
Dissonances		Major seconds, and their inversions, minor sevenths;
		Minor seconds, and their inversions, major sevenths;
		and also all augm. and dim. intervals, on account of their obliquity to the scale.

*1) Major and minor 3ds and 6ths, being no longer perfect intervals, are distinguished as *imperfect* consonances.

CHORDS.

24. Chords are associations of *more than two* tones, in exclusively, or at least preponderantly, consonant interval-relations. Giving first preference to the perfect 5th, as a matter of course, the skeleton of a chord erected upon the tone *g* (for example) would be

This is the ratio 2 : 3 (or 4 : 6, which will prove more convenient). The third tone, necessary to develop the "interval" into a complete "chord," must be in consonance with each and both of these tones, therefore the simplest ratio for the three tones together is 4 : 5 : 6, which mathematically determines what the ear also unhesitatingly sanctions, namely, the addition of the tone *b*-natural:

This is the primary three-tone chord-form and furnishes the incontestible model of all

primary or fundamental chord-structure, namely: Any tone as given basis, with its major third and perfect fifth.

25. Other, externally different, forms can be erected, in which again all the intervals are consonant. Thus:

Ex. 14.

But these are all readily recognizable as modifications of the original form, *obtained solely by means of the octave-relation*, which never alters the harmonic significance, but simply effects a more or less complete **inversion** of the **chord.**

26. No other forms than these can be constructed without marring the consonant condition of the chord; in other words, *consonant chords, or Concords, are limited to three tones.* Still, the fundamental principle of chord-structure here revealed may be extended, in order to give the chord a more copious form. Thus, the structure of ascending thirds may be extended to a new tone,

but this new tone (in this case *f*) must necessarily constitute a *dissonant interval* (7th) with the fundamental tone, for which reason chords of four tones will invariably be *dissonant chords or Discords.*

A three-tone chord with one or more duplicated tones (as *g-g-b-d*, *g-b-d-d*, etc.) evidently does not belong to this species of genuine "4-tone" chords.

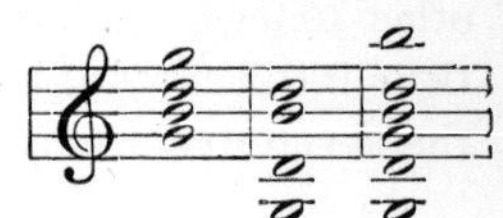

Still another upper third may be added, thus:

but the new tone (in this case *a*) gives rise to two additional dissonant intervals, namely, a 7th with *b*, and a 9th with *g* (see Ex. 6, note *3).

27. Dissonant chords are not only admitted, but even deemed necessary in music, on account of their contrast with consonant harmonies, and the peculiar quality of activity which their dissonances involve. But the following limitations are dictated by wisdom: first, as discords are merely extended forms of the concords, their application should be deferred until the relations and progressions of the primary three-tone forms have been thoroughly mastered; and second, the dissonant intervals must be introduced in moderate and judicious proportion to the consonances; hence, while 4-tone chords may be unexceptionable, those of 5 tones are more rare, and the addition of still more dissonances (as six or seven-tone chords) is obviously out of the question.

It is true that dissonances are often multiplied, so that occasionally even all seven letters of the scale are associated simultaneously — for example, at ×,

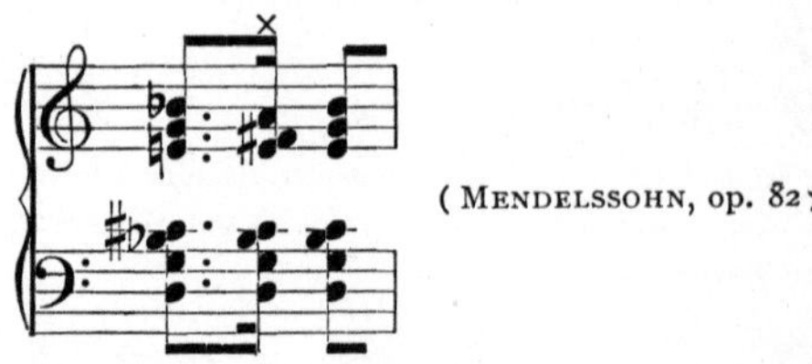

(MENDELSSOHN, op. 82)

But such dissonant clusters are never "chords." Their demonstration will appear in due time.

28. The concise definition of a chord is, then:
the combination of three (or four, or five) tones in thirds, or in inverted forms reducible to thirds (see par. 25).

29. The structure of *thirds* is the **fundamental** chord-form:

In *this* form the lowermost tone is the **root** of the chord, from which the latter takes its name, according to the name of the letter, or of the scale-step. Thus:

is the chord of *C*, or, in C major, the *tonic* chord, because *C* is its root. The other tones (*e* and *g*) are called the **third** and **fifth** of the chord, according to their interval-relations with the root. Two additional tones would be called the **seventh** and **ninth.** Thus:

30. Three-tone chords are termed **triads;**
Four-tone chords are termed chords of the **seventh;**
Five-tone chords are termed chords of the **ninth.** Thus:

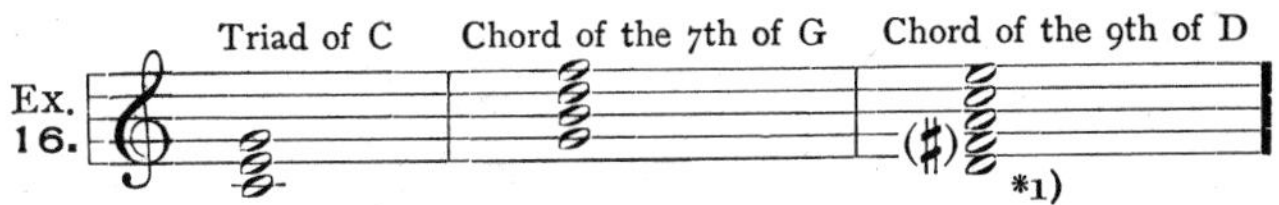

*1) Why the ear prefers F-sharp to F-natural in this case will shortly be deduced from the simple principles of chord-relation.

RELATION OF TRIADS WITHIN ONE KEY.

31. Any step of the diatonic scale (*excepting the leading-tone*) may be a root, and develop into a triad by uniting with its third and fifth. And, as already stated, each chord derives its harmonic name *from the step of the scale which its root occupies.* For illustration, in C major:

For convenience, the triads are also designated by Roman numerals, coinciding with the number of the step on which their roots stand, and are named accordingly: The **One,** the **Two,** the **Three,** etc.

Ex. 18.

I II III IV V VI

32. The relative importance of each of the six triads of a key corresponds exactly to that of the respective scale-step, and depends

upon the distance of its root from the tonic in perfect fifths;
or, upon its location in the "natural" scale (Ex. 2).

Assuming, as self-evident, that the tonic triad is of first and fundamental significance, the next in importance is the dominant triad, then the sub-dominant triad, and so on, precisely in the order of Ex. 17.

33. The tonic triad and its two nearest relatives, the dom. and subdom. triads, are the **principal** chords of the key (see par. 14), and represent

THE THREE ESSENTIAL ELEMENTS OF HARMONY,

among which the other three triads (the Two, the Six, and the Three), called **subordinate** chords, are interspersed only for the sake of variety, contrast and embellishment.

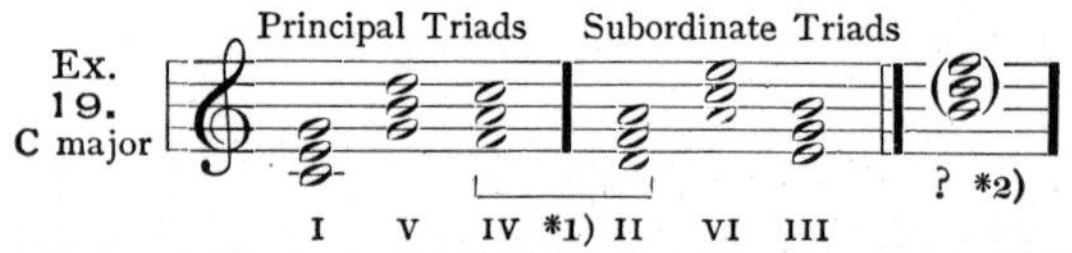

*1) A fine distinction in the relative importance of the IV and the II will be discussed later on. — *2) To the "Leading-tone triad" no name or rank can be assigned at present; see par. 162. From this a significant inference can be drawn in regard to the choice of *f-natural* instead of *f-sharp* for the key of C (Ex. 2, note *1). *F-natural* can be a *root* in that key; *f-sharp* cannot. B, which cannot be a root, is the last tone admitted in C major.

34. These two classes of chords (Ex. 19) will be found, at the pianoforte, to differ in sound. The principal triads have a *major* third and perfect fifth, wherefore they are called major triads. On the contrary, the subordinate triads have a *minor* third and perfect fifth, and are termed minor triads. *This accidental difference in effect is owing only to the situation of the chords in their key, and does not in any wise influence their movements or significance.*

LESSON 3.

A. Write the major triad (as the I) on every possible tone in the octave, adhering throughout to the *fundamental* form (par. 29). B. Write the six triads of the twelve diatonic scales, in the order of Ex. 19. C. Name, mentally, the I of every key; the V of every key; the IV; the II; the VI; the III. D. Find and play these chords at the pianoforte. (The practice of 4- and 5-tone chords is deferred till later.)

CHAPTER IV.

RHYTHM AND MELODY.

35. The images of musical art, unlike the *stationary* creations of the arts of painting, architecture and sculpture, are *progressive;* as in the art of poetry, the impressions in music succeed each other by *progressive motion.* Therefore, *time* is absorbed in the expression of a musical thought, and it is the province of **Rhythm** to define and regulate the divisions and subdivisions of this passage of time.

Rule I. The time is divided into **absolutely equal** units (*beats*, fractions of beats, or measures, as the case may be); i.e., the respective units are of exactly equal *duration* (like the uniform divisions of a 12-inch rule).

Rule II. Though the units are alike in duration, they **differ in force;** i.e., some are heavy and others light (as certain lines on a 12-inch rule differ from others in length or heaviness).

36. The primary units (or beats) are grouped, in conformity to these rules, in uniform *Measures,* of which there are but *two fundamental species;* either a succession of one heavy and one light beat, in regular alternation; or a succession of one heavy and *two* light beats, in irregular alternation. The former is called **Duple** time, or rhythm, or measure; the latter is called **Triple** rhythm. *There are no other species.*

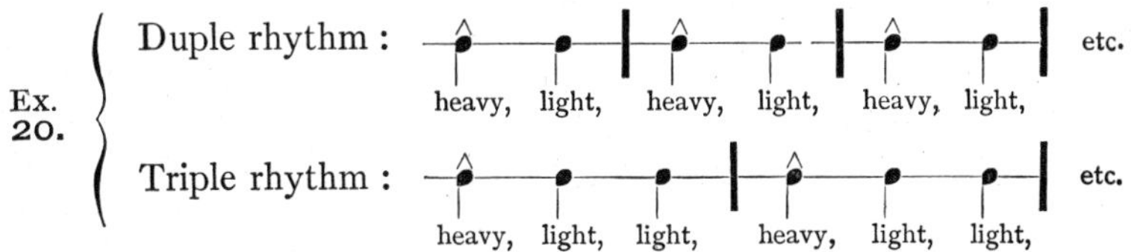

37. Rule III. The heavy beat (called *Accent*) should indicate the *beginning of a measure.* If a heavy impression is created by any means at *any other* point in the measure, the rhythm is "*irregular,*" though not necessarily wrong. For illustration:

Both of these examples are perfectly regular, because the heaviest (longest) beat, or tone, stands in every case at the beginning of the measure.

On the contrary:

*1) This is an example of irregular rhythm, because the heavier tone is where a *light* unit should stand. — *2) Irregular because of the *sf*, which transforms a light unit into a dynamically strong one. — *3) Like note *1). It will be noticed that in each of these three examples the irregular rhythmic figure is *repeated*. In No. 1, for instance, the second measure has the same irregular formation as the first; see also Ex. 23, No. 2. Such confirmations are almost invariably present, and they *fully justify* the rhythmic irregularity.

38. RULE IV. The necessary subdivision of beats into fractions, and the addition of beats, or parts of beats, into notes of greater value (Ex. 23, No. 1), must consequently be so effected that the heavy beats retain the *comparatively longer* tones; i.e., subdivisions must take place on comparatively *lighter*, as a rule not on comparatively *heavier* beats, and vice versa.

*1) Regular; 3d (light) beat subdivided. — *2) Irregular, the *heavy* beat being so subdivided that the following (light) unit becomes more weighty. The measure seems to begin with the second eighth-beat. — *3) An unusual example of irregular rhythm. Without its rhythmically definite accompaniment, it sounds like 3-4 measure, thus:

39. RULE V. For these reasons, the repetition of a chord from an unaccented beat to an accented one (i. e., *over an accent*) gives rise to irregular rhythm, and should be avoided.

40. All larger measures than those which comprise but two or three beats, are called *Compound*, and contain *as many accents as there are groups*. Thus:

Ex. 24. $\frac{4}{4}$ or C — $\frac{6}{4}$ — $\frac{9}{8}$ — etc.

Acc. Acc. Acc. Acc. Acc. Acc. Acc.

The *upper* figure of the time-signature always indicates whether the measure is simple or compound. In the former case it is 2 or 3 ($\frac{2}{2}, \frac{2}{4}, \frac{3}{4}, \frac{3}{8}$, etc.); in the latter case, 4, 6, 9, or 12 ($\frac{4}{4}, \frac{4}{8}, \frac{6}{8}, \frac{6}{4}, \frac{9}{4}, \frac{9}{8}, \frac{9}{16}, \frac{12}{8}$, etc.)

MELODY.

41. Any succession of single tones is a Melody. Its quality depends upon the *choice* of the tones, and their *rhythm* or time-values.

Melody is a manifestation of tone-relations in horizontal or *progressive* association, whereas Harmony associates tones vertically or *simultaneously;* the two partly similar processes are subject to the same natural laws only in a limited sense. The principles of Harmony, in the broad sense of chord-succession, are very distinct; those of Melody far more vague. Harmony is the substratum of all music, and its few sturdy laws fix themselves upon the mind easily, and so firmly, that their fulfilment soon becomes almost automatic, and indeed is often intuitive; but melody is guided by more veiled and subtle conditions, which can hardly be reduced to a system, but must be left largely to the individual talent, native sagacity, or acquired skill of the composer. Largely — but not altogether: As far as the natural decrees of harmonic combination and succession influence and determine the ruling conditions of melody, the latter *can be* reduced to apprehensible form, and this should be faithfully observed until essentially fastened on the mind.

42. Rule I. The general requirements of *good* melody are: *a.* smooth and natural undulation (to the exclusion of awkward interval-successions); *b.* rhythmic variety; *c.* definite and symmetrical delineation — including frequent confirmation of the melodic figures, either upon the *same* steps (as direct repetition), or upon other, *higher or lower steps* (as sequence — par. 128 *b*). For illustration:

*1) An example of bad melody, in which all the above-named requirements are wanting.
*2) A good melody, fulfilling all the given conditions.

ACTIVE AND INACTIVE SCALE-STEPS.

43. The seven steps of every scale are divided into two classes: **active** (or leading) tones, which possess a natural inclination to progress, upward or downward, into other tones; and **inactive** (or central) tones, which have no melodic tendency, but represent the aim of the active tones. The inactive tones are the 1st, 3d, and 5th scale-steps; that is, the *tonic* or stationary centre of the whole key, and its two harmonic associates, which naturally share this central quality with it. They are *interior* tones, within the circle of rest. The active tones are the 7th, 6th, 4th and 2d steps, or, in other words,

> **those exterior steps which lie not within but without the inner circle of harmonic repose, and which therefore strive to gain (or regain) the condition of rest. For illustration:**

44. Rule II. The direction of each active step is defined by its proximity to an inactive step, *each being attracted most strongly by that inactive tone which lies nearest.* Hence, the *7th step* progresses *upward* to the tonic; the *6th step downward* to the dominant; the *4th step downward* to the mediant; and the 2d step either upward or downward, to the tonic or mediant, from either of which it is *equally* distant. Thus:

45. This duality of melodic quality in a key — the opposed positive and negative conditions of animation and repose — underlies all harmonic and melodic life. Like the coil and recoil of the hairspring of a watch, the melodic and harmonic factors swing to and fro between these two groups, with more or less regularity. And it will be seen (Ex. 28) that their fundamental tones are respectively *tonic and dominant;* this again proves the basic significance of the perfect-fifth relation, and, further, illustrates the dominating quality of the "dominant," which is the common tone, or connecting link, of the two groups. For example:

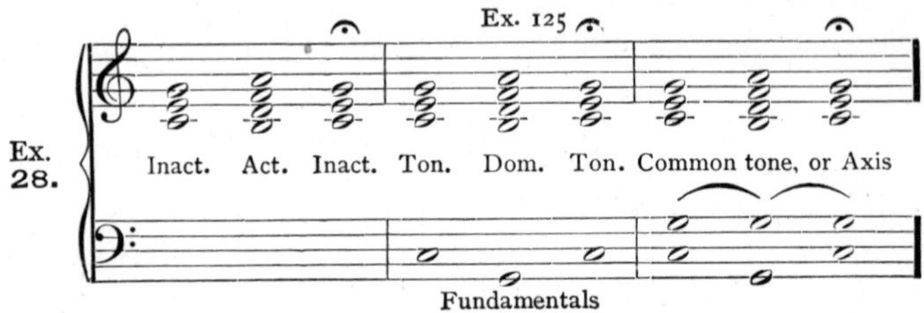

Further illustration:

Since step 2 may move in either direction, no attention is paid to it.

46. RULE III. The direction of the active steps 7, 6 and 4, may be counteracted by approaching them *along the scale* from the opposite side. Thus, step 7 may descend diatonically if preceded by step 8; and the same rule applies to the others. That is, steps 8–7–6–5, or 5–6–7–8, or 3–4–5 are permissible.

47. RULE IV. The "narrow" leap (a third) is always good. See Ex. 29, measure 2, beats 3 and 4.

Any leap beyond a third is called "wide." Wide leaps are always good when both tones belong to either one of the three *principal triads* (I. V or IV, par. 33). Thus:

48. RULE V. After a *wide* leap the melody usually *turns*:

49. The chief exceptions to this rule occur:

a) When the melody continues in the same direction along the *same good* chord-line.

b) When the melody turns after the *next* beat.

c) The rule is not imperative after the inactive steps 1, 5 and 3.

50. *Any* wide leap is permissible (whether in the good chord-line or not) *down* to step 7, or *up* to steps 6 or 4, on condition that these active steps then *turn* and follow their natural tendency. Thus:

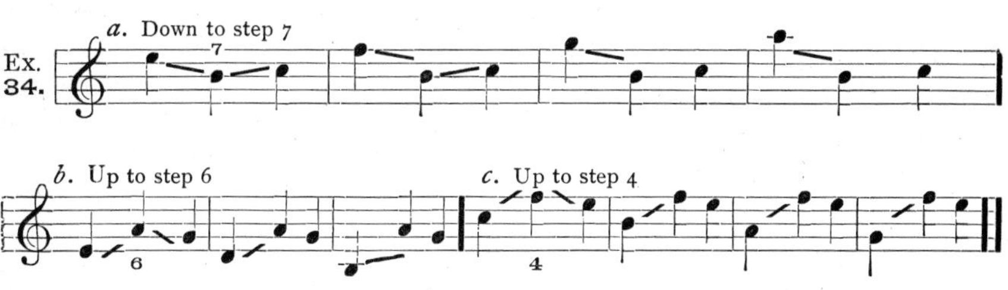

51. The following wide leaps are faulty (C major):

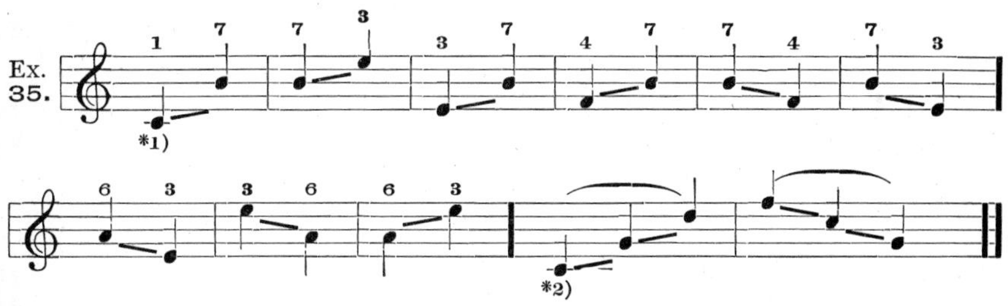

*1) The first nine progressions are wrong, because the two tones do not lie in a good chord (par. 47), and the *direction* of some of the leaps is contrary to par. 50.

*2) Successive skips *in the same direction* must follow the line of *one and the same* good chord (Ex. 33, *a*).

52. The arrangement of melodic *figures* in uniform repetitions, or sequences, generally justifies any reasonable irregularity. Compare Ex. 22, note *3); Ex. 25, No. 2; and the following:

*1) At each bracket there is a faulty leap, but the relation of the *melodic groups* justifies them.

*2) The octave leap, and the repeated tone, are always good.

LESSON 4.

A. Write out Ex. 27 and Ex. 28 in every major key.

B. Write a large number of melodies in different *major* keys, according to the **above rules,** and the following:

a) Each melody is to be *four measures* in length (as Phrase; see par. 65).

b) The melody may begin with the first, third or fifth scale-step (the tones of **the tonic** chord); the first tone may stand upon an accented beat (as in Ex. 30, and Ex. 36), or upon the unaccented beat preceding the first measure (as in Ex. 29). See par. 66.

c) The melody must end upon the keynote, on an accented beat of the fourth measure (as in Ex. 29 and Ex. 30; Ex. 36 is an incomplete sentence, as it ends on the fifth step). See par. 67.

Examples of the four-measure phrase will be found in Lessons 10, 13, 16, 18, etc.

CHAPTER V.

PARTS (VOICES). ERECTION OF CHORDS.

53. All music is based upon *chords*, which succeed each other in *Harmony*, as single tones succeed each other in *Melody*. These chord-successions (chord-combinations or chord-progressions) are effected by means of a number of *simultaneous melodic Parts* or voices, each of which assumes one of the chord-tones, and serves, in conjunction with the rest of the voices, to unite the chords in horizontal order, interval by interval. See Ex. 42.

54. The number of parts or voices generally employed is four. The following example indicates their respective *names*, their average *compass*, and their *notation:*

Bass and tenor (male voices) are written together on the F-staff, and distinguished by turning the stems of their notes respectively down and up; alto and soprano (female voices) both on the G-staff, stems respectively down and up. Ex. 38. Bass and alto, the lowest of each class, are called *parallel* parts or voices; tenor and soprano likewise. Bass and soprano are *outer* voices, tenor and alto *inner* voices.

55. The distribution of the chord-tones among the 4 parts or voices is called *erecting* the chord.

RULE I. The parts must not cross.

RULE II. The alto should not lie more than an octave from either of its two neighbors (i.e., soprano or tenor); but the lower adjacent voices, bass and tenor, are not limited by this rule. For illustration:

Ex. 38. I of C.

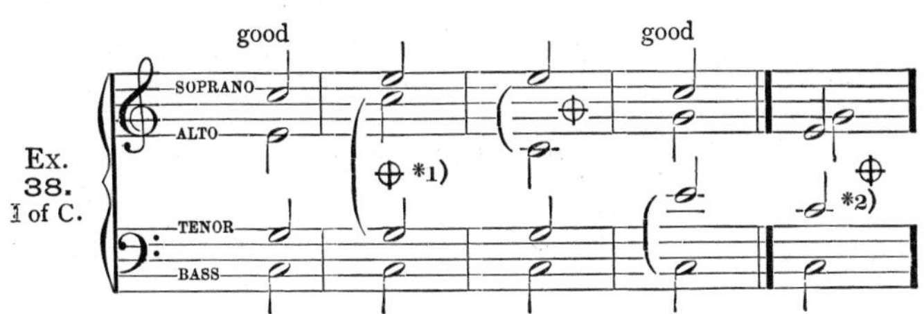

*1) This sign ⊕ will be used to indicate bad (wrong) examples. Chord 2 is wrong, because the alto and tenor are more than an octave apart. In chord 3, alto and soprano are too far apart. — *2) According to the notation, the soprano note *e* lies *below* the alto note *g*. This violates Rule I.

56 a. In 4-part harmony, all triads (3-tone chords) have to be enlarged by *duplicating* one of their tones.

> **RULE. The best tones to double are the principal steps of the scale, i.e., tonic, dominant and subdominant, especially when they are roots.**

Thus, in C major, the tones *c*, *g* or *f*:

Ex. 39. C major

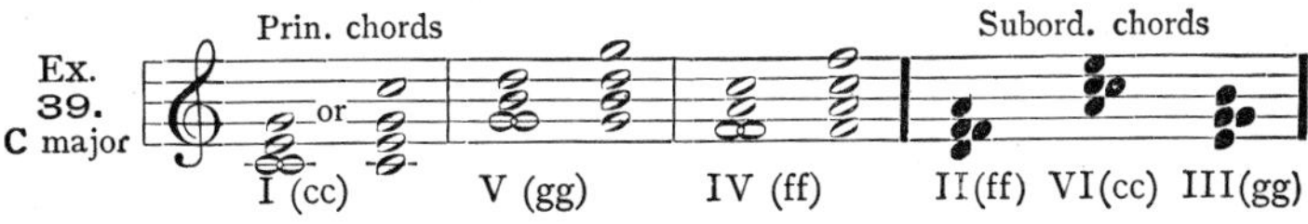

b. From which it appears that, as a rule, the *root* is doubled in each *principal triad;* and the *third* is the best interval to double in each *subordinate triad*. Further, by inference, it is unwise to double the *fifth* in any fundamental chord.

57. It is possible to *omit the fifth of any principal triad* (if found necessary), in which case the root of the chord is *tripled*. Thus:

Ex. 40. C major

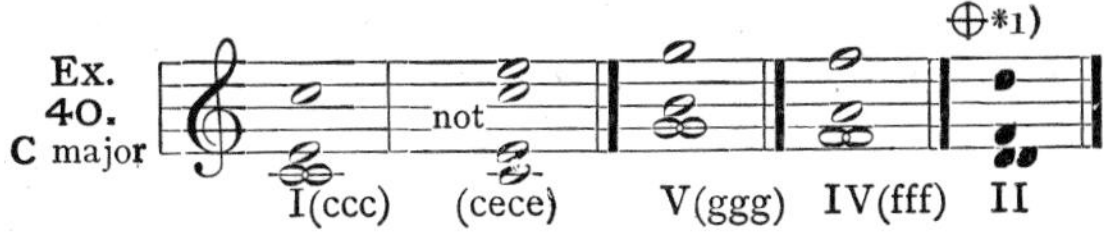

*1) The fifth is never omitted, however, in a *subordinate* chord.

58. It is always justifiable to double a root, because of its importance in its chord. Therefore, it is also possible to double the *root* in a subordinate triad. Thus:

LESSON 5.

Erect (in writing) the I of the following major keys, in as many forms as possible: F, G, D, A, E, B, F♯, B♭, E♭, A♭, D♭. Study the given model (the I of C), and observe the following rules: Always place the root in bass; double the root; place either root, third or fifth in the soprano; see par. 54; par. 55; and par. 57.

CHAPTER VI.

RULES OF PART-WRITING.

59. Part-writing means " writing in parts "; that is, tracing the **tone-line** which each one of the four parts (or voices) describes in passing from one chord into another. Comp. par. 53. In this, which is the vital and fundamental operation throughout the art of music composition, the following rules should be observed — by the beginner very strictly.

60. Rule I: The parts, each and all, should move as evenly, smoothly (as nearly horizontal) as possible.

Wide leaps should be avoided.

Diatonic movement (along the scale) is best.

The *narrow* leap is always good.

A tone which is common to two successive chords is *generally* (by no means always) retained in the same part.

The bass, which is obliged (at present) to take the root of each successive chord, is privileged to make wide leaps.

For illustration, the connection I–V in C major:

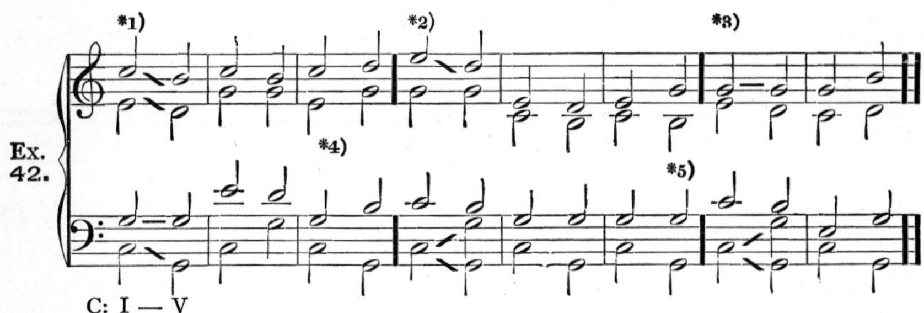

N.B. Each of these "measures" is an example by itself, and not connected with the next.

*1) Beginning with the root in soprano. The following tone in that part is either *b*, or *d* (measure 3), because *these are the nearest tones.* The alto also moves to the nearest tone (*e* to *d*, along the scale). The tenor holds the common tone, *g*. The bass is obliged to make a wide leap, from root to root; either up or down.

*2) Beginning with the third in soprano, *e*, which moves along the scale to *d*, or up to *g*.

*3) Beginning with the fifth in soprano, *g*, which is either held, or makes the narrow leap to *b*.

*4) Narrow leaps in alto and tenor. — *5) Omitted chord-fifth.

61. Rule II: Successive perfect fifths, and successive octaves (or unisons) in any pair of parts, in parallel direction, are prohibited.

Successive perfect 5ths *sound disagreeable*, in the majority of cases.

Successive octaves are forbidden in *part-writing*, because they reduce the number of independent tone-lines (voices) and create a blundering impression. For illustration:

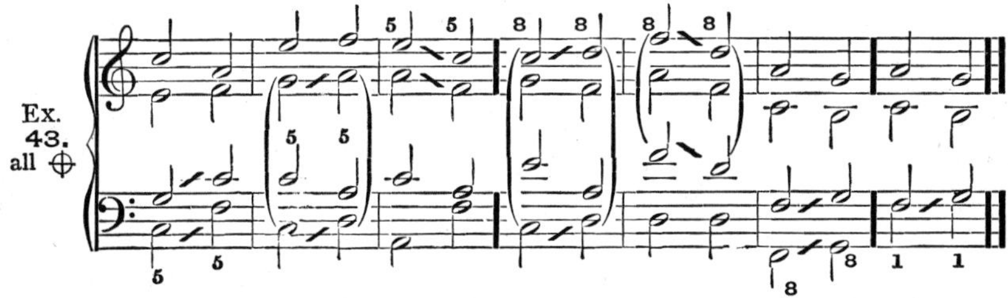

It is significant, that almost all of the above erroneous progressions are due, primarily, to the violation of other simple conditions, especially that of Rule I. In measure 1, tenor and bass progress parallel from one perfect 5th to another. The real cause of the error is, however, the wide leap in the tenor. — Measure 2: bass and alto run parallel in perfect 5ths; at the same time, the *a* in alto is a faulty duplication of the fifth of the chord (par. 56*b*). — Measure 4: soprano and bass progress in parallel octaves; at the same time, the tenor makes a wide leap. — Measure 5: tenor and soprano run parallel in octaves; at the same time, the fifth (*a*) of the subordinate chord (II) is omitted. — In the last measure there are consecutive unisons in tenor and bass, whereby the loss of one of the four tone-lines is clearly shown.

N.B. It must be remembered that successive octaves and fifths are wrong in *any* two parts, but only when they follow each other in the *same pair* of parts. In Ex. 42, meas. 1, the perfect 5th *c–g*, in tenor and bass, does not progress into the next perf. 5th *g–d*, in tenor and alto.

62. As these erroneous parallels are induced by leading the parts in the same direction (upward or downward), it is generally preferable to carry the *soprano*, at least, in contrary direction to the bass.

63. Rule III: The leading-tone should ascend, to the tonic if practicable, in each of the four parts.

The downward tendency of the 6th and 4th steps should be respected *in the soprano;* but this is not so necessary (though always better) in the other parts. The 4th step *in bass*, as root, frequently ascends (Ex. 45, meas. 7). For example:

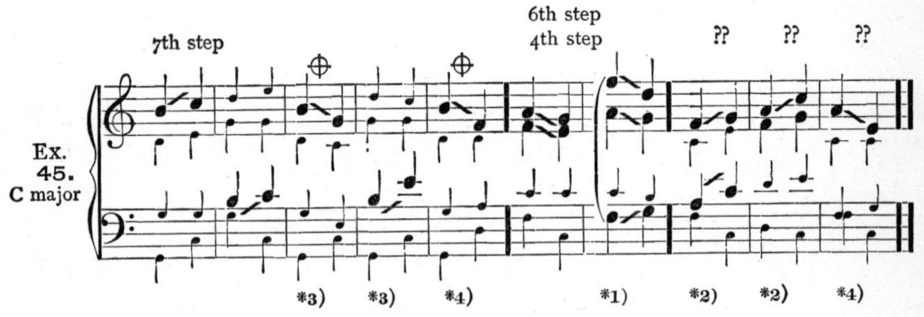

*1) When the 4th step is doubled, as here, it is likely to ascend in *one* of the parts. The *correct progression* however (downward) is given to the most prominent or *most melodious* voice. In this case the soprano descends, correctly.

*2) Here the 4th step and 6th step ascend in soprano. This is faulty. The ascent of these same steps in tenor and alto is not noticeable (as inner parts) and therefore permissible.

*3) Faulty progression of the leading-tone. — *4) Bad leap in soprano (Ex. 35).

64. A general exception to all these rules of part-writing is applicable (and often almost obligatory) in case a chord is simply repeated, instead of being exchanged for a new chord.

Hence, *when the chord remains the same,* wide leaps are good, and even desirable; the tendency of active steps is not urgent; and "parallel" 5ths are impossible. For example:

Measure 1 is monotonous; meas. 2 is far better. The successive octaves in meas. 1 and 2, and the successive 5ths in meas. 3 (in bass and tenor), are not "parallels."

LESSON 6.

Connect (in writing) the I with the V in C major, in as many ways as possible — but always with root in bass — according to the foregoing rules. See Ex. 42, and the model, below. — Connect the I with the IV in the keys of G, E, and B major. — Connect the V with the I in F, B-flat and G-flat major (with especial vigilance in regard to the first clause of Rule III, par. 63). — Connect the IV with the I in D, A-flat, and E major (observing the second clause of Rule III). — Find and play these chord-successions at the **pianoforte,** the three upper parts in the right hand, and the bass alone in the left.

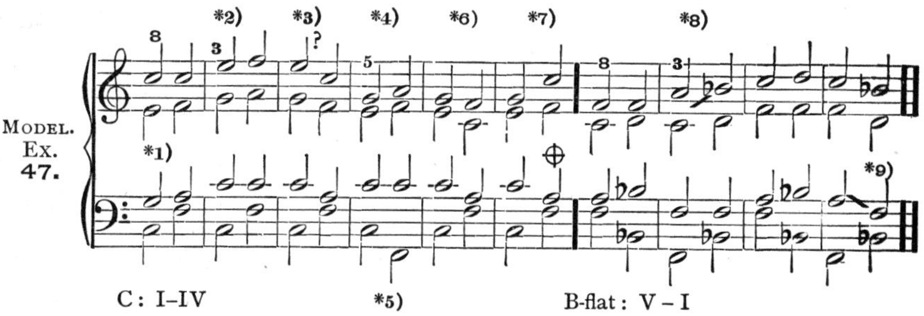

*1) The choice of triads determines the bass progression; here *c–f*, because **I–IV of C.** The soprano takes first the *root* or "octave"; its progression is a repetition, *c–c*, as ***no other*** *tone of the second chord (f–a–c) lies as near as this.* The same is true of the alto (*e–f*); and the tenor moves with similar smoothness from *g* to *a*. — *2) The soprano starts here from the *third* (*e*) and moves to *f*, the nearest tone. — *3) The leap from *e* to *c* is doubtful. — *4) The soprano starts from the *fifth* (*g*), and reaches either *a* or *f* (note *6) smoothly, while the leap to *c* (note *7) is wrong, making parallel perfect 5ths with the bass. — *5) The bass may rise or fall; see Ex. 44. — *6) and *7), explained in *4). — *8) The *a* is leading-tone, and must, when in the soprano, ascend to *b-flat*. — *9) In an *inner* voice this descent of the leading-tone is not distinctly noticeable, and therefore not strictly forbidden.

CHAPTER VII.

PERFECT CADENCE AND PHRASE.

65. The **phrase** is the smallest complete musical sentence. It is usually *four measures* in length; much more rarely two measures, or eight measures.

66. A phrase which is to represent an independent, complete sentence, begins with the *tonic triad*, either upon the first accented beat, or upon the unaccented beat preceding this accent. The root is in bass, as usual; but the soprano may take either root, third, or fifth of the chord. The body of the phrase consists of successive chords, ending with the *Perfect Cadence.*

67. The **perfect cadence** is made upon the *tonic triad*, with its root in bass *and in soprano;* upon an *accented beat* of the fourth measure (possibly second, or eighth, measure). And this final tonic chord is preceded by the *dominant triad* (root in bass, but the soprano optional). Thus:

*1) The cadence chord (I) may fall upon *either* accent, in compound measure (par. 40). — *2) Comp. Ex. 47, note *9). When the leading-tone is in an *inner* part, and is *approached from above*, as here, it may make the narrow leap down to the dominant (in order to redeem the fifth of the I).

68. The skeleton of a 4-measure phrase in triple measure, is, then, as follows:

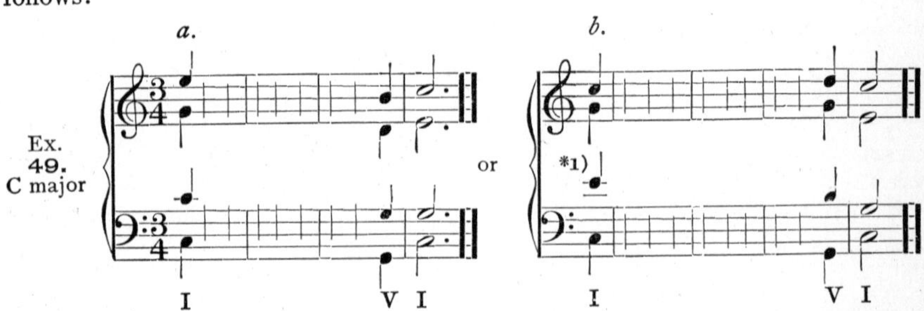

*1) The light beat (unaccented), upon which this Phrase begins, is called a *preliminary* beat, and must be subtracted from the cadence measure. Therefore, the final half-note has no dot here, as it had in the preceding case.

69. The vacant beats (marked | | |) may be supplied with chords in an infinite variety of successions, and it is therefore first necessary for the student to learn the rules of chord-succession. For chords have their tendencies (like the active scale-steps), and not every progression is legitimate. The rules for the **three principal triads** are as follows:

Rule I: The tonic triad can progress, under all harmonic circumstances, into any other chord of its own, or of any other, key. This is its prerogative as chief of the harmonic system. Therefore I–V and I–IV are good.

Rule II: The subdominant triad (IV) may progress either into the I or the V. Thus: IV–I or IV–V.

Rule III: The dominant triad (V) may progress, legitimately, **only into the tonic chord.** Therefore V–I is good; but V–IV must be avoided.

Rule IV: Any bass tone (or fundamental chord) may be *repeated* after an accent, but not over *into* an accent — as a rule, not over the bar. See par. 39.

THE CHORD-PROGRESSIONS I–V–I, AND I–IV–I.

70. According to the above rules, the phrase-skeletons in Ex. 49 may be filled out as follows, employing only the direct connections of the I with the V and IV (not IV with V, at present):

Any key. $\frac{3}{4}$ *a.* I I V | I IV I | V V V | I || Or: *b.* I V I | IV IV I | V I V | I ||

Or: *c.* I V V | I IV IV | I V V | I || Or: *d.* I I I | V I I | IV I V | I ||

Or, beginning unaccented: *e.* I | V I I | IV I I | V V V | I || And many more.

71. In working out these harmonic formulæ, in complete four-part phrases, it is necessary first to choose a key; then to write out the bass part (in each case with the root of the chord); then, as a rule, the soprano; and then the inner parts. Thus, with formula *a*, in F major:

*1) Note the wide leaps during *chord-repetition* (Ex. 46). Everywhere else (excepting in bass) the movements are smooth. — *2) The chord-fifth is omitted.

These are but two of very many different solutions.

LESSON 7.

A. Work out the formulæ given in par. 70, as shown in Ex. 50, in as many different major keys, and different ways, as possible.

B. Construct a number of additional (original) formulæ, using only the progressions I–V–I and I–IV–I, and chord-repetitions; and employing $\frac{3}{4}$, $\frac{3}{8}$ and $\frac{3}{2}$ measure.

N.B. This work must all be done away from the keyboard. The text, and the given Examples, may and should be studied at the piano; but the student's work *must be mental*, unassisted by the external tone.

CHAPTER VIII.

THE PROGRESSION IV–V.

72. The progression IV–V is called *Foreign*, because here there is no common tone. That is, in passing from IV to V every tone changes. In this succession:

a) *Wide* leaps are wholly excluded. And

b) The *three upper parts* must progress *downward* (opposite to the progression in bass). For example:

Ex. 51.

*1) This is wrong, because of the faulty soprano progression (Ex. 27, and par. 63). The 6th scale-step should descend (in *this* chord-succession, at least). And there is a wide leap in the tenor. — *2) Parallel octaves in soprano and bass. — *3) Parallel fifths in soprano and bass.

73. By adding this progression, the phrase-formulæ given in par. 70 may be multiplied almost without limit. Thus (still in triple measure):

Any key: $\frac{3}{4}$ *a.* I I V | I IV V | I V V | $\overset{\frown}{\text{I}}$ || *b.* I V I | IV IV V | I IV V | $\overset{\frown}{\text{I}}$ ||

c. I | V I I | V I IV | V I V | $\overset{\frown}{\text{I}}$ || *d.* I | IV IV V | I I IV | V V V | $\overset{\frown}{\text{I}}$ ||

And many more.

74. Formula *a* may be solved as follows (in G major, $\frac{3}{2}$ measure):

75. The following solution, while technically faultless, would be unmusical, because of the monotony of the soprano.

Such versions must be avoided. It is of the first importance to obtain a good, interesting, soprano; for this is the chief melodic part, and *melody is the soul of music.*

76. In duple measure the possibilities are again greatly multiplied. For example:

a.

Any key: $\frac{4}{4}$ I | V I V I | IV IV V V | I IV V V | $\overset{\frown}{\text{I}}$ ||

b.

I I IV V | I IV V I | V V I IV | V V $\overset{\frown}{\text{I}}$ ||

c.

$\frac{2}{4}$ I | IV V | I IV | V V | $\overset{\frown}{\text{I}}$ || And many more.

A solution of *a* (in B-flat major, $\frac{4}{8}$ measure):

*1) Here there is a wide leap in the tenor; but it is a permissible leap (*down* to step 7 — Ex. 34); and it obviates other awkward conditions that are worse than the leap. An *occasional* wide skip may, therefore, be justified.

77. A few exceptional connections, permissible for variety; or in order to avoid worse conditions; or as a means of securing a better melody in the soprano:

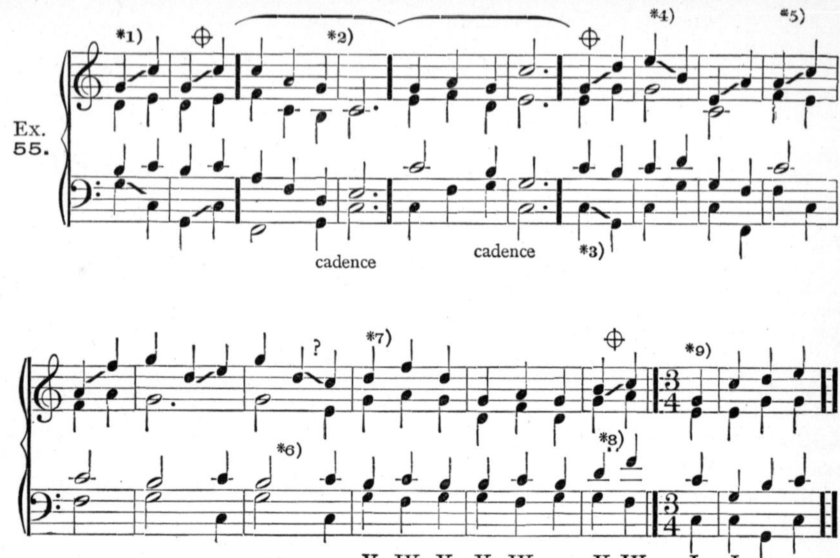

*1) The leap in soprano (from *g up* to *c*) makes octaves with the bass; but they are not *parallel* octaves, because the bass moves *down* from *g* to *c*. Therefore they are permissible. In any case, if there is, as here, a wide leap in both soprano and bass, it is important to make the leaps in *opposite direction*. The second measure is wrong, because the octaves are parallel. *2) This leap in the soprano is most common at the perfect cadence. See Ex. 57, *a*, ending. — *3) Here there are successive fifths in soprano and bass; this is wrong, although they are *not parallel*, because fifths are more sensitive than roots, and are always objectionable *in proportion to their prominence*. Opposite 5ths may be excusable in inner parts, but not in the outer ones. — *4) This is like Ex. 54, note *1); not wrong, even in soprano, but to be avoided. The next measure is similar; the leap in soprano from step 3 *up* to 6 is permissible. *5) Here the 6th scale-step ascends in *soprano;* permissible, but not good. Comp. par. 63. The next measure is faultless, because the chord remains the same. — *6) This measure is unmelodious, in soprano, according to the rule in par. 48. The preceding measure is good. — *7) Here the V progresses into the IV, contrary to par. 69, Rule III. It is rare, but possible; best when, as here, the V immediately returns. Note the soprano. — *8) In this soprano position the progression is not good, because *c* in the soprano, as fifth of the IV, does not sound enough like a tonic to satisfy the progression of the leading-tone. — *9) The I may be repeated over the *very first* bar in a phrase, as here, since the unaccented beat is only "preliminary." See par. 69, Rule IV; and Ex. 49, note *1).

LESSON 8.

A. Work out the formulæ given in par. 73, and par. 76, in a number of different major keys, and with different soprano.

B. Construct a number of additional original phrases, in all kinds of measure. Review Lesson 7, N. B.

CHAPTER IX.

RHYTHMIC PHRASES.

78. By altering the *time-values* of the chords (instead of the uniform values used in the preceding Lessons), still more variety, harmonic and melodic interest, can be obtained.

The student should realize that these three principal triads constitute the broad, and only, basis of all music composition. No chord, or group of tones, can be found, which is not a derivative of one or another of these three; precisely as there is no shade of color in the universe that does not originate in the three primary colors. See par. 33. Of all the various methods of treating these fundamental chords, which result in the infinite variety of styles of music, the most significant and prolific is diversified **rhythmic** manipulation. The work of this chapter is therefore directed to the very fundament of the whole musical structure, and no amount of time spent upon it can be considered wasted. Review the chapter on Rhythm (par. 35 to 40) very thoroughly.

79. Rhythmic animation is secured simply by the use of *different time-values.* For illustration:

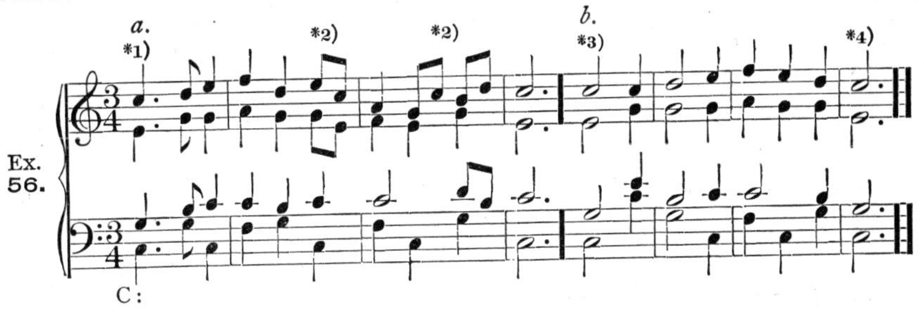

*1) The dot, applied to the accented beats (par. 38), represents one of the simplest means of modifying the rhythm. — *2) Here the beat is divided, the chord remaining the same. This is applied to the unaccented beats (par. 38). — *3) Chords which represent the sum of two or more beats should occupy accented beats. — *4) The cadence-chord is usually more than one beat in length.

In duple measure:

*1) See Ex. 55, note *2). — *2) The chord-fifth must be omitted, because the leading-tone, *g*, must, in this case, ascend. — *3) See **Ex.** 55, note *7).

LESSON 9.

Construct a large number of original phrases, in different major keys, in triple and duple measures, and with rhythmic diversity (*regular*), imitating the above examples.

CHAPTER X.

HARMONIZING OF MELODIES.

80. As stated in par. 41 (which review), Harmony or Chord-succession is the substratum of all music; *it is the source from which all melody is derived*, be it with or without direct and conscious intent. Hence, the system adopted in the above Lessons, of constructing phrases upon the basis of primary chord-succession, is obviously the most natural and correct one. Nevertheless, the process is often reversed; that is, the melody is generally conceived first, off-hand, *apparently* without reference to the underlying harmony; especially in the actual practice of composition, when the observance of harmonic conditions has become, so to speak, automatic.

81. In working out a phrase *from the melody downward* (i.e., in harmonizing a given melody), the following facts must be recalled: The melody will not contain, at present, any other tones than the seven steps of its scale. Of these,

the 1st, 3d and 5th scale-steps belong to the I of the key;
the 5th, 7th and 2d scale-steps belong to the V; and
the 4th, 6th and 1st scale-steps belong to the IV. Thus:

82. The tonic and dominant tones (steps 1 and 5) each belong, as is seen, to *two different prin. triads*, while each of the other steps represents but one. The choice between the two chords, at these points, will be dictated by the rules of par. 69, and other familiar established principles. For example, applying Ex. 58 to the following given melody:

*1) Of these two chords, the I must be chosen (par. 66). — *2) The choice falls upon the I; the V should not progress into the IV of the next beat (par. 69, Rule III). — *3) May be either I or V, because the following beat will be the I, chiefly because of the wide leap in soprano, which almost always calls for chord-repetition. — *4) The IV is not possible, as it would give rise to successive 5ths (sopr. and bass) with the following V. Comp. par. 72 *b*. — *5) The IV is canceled by par. 67.

83. The chords (and the bass part) will therefore be as follows:

*1) Ex. 55, note *9).

84. Another illustration, in duple measure:

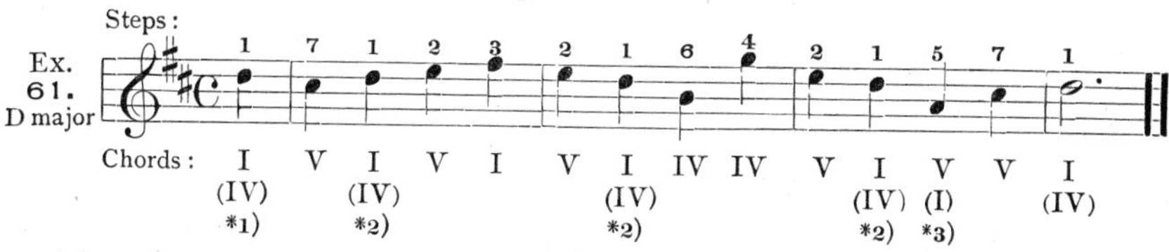

*1) The triads in parenthesis are canceled. — *2) The IV should not follow the V. — *3) This may be either the I or the V; the I, because of the wide leap in soprano; or the V, which is the better of the two, because it is wiser to *change the chord at an accented beat* — though not imperative at the *secondary* accent.

LESSON 10.

Harmonize the following major melodies, according to the above directions:

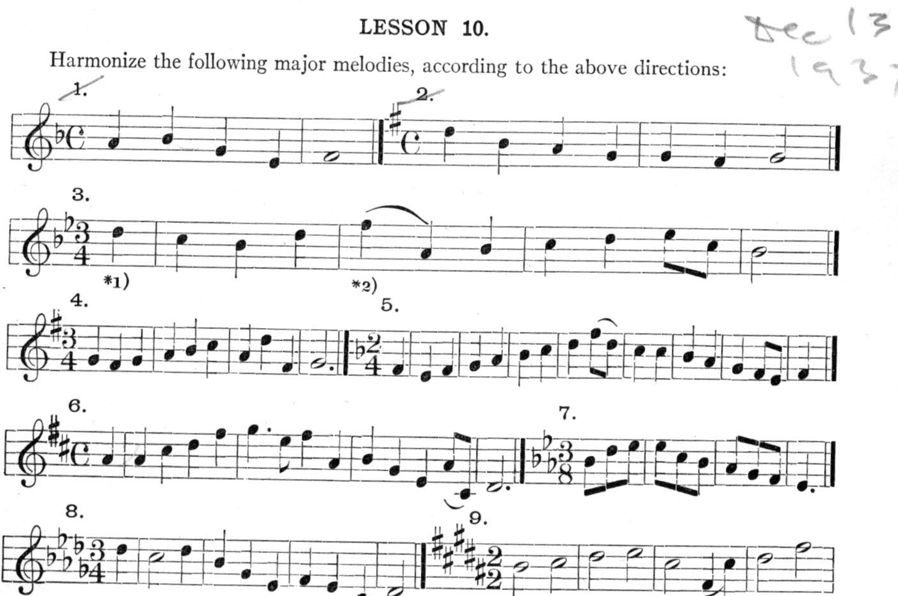

*1) Turn all stems upward. — *2) The wide leap (and slur) *usually* indicates that the chord remains the same. — *3) At this wide leap the chord must be changed, because of the scale-steps represented. — *4) Here the chord must be changed, despite the wide leap in the melody, in keeping with par. 69, Rule IV. Beware of parallel octaves in soprano and bass. Review Ex. 55, note *1). — *5) Here, also, the wide leap must be harmonized with *different* chords, because the phrase should begin with the I. Again, see that the bass skips in opposite direction to the soprano. — *6) See Ex. 55, note *9). — *7) When the leading-tone descends, as here, with a narrow leap to the 5th step, it is evident that the chord must remain the same; for only chord-repetition justifies the melodic licence; see Ex. 46, meas. 4. *8) Compare Ex. 46, measure 1. The chord should be changed for each of these four beats. — *9) In this chord it will be found necessary to *double the third* (*b-flat*). This licence is the only means of counteracting the very unusual wide leaps in the soprano (which cannot be harmonized with the same chord).

CHAPTER XI.

THE HARMONIC MINOR MODE.

85. The line of research and argument in Chapter I, leading up to paragraphs 11 and 12 (which see), proves that, of the two modes recognized and employed in modern music, that one known as **major** (because its prin. triads have a major third) is the **natural** one.

86. The other, i.e., the **minor** mode, is consequently to be regarded as an unnatural or **artificial** mode, and is accounted for as an *arbitrary modification of the natural major mode.*

87. This modification affects the two mediants, namely:

The third and sixth steps of the major scale, which are lowered (by an accidental) so as to transform the corresponding major intervals into minor intervals. No other steps are changed.

In other words, the minor scale is derived from the corresponding major scale by lowering the third and sixth scale-steps of major. Thus:

88. The scale thus obtained is called the **harmonic** minor mode. It is the only theoretically accurate minor scale, and is the same in both ascending and descending succession. Still other alterations, rendered necessary by *melodic* considerations (to be explained in due season), are based upon this harmonic minor mode, which must therefore be first thoroughly mastered.

89. It appears, then, that a minor scale is derived *from the major mode of the* **same keynote** — C minor from C major; A minor from A major, etc. And the lowering of the 3d and 6th steps results from transforming the prin. chords I and IV *from major into minor triads* (comp. par. 34). Thus:

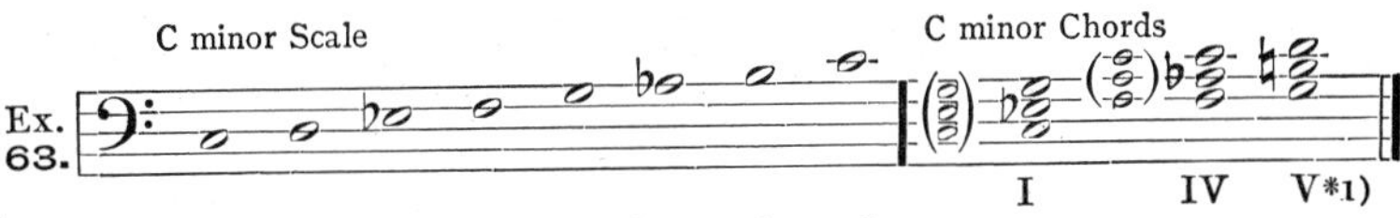

*1) Observe that the dominant chord is not changed.

N. B. The best reason that can be given for the lowering of these particular scale-steps (3 and 6), is, that these alterations do not impair the essential consonant quality of any one of the three principal triads, and therefore do not interfere with any legitimate function of the scale and chords — as *any other changes* would. It is true, the 7th step might also be lowered without injuring the dominant triad, but it would interfere with the significant function of the leading-tone, and therefore it is not done in the *legitimate, harmonic,* minor mode. (The lowering of the 7th step, and other alterations, belong to the domain of Altered chords.)

90. It is significant that, while the tonic and sub-dominant chords are major in major, and minor in minor, *the dominant chords remain the same (major) in both modes.*

SIGNATURE OF MINOR.

91. The minor mode has no specific signature. For convenience (and for that reason *only*), signatures for minor are borrowed from major, and the choice falls upon the *third scale-step* of the minor scale, that proving to be the most convenient. That is, the signature of a minor mode is taken from *its third step:* For *c* minor, the 3d step being *e-flat*, three flats are adopted. Thus:

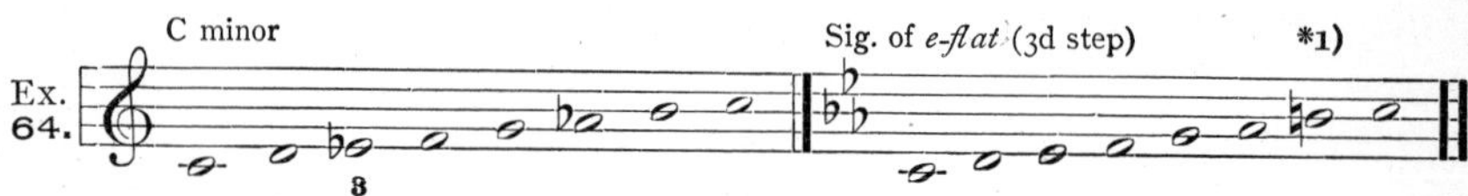

*1) The accidental before *b* (the leading-tone) shows that the adopted signature, though the most convenient one, does not exactly fit the scale. It must be remembered, then, that in the notation of the minor mode with its customary signature, *an accidental is necessary at the 7th scale-step.*

N. B. The *major* key represented by this minor signature, is called the **relative** major — in this case *C* minor and *E-flat* major. The relation is significant, as will be seen; but it must not be confounded with the still closer relation of *derivation.*

92. The treatment of the principal triads in minor corresponds in every respect to that of major, excepting only that *the succession of the 6th and 7th scale-steps* (in either direction) should be avoided, as it is an interval of the augmented second — an unnatural melodic movement. For example:

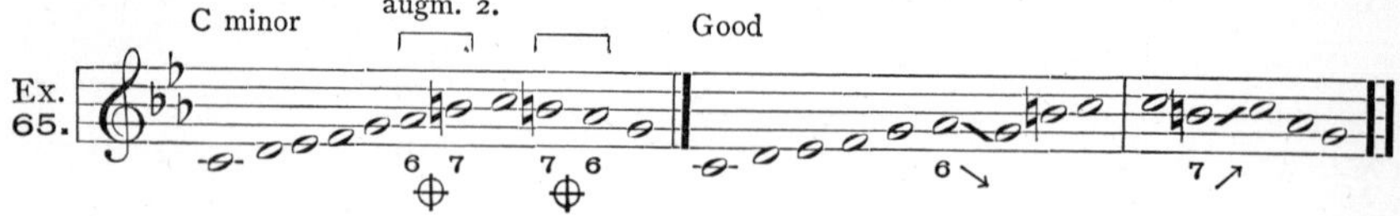

93. This succession (6–7 or 7–6), *has not appeared in any of the foregoing exercises in major* (comp. Ex. 51, note *1); therefore, any phrase in the preceding chapters may be transformed from major into minor with no other changes than those of accidentals. For illustration, Ex. 52:

*1) Compare these at the piano. — *2) The signature is that of *B-flat,* that being the third step of the *G* minor scale. — *3) The leading-tone of G (major or minor) is *f-sharp;* as this is not in the adopted signature, the accidental is everywhere necessary.

LESSON 11.

A. Write out all the major scales (excepting D flat and G flat) and place *their corresponding minors* below them, using no signatures, but accidentals, as follows:

C major
3
6
C minor
etc.

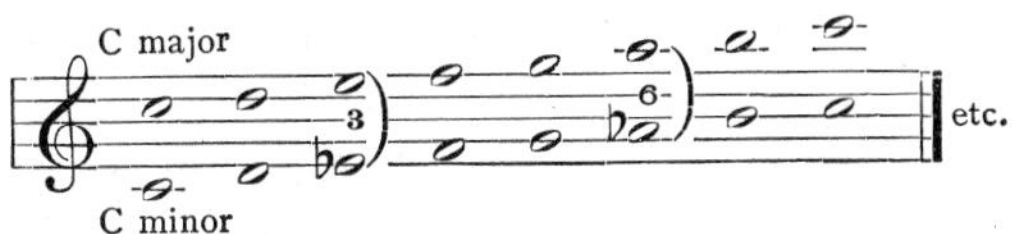

The minor scales of *c-sharp, g-sharp* and *d-sharp* are derived from the corresponding major scales, in the same manner. This is a little more difficult than the process with the more familiar scales, but must also be included in the lesson.

B. Harmonize the following melodies, as before. The choice of chords is governed by the selfsame rules (Ex. 58). Do not neglect the accidental before each leading-tone:

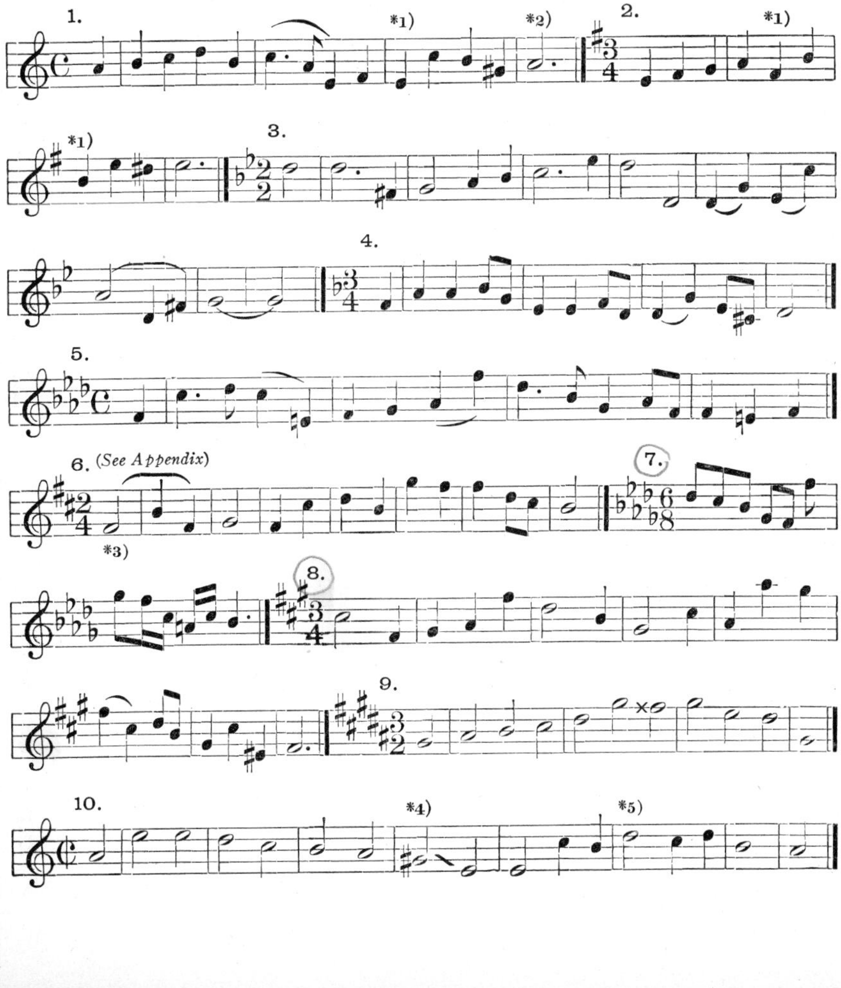

1.
*1)
*2)
2.
*1)
*1)
3.
4.
5.
6. (See Appendix)
*3)
7.
8.
9.
10.
*4)
*5)

*1) As a rule, the wide leap is harmonized with the same chord. — *2) Since the last tone is *a*, as keynote, this phrase is in *A* minor, which is treated like *A* major. — *3) There is no alternative here but to use the same chord for both measures (an exception to par. 69, Rule IV, induced by the skips in soprano). — *4) Like Lesson 10, note *7), which see. — *5) Here the IV must follow the V, because of the succession of steps in the melody.

C. Construct a number of four-measure Original phrases in minor, exactly as in Lesson 9.

CHAPTER XII.

SUBORDINATE TRIADS IN MAJOR.

94. The triads upon the subordinate scale-steps (the II, VI, and III — see par. 33), are not to be regarded and employed as new and independent chords, but as the

parallels of the three principal triads, in the place of which they are respectively used, chiefly for the sake of variety.

95. The relations are as follows:

The VI is the parallel of the I (Tonic element);

The II is the parallel of the IV (Subdom. element); and

The III is the parallel of the V (Dominant element).

In other words, the VI is the subordinate representative of the **tonic** element; the II is the subord. representative of the **subdom.** element; and the III the subord. representative of the **dominant.** For illustration:

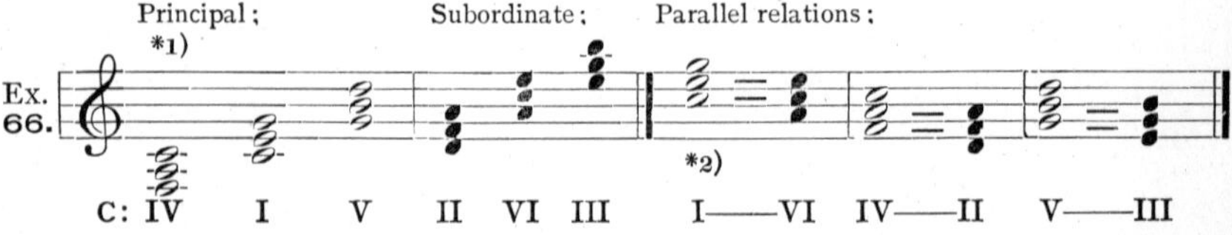

*1) Comp. Ex. 19. — *2) It will be observed that the parallel chords represent *relative* major and minor keys (Ex. 64, N. B.) — that is, keys with corresponding *signatures* (*C* major — *A* minor, etc.).

THE II.

96. The strongest of the subordinate triads is the II, because it follows the V, in perfect-fifth succession, as second-dominant (see Ex. 5). Assuming the I and V to be the two vitally important chords of the key, it follows that the perfect-fifth relatives of these, on either side, constitute the most important secondary rank. For illustration:

The II is thus very closely allied to the IV, and is very nearly, if not wholly, equal to the latter in importance — though perhaps somewhat less frequent. The II is therefore a semi-principal chord, and has, in its treatment, many of the traits and privileges of the principal triads. This will be more clearly seen further on.

97. The best interval of every subordinate triad is its **third**. The triad is at its best when *the third is in the soprano*. And, as shown in par. 56*b* (which review), it is usually best to *double the third*, although the doubled root is always good (par. 58).

98. The II often takes the place of the IV before the perfect cadence. Thus:

*1) Doubled root. — *2) Third in soprano, and doubled third; this is better. The 4th step, *in soprano*, should descend. — *3) A good leap, according to Ex. 34. — *4) This is one of the very rare cases where the 6th step ascends to the 7th *in the soprano*. Note the chord-succession, II-V. — *5) Like Ex. 55, note *3).

99. The progressions of the II, in the order of preference, are as follows:

*1) The best progressions from the II are a perfect fifth down and up: II-V and II-VI. — *2) This is a "Foreign" progression (par. 72). It is stiff, and uncommon, and should be avoided. — *3) No subordinate chord can legitimately *precede its own principal triad*. Therefore II–IV is not good. — *4) This, on the contrary, is an excellent progression, almost equivalent to chord-repetition, since IV and II are parallels. — *5) The I can progress in all directions (par. 69, Rule I); therefore this foreign progression is perfectly good. — *6) Similar to the doubtful progression V–IV. Compare par. 69, Rule III.

N.B. This table of chord-movements must be thoroughly memorized.

100. The connections of the II, in four-part harmony:

The best progression, II–V, is illustrated in Ex. 68.

*1) Doubtful, because the II rarely sounds well with its *fifth in soprano*. And the soprano progression is inferior. — *2) This is the only plausible form of the very rare progression II–I; each chord has its third in the soprano. — *3) The wide leap in soprano is perfectly good, because the connection of parallel chords (here IV–II) is practically the same as chord-repetition. — *4) The strict rules of the foreign progression IV–V, given in par. 72, are somewhat less rigorous here, because one of the chords, being a subordinate, may have either a doubled root or doubled third. In this measure, the soprano moves upward, *in 3ds with the bass*. In the last two measures, *all three* upper parts run contrary to the bass.

THE VI.

101. The VI is the counterpart of the I, and is used exclusively as inferior representative of the tonic harmony.

102. As in the II, the best interval is the **third** of the chord, which is usually doubled, and which appears most frequently in the soprano.

103. Being a *tonic* chord, the VI can also progress into every chord of its key (par. 69, Rule I), *excepting into the* I (Ex. 69, note *3).

Therefore, the VI may also precede the perfect cadence. Thus:

*1) In the first measure, the third of the VI is doubled; in the next measure, the root. — *2) Extremely rare, and scarcely permissible. The VI should never be used with its *root in soprano*. — *3) A faulty leap in soprano; and inexcusable, because a foreign chord-progression (par. 72*a*).

104. The full table of connections of the VI is as follows, in the order of preference:

*1) A subordinate triad preceding its own principal chord. See Ex. 69, note *3). — *2) This progression is correct, according to par. 69, Rule III, because the VI is a tonic chord.
N.B. This table, also, must be thoroughly memorized.

105. The connections of the VI, in 4-part harmony:

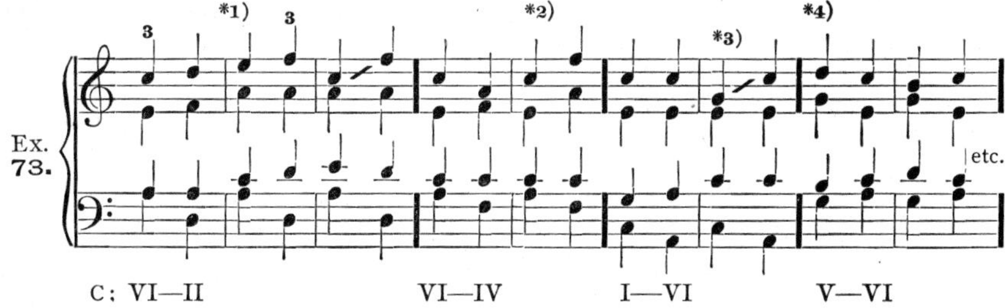

*1) The fifth of the VI is rarely used in soprano. — *2) Two wide leaps in parallel motion (soprano and alto); good, in this case, because they are *parallel sixths*. — *3) Compare Ex. 70, note *3). This, again, is practically chord-repetition. — *4) A foreign progression. Note that *two* upper parts run contrary to the bass. Compare Ex. 70, note *4).

LESSON 12.

A. Write out the following chord-successions in the usual manner, without regard to rhythm (uniform quarter-notes or half-notes), in a number of different major keys:

IV-II-V-I || VI-II-V-I || I-II-V-I || IV-II-VI-V-I || $\overset{3}{\text{I}}$-II-VI-II-V-I ||

I-V-$\overset{3}{\text{II}}$-V-VI || $\overset{3}{\text{I}}$-VI-IV-V-V-I || I-$\overset{8}{\text{V}}$-$\overset{5}{\text{VI}}$-$\overset{3}{\text{VI}}$-V-I || $\overset{5}{\text{I}}$-IV-II-VI-$\overset{5}{\text{VI}}$-IV-V-I ||

N.B. A part of the Lesson may be done at the keyboard, the three upper parts together in the right hand.

B. Construct a number of Original 4-measure phrases, in different major keys, similar to Lesson 9.

CHAPTER XIII.

SUBORDINATE TRIADS. MELODIES.

106. In applying the subordinate triads to the harmonization of melodies, the following facts must be recalled: that the VI takes the place of the I (par. 95) and therefore harmonizes the *1st step* of the scale (more rarely the 3d step); that the II takes the place of the IV, harmonizing the *4th* *step*, (rarely the 6th step); and that the II may also be used as *independent* harmonic factor (par. 96), harmonizing its own step — *the second* — (just as the I harmonizes the 1st step, the IV the 4th step, and the V the 5th step). Thus:

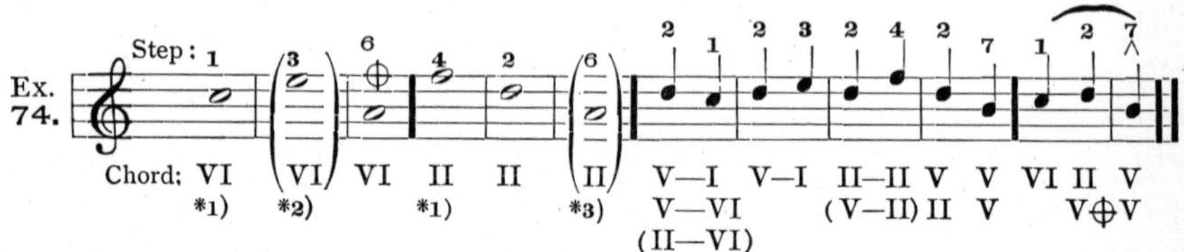

*1) Always the best step for this chord. — *2) Rare; Ex. 73, note *1). — *3) Very rare; but see Ex. 68, note *4). And remember that almost *any* condition is possible, *when the chord remains the same.*

107. Applying these rules to Melody 18 of Lesson 10, the following substitutions may be made:

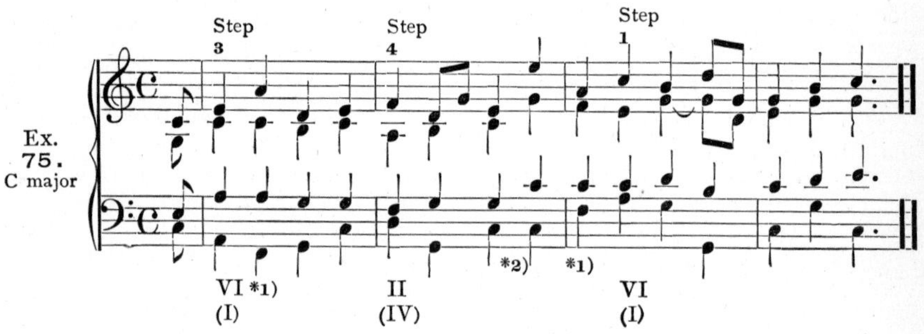

*1) Not the II. — *2) Not the VI.

108. Furthermore, with special reference to the second scale-step:

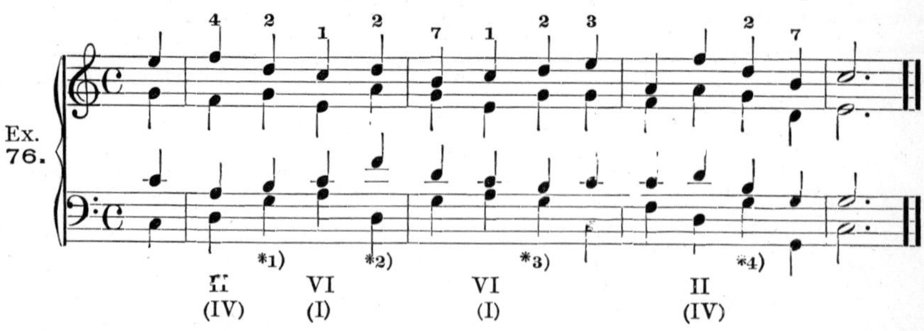

*1) Whether the 2d step is to be harmonized with the V, or with the II, depends largely upon the *next* melody-tone. This *d* might be either V or II, as the VI follows. — *2) This *d* cannot be a V, because the latter would not be repeated over the bar. — *3) The following tone (*e*) must be harmonized with the I; therefore choice falls upon the V for *d*, as II–I is objectionable (Ex. 69, note *2). — *4) Must be the V, as the II should not be repeated from the preceding (light) beat.

THE III.

109. As shown in par. 32, and Ex. 19, the III is the last, and weakest, of all the triads of its key, as it lies most remote from the tonic centre, in the chain of perfect fifths. It is therefore very rare, and limited in its connections.

The only way in which it may safely be used (and, in fact, must be chosen) is in harmonizing the **leading-tone**, when the latter **descends into the 6th scale-step.** In this case the III is followed by the IV.

In very rare cases it harmonizes the 5th step, and may then be followed by the VI or the IV. For example:

110. The following table shows the application of principal and subordinate triads to the seven steps of the scale:

*1) Note that steps 3, 6 and 7 are limited almost entirely to the *principal* triads I, IV and V respectively (each with its third in soprano). — *2) These irregular melodic progressions are explained in par. 46. Each of the melodic irregularities is attended by a corresponding *harmonic* irregularity; steps 6 and 7, *when they progress properly*, are always harmonized with the IV and V; but when they move improperly, the *parallel* triad of each (II and III respectively) must be taken.

LESSON 13.

A. Re-harmonize, with the material of this chapter, Lesson 10, Nos. 1, 2, 3, 4, 7, 10. Refer constantly to Ex. 78.

B. Harmonize the following melodies:

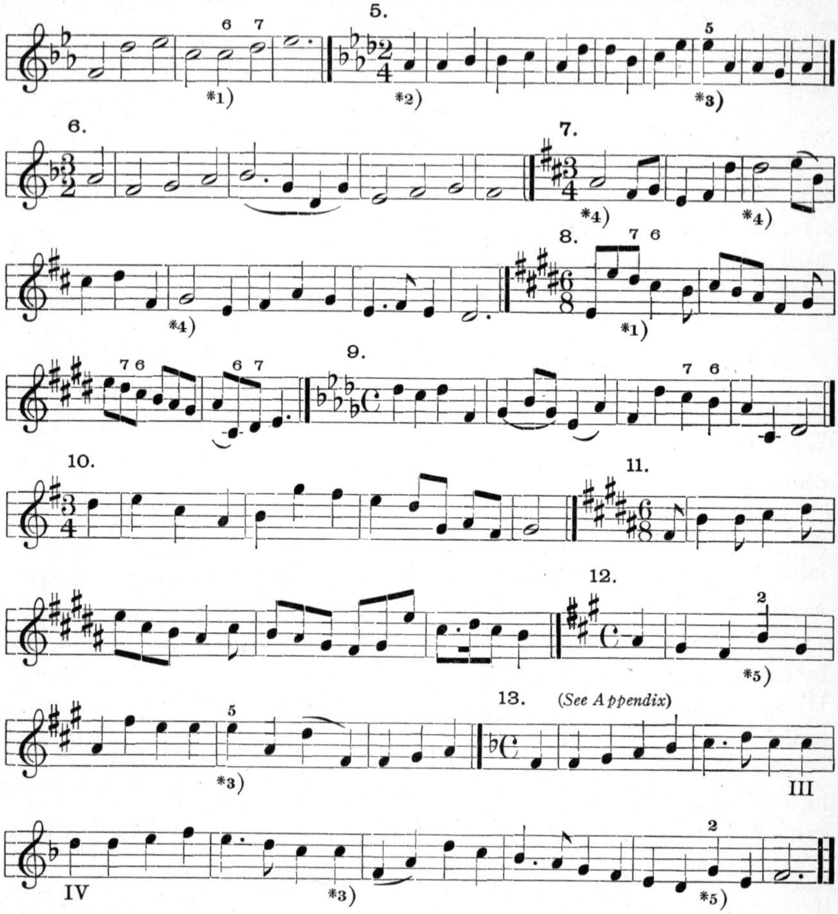
5.
6.
7.
8.
9.
10.
11.
12.
13. (See Appendix)
III
IV

*1) Ex. 78, note *2). — *2) At each of the *repeated* notes in this melody, the chord must be changed. — *3) The III is *possible* here (followed by the VI). — *4) Each of these half-notes may be harmonized either with one chord, or with *two* (as quarter-notes), at option. — *5) This second step must be harmonized with the II (not with the V, because of the wide leap, and foreign progression).

CHAPTER XIV.

SUBORDINATE TRIADS IN MINOR. THE PERIOD-FORM.

111. The notation of the II, VI and III in minor must conform to the harmonic minor scale. Thus:

Ex. 79. C minor

II
VI
III

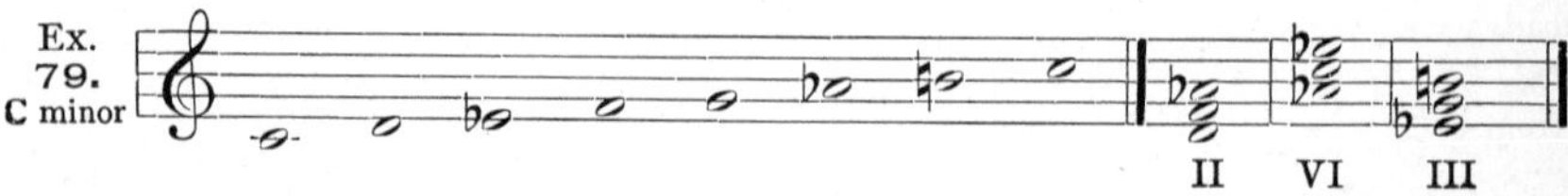

a) The II, having a diminished fifth, is a *diminished* triad. It occurs very rarely in its *fundamental* form (as triad, with root in bass).

b) The III, having an augmented fifth, is an *augmented* triad. It is even less frequent in minor than in major.

c) The VI is a *major* triad, and is of equal importance in both modes.

Review the notes to Ex. 63, N.B., and observe the effect upon the *subordinate* triads of lowering the 3d and 6th steps.

112. The II and III in minor are, therefore, Discords, and cannot be used here. Of the three subordinate chords in minor **only the VI may be used at present.** See par. 92, which applies also to the VI.

THE PERIOD-FORM.

113. When a musical sentence is eight measures in length, it usually separates into *two* four-measure phrases. The first of these is called **the Antecedent** phrase; the second, the **Consequent** phrase.

114. The division is made by a cadence in the middle of the sentence (on an accent of the fourth measure), which is called the **Semicadence**, and differs from the perfect cadence in being made upon some lighter form of harmony.

115. The semicadence is most frequently made **upon the V** (preceded by the IV, II, VI, or I). But any other chord may be chosen, excepting the III; and it is sometimes the I itself, with *third or fifth* in soprano (not with the root).

The semicadence chord must be *longer* than the adjacent chords (similar in length to the perfect-cadence chord), in order to interrupt the rhythm, and mark the end of the Antecedent.

More rarely, the whole Period is only four measures long, in which case the Antecedent phrase will contain only two measures. Comp. par. 65. The following illustration is a small (two-measure) Antecedent; that is, the semicadence falls in the second measure:

Ex. 80.

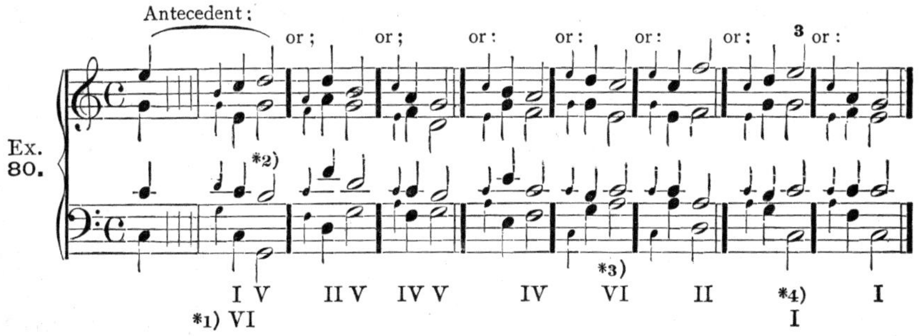

*1) Or the VI, by taking *a* in bass. — *2) The semicadence chord. — *3) The semicadence on the VI is called "deceptive," because V–VI is substituted for the *expected* V–I. — *4) This semicadence, on the I, is sometimes called an "imperfect cadence," as it is prevented from being a perfect cadence only by the absence of the *root in soprano.*

116. The second phrase (the *Consequent*) should begin on the same beat as the Antecedent (with any convenient chord), and must close with the perfect cadence, on the same accent as the Antecedent, which it must exactly equal in length. The Antecedent sketched in Ex. 80 might be continued as follows:

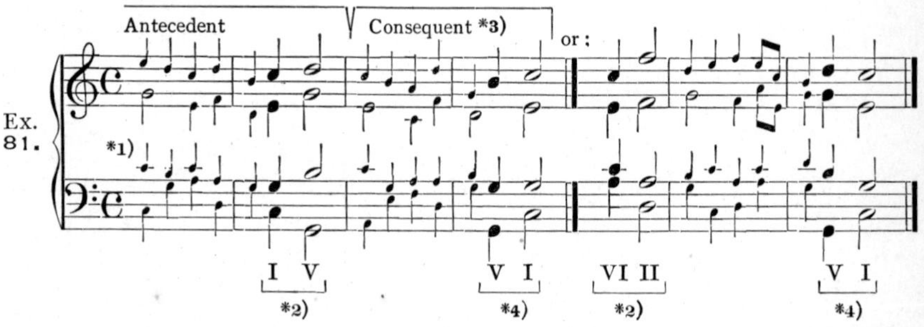

*1) Compare these 4 measures with the 4-measure melodies of Lessons 10, 11 and 13, and observe the distinction between the Phrase (as *uninterrupted* chord-series), and the Period (or Double-phrase), with its semicadence in the middle. Not the number of measures, but the presence or absence of a semicadence defines the form. — *2) Semicadence. — *3) The melody of this Consequent phrase runs parallel with that of the Antecedent. This is favorable, but not obligatory. Comp. par. 42*c*. — *4) Perfect cadence.

LESSON 14.

A. Re-harmonize Lesson 11, Nos. 6, 7, 9, 11, 12 — introducing the VI at least once in each melody.

B. Write a number of Original 8-measure Periods, in *major;* and a few in *minor*, with the three principal triads and an occasional VI.

C. Write out the following series of chords, in 4-part harmony as usual, formulated in Phrases of 4 measures:

I-V-VI-IV-V-I-V-I

Use the following forms (the *rhythm*, *location of bars*, and *chord-repetitions* being optional):

1. C minor, 2-4 measure, beginning on heavy beat;
2. A minor, 3-4 measure, beginning on light beat;
3. F-sharp minor, 4-4 measure, beginning on heavy beat.

Directions: 1. First fix the *bars*. These may be drawn between *any of the given chords*, almost unlimited option being possible. But care must be taken to preserve the sum of four measures, and to locate the Cadence properly. 2. Determine the number of *melody-tones* for each measure; this will decide the number of *chord-repetitions* that may be necessary, and the *rhythm*. 3. Write out the bass; then the soprano; and then finish.

CHAPTER XV.

CHORD-INVERSION.

117. The fundamental forms hitherto employed (with the root in bass) are naturally strong and heavy, but also to a certain degree inflexible and ungraceful. Therefore it is not only admissible, but often desirable, to modify the form of a triad *by placing either its third or its fifth in the bass, instead of the root, thus effecting the* **inversion** *of the chord.*

This is touched upon in par. 25, which see.

118. This alteration of the lowermost part *affords the bass similar opportunities for smooth and graceful melodic progression* (instead of the almost constant succession of wide leaps).

119. When the bass thus assumes the **third** of the triad, the latter stands in the **first inversion.** For illustration:

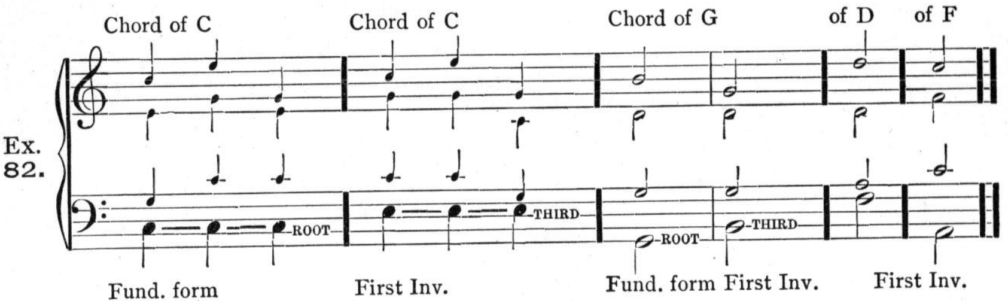

120. The first Inversion of a triad is designated **"chord of the sixth,"** because the *shape* of the triad (as regards its component intervals from the *bass tone upward*) has changed from "root—3d—5th," to "bass tone—3d—*6th*":

The figure 6, when attached to any bass note (usually below it) will therefore serve to indicate that the *first inversion* of the chord is required; or, in other words, that the bass note in question is not the root (as hitherto), but the **third** of the chord;—the root must therefore be sought *a 3d below* the given bass tone:

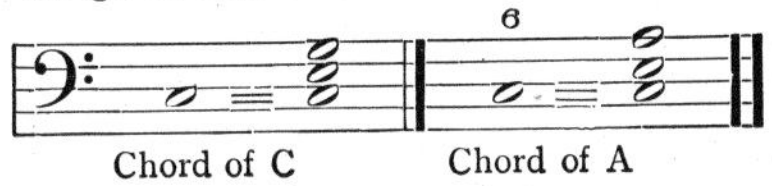

CHORDS OF THE SIXTH.

121. Rule I. In a chord of the 6th, the *soprano usually takes the root*—or, if more convenient, the *fifth* of the chord. But rarely the *third*, which should not appear simultaneously in both soprano and bass. Ex. 84*a*.

Rule II. Double, as usual, *any of the principal tones of the scale* (tonic, dominant, or subdominant—par. 56*a*). That is, either the root or the fifth; or even the third, in a subordinate sixth.

In other words, the rules of duplication, in the first inversion, are less strict than in the triads, and subserve, chiefly, the purpose of *good, smooth melodic progression.* Ex. 84*b*.

RULE III. In an inversion, *no interval should be omitted.*

RULE IV. Change the *bass tone* at each accent, and change the chord also if possible. For illustration:

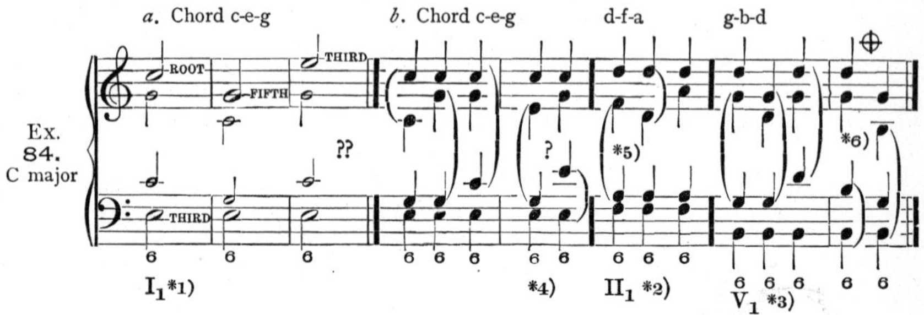

*1) In C major, c-e-g is the tonic chord, or I. With *e* (the third) in bass, it is the 1st inversion; this is indicated by I_1 (spoken: **One-one**), and figured 6. — *2) The II (d-f-a) with *f* in bass; hence II_1 (**Two-one**). — *3) The V (g-b-d) with *b* in bass, hence V_1 (**Five-one**). — *4) Doubtful, because *e* is doubled. — *5) These three duplications are all admissible. — *6) Doubled leading-tone — always wrong.

122. The first inversions of the I, V, IV and II are excellent, and should be freely used. But the first inversion of the subordinate VI and III must be shunned.

123. Applying the principle of first inversion to the following chord-series,

I | V–I | IV–II | V–V | I ||

the results would be:

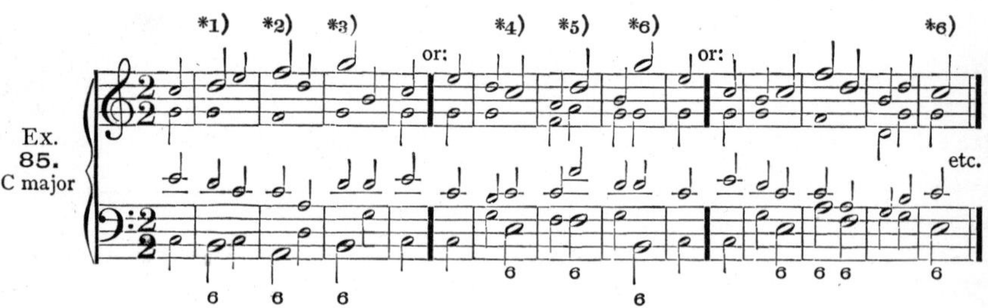

*1) The V (g-b-d), with the third in bass and fifth in soprano. — *2) IV (f-a-c), third in bass, root in soprano. — *3) V_1 — root in sopr. — *4) I_1 — root in sopr. — *5) II_1 — root in sopr. — *6) In a *complete* phrase, neither of the two cadence-chords should be inverted.

Furthermore (the bass alone):

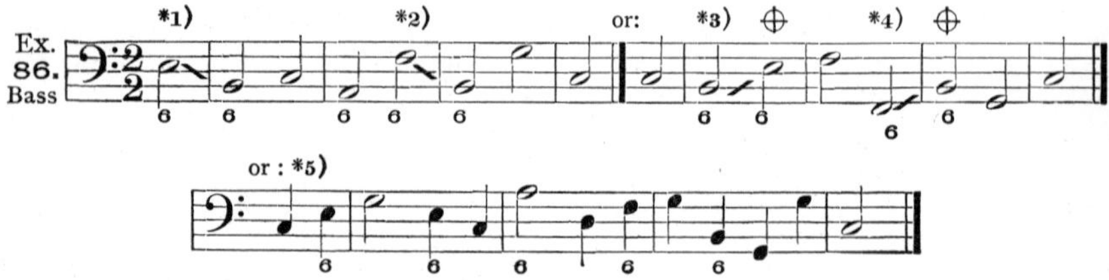

*1) In a complete phrase, the *first* chord is not inverted. *2) This *descending* leap to the leading-tone is admissible. See Ex. 34. — *3) This progression violates par. 63. — *4) The *ascending* leap to the leading-tone is wrong. Comp. note *2). — *5) This version illustrates how *both* chord-forms may appear, as repetition, during the same beat.

LESSON 15.

A. Construct complete 4-measure phrases in A major, E-flat major, F major and D major, 3-4 measure, with the following chords:

I | I-I-VI | V-I-IV | I-II-V | I ||

using occasional chords of the 6th (i.e., the third in bass) as shown in Exs. 85, 86. Remember that the VI is not to be inverted. Also, that the first chord and the last two chords are not inverted. Place the figure 6 below the bass at each first inversion, as in Exs. 85, 86.

B. Construct complete 4-measure phrases in E minor, D minor, B minor and F minor, 4-4 measure, with the following chords:

I | V-V-I-I | IV-IV-V-V | I-VI-IV-V | I ||

utilizing the first inversion as before.

CHAPTER XVI.

CHORDS OF THE SIXTH. MELODIES.

124. The chord-basis of the given melody is defined in the usual manner, according to the Table in Ex. 78, without reference to inversion. This being done, choice is made between the root or the third of the chord, *in bass*, as shown above.

The root is generally chosen in bass when the soprano has the *third* (or fifth) of the chord; *the third is taken in bass most commonly when the soprano has the root of the chord* — more rarely, when the fifth is in soprano. Review par. 121, Rule I.

125. Assuming the chord-basis of melody No. 1, Lesson 13 (slightly modified) to be as follows,

the bass voice might run thus:

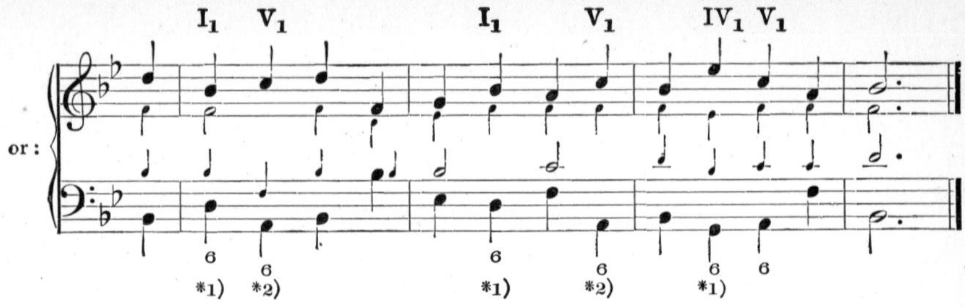

*1) Root in soprano, *third in bass.* — *2) Fifth in soprano, third in bass; good, but less common, and only in *principal* chords.

126. Another important advantage of inversion is, that it facilitates the chord-progressions.

All objectionable triad-progressions become possible when the second chord of the succession is inverted.

For example:

SUCCESSIVE SIXTHS.

127. From the above it follows that chords of the sixth may be connected *with each other, in any order.* Such "lines of 6ths" are common in music, and very effective; but they are subject to the following rules:

a) The bass should move smoothly *along the scale,* or, at most, with a narrow leap. A wide leap, from one 6th to another, is very rare (but see Ex. 85, third version, chords 3 and 4; and Ex. 86, chords 1–2, 4–5–6).

b) The root should always be in the soprano, so that *bass and soprano run parallel in 6ths.*

c) Care must be taken to avoid *absolute* parallel movement in all four parts.

d) Further, even the forbidden VI_1 and III_1 (par. 122) may appear in such a line of 6ths — that is, when *followed* by another chord of the 6th. Thus:

*1) This might also be a 6th (I_1), but the triad is better, after so many inversions; and the progression III_1–VI is correct. — *2) Par. 127*d*. — *3) Par. 127*b*. — *4) Par. 127*c*. Note how the tenor is obliged to leap, in order to avoid parallel octaves and fifths with the other parts. — *5) Par. 127*c*. Such absolute parallel movement in *all four parts* is tempting, but wholly wrong in strict part-writing. — *6) Par. 127*a*.

SEQUENCES.

128. *a.* The reproduction of a cluster of tones on the *same steps* constitutes a simple **repetition:**

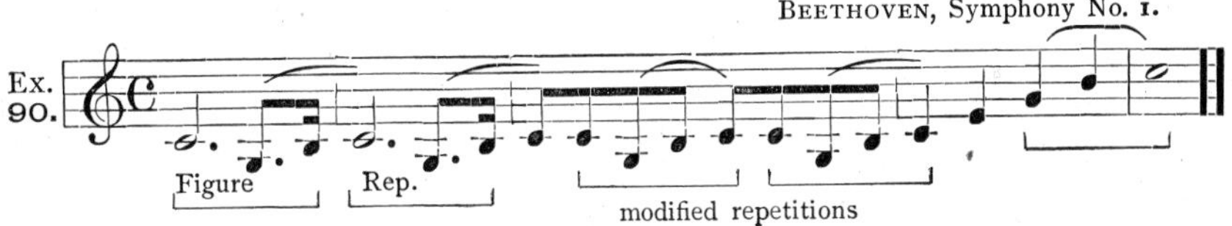

b. The reproduction of a figure or cluster of tones upon other, *higher or lower*, steps, is called a **sequence:**

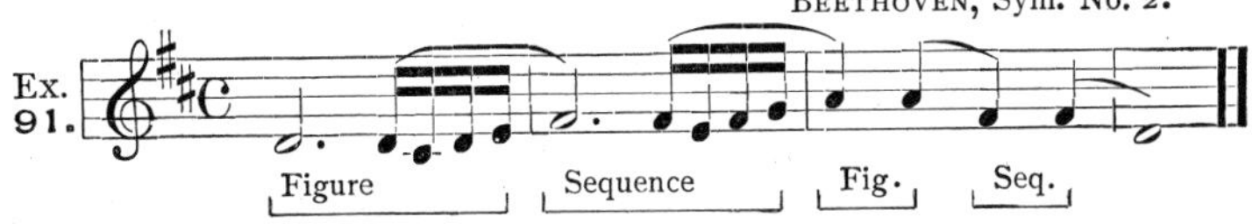

129. Such symmetrical recurrences as these *justify any reasonable irregularity of melody, harmony, or rhythm.* See par. 52. For example:

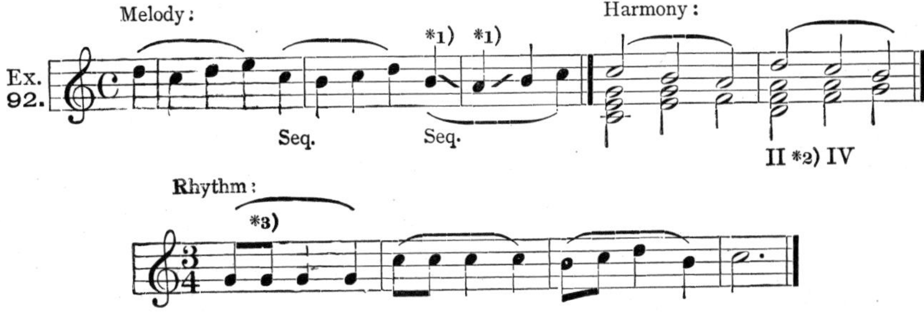

*1) This extremely irregular melodic progression (7–6–7, see par. 63) is justified by the sequence. — *2) An exception to Ex. 69, note *3), permissible because of its sequential relation to the preceding measure. — *3) Like Ex. 22, note *3), which see.

130. When the sequential form is adhered to in *all four parts*, the result is a complete *harmonic* sequence.

Such chord-clusters in sequential succession are generally good, regardless of the rules of regular chord-progression, excepting when the triad on the leading-tone (Ex. 19, note *2) is involved. When this occurs, the sequence is either abandoned, or altered.

Sequences rarely extend beyond three (or four) recurrences.

In minor they are less common than in major.

For illustration (sequences, with triads and chords of the 6th):

*1) Leading-tone triad. In this case the sequence would be altered to the next higher step. — *2) This is the connection of a triad and 6th upon the same bass tone. The figure 5 (before 6) is necessary, to indicate the change in shape, and the progression 5-6, which occurs in the soprano. — *3) Here the sequence is shifted to an unexpected *higher* step. At the same time, the relative position of the inner parts is altered; but the harmonic form as a whole remains the same as in the first group. — *4) The inner parts are altered.

LESSON 16.

A. Re-harmonize, with triads and chords of the 6th, Lesson 10, melodies 1, 2, 3, 4, 8. — Lesson 11, melodies 2, 4, 6. — Lesson 13, melodies 2, 3, 5.

B. Harmonize the following:

4.
*1)
*2)
II1
5.
*3)
*2)
II1
6.
7.
*2)
*4)
6 6 6 6
8.
*4)
6
9.
*4)
6 6 6 6
6 6 6 6 6 6
*1)
6
*5)
10.
*2)
6 6 6 6 Seq. Seq.
*6)
*1)
V-II1
I-V1
11.
II1
6 6 6 6
12.
*5)
6
II1
I I1 IV Seq. Seq. I IV1 II1 Seq.

*1) The semicadence (par. 115). — *2) The II may be freely used in minor, **when inverted.** See par. 112, and comp. par. 126. Also par. 166*a*. Even the inverted III is available in minor, but the occasion for it is very rare. — *3) This may be the VI_1, if the following chord is the V_1. See par. 127*d*. — *4) The tones under the bracket are to be harmonized with successive 6ths. Review par. 127. — *5) To be harmonized as harmonic sequence of the preceding figure. — *6) An example of irregular rhythm, justified by recurrence in the following measure, and in measures 5 and 6 (par. 129). — *7) A different *bass tone* for each repeated tone, throughout this melody.

C. Extend the following measures in exact sequences, at the keyboard:

CHAPTER XVII.

CHORDS OF THE SIX-FOUR.

131. When the bass assumes the **fifth** of the triad, the latter stands in the **second inversion.** Compare par. 119. For example:

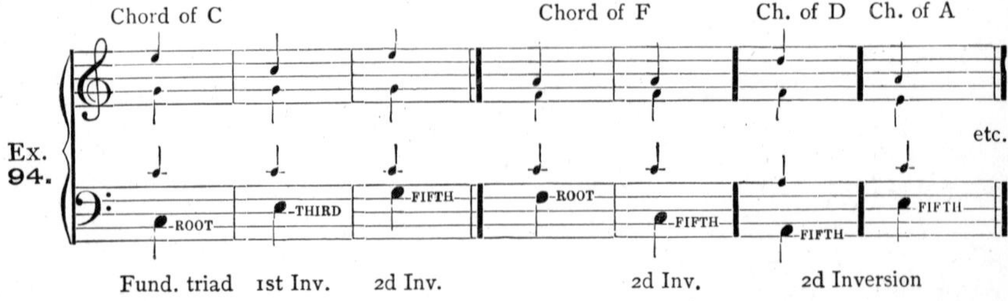

132. The second Inversion of a triad is designated "**chord of the six-four**" because the *shape* has changed from "root — 3d — 5th," to " bass tone — 4th — 6th":

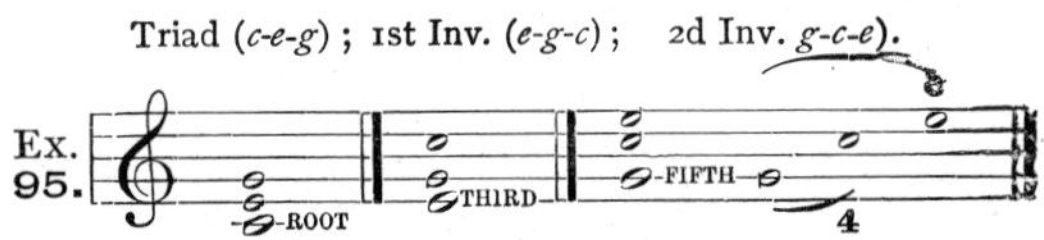

The figures 6-4, when attached to any bass tone, therefore serve to indicate that the *second inversion* is required; i.e., that the bass note in question is not the root, nor the third, (as hitherto), but the **fifth** of the chord. The root must therefore be sought *a 5th below* the given bass note:

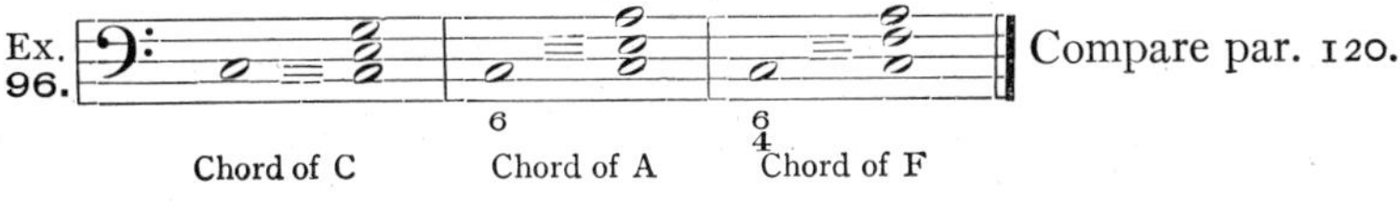

THE TONIC 6-4 CHORD.

133. The second inversion is the *weakest* (though not the least useful) form of a chord, and is therefore subject to many restrictions. A second inversion is never employed to represent or substitute its own fundamental chord, but only for the purpose of *harmonic embellishment.* The best six-four chord is the second inversion of the **tonic triad**; i.e., the I_2 (I in second inversion; or "**One-two**"; comp. Ex. 84, note *1).

134. The tonic 6–4 chord may be connected (preceding or following):

With the triad on the same bass tone, namely, the V.

This may occur anywhere in the course of a phrase or period, but it is of peculiar importance at the semicadence, and at the perfect cadence. For illustration (both major and minor):

*1) This chord does not produce a genuine tonic impression, but merely that of a casual embellishment of the dominant harmony. — *2) Note the figuring. When the *shape* of a chord changes while the *bass tone is held,* sufficient figures must be used to indicate the change, and where it takes place. Here, 5/3 denotes the triad form. — *3) The bass tone is repeated over the bar, contrary to par. 121, Rule IV. It is therefore evident that this connection, V–I_2–V, can not take place *over an accent.*

135. The use of the connection I_2–V at (or near) the cadences, is shown in the following 4-measure period:

136. The tonic 6-4 chord is furthermore connected, before or after: **With any other form of the same chord, as repetition.**
Thus (major and minor):

This, and the preceding connection, together:

137. The tonic 6-4 chord may, finally, be also connected, before and after: **With the triad, or chord of the 6th, upon the next higher or next lower bass tone; that is, along the scale, in bass.**
For illustration:

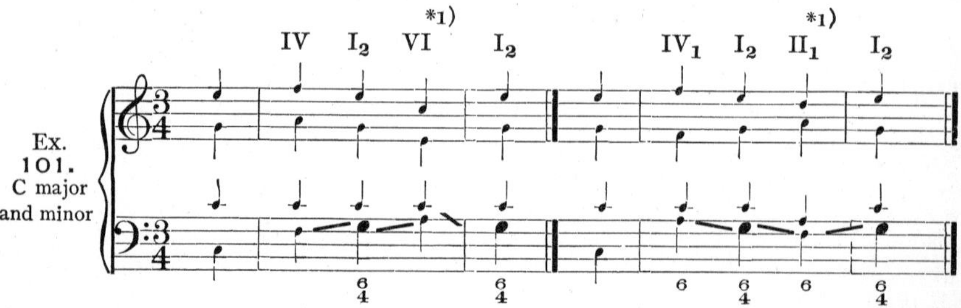

*1) VI–I_2, and II_1–I_2. Both exceptional chord-progressions, justified by inversion. — *2) These parallel 5ths are very insidious. More than ordinary caution must be exercised in *all* connections of I–II or II–I in major. In **minor,** however, one of these 5ths is "imperfect" (the diminished 5th in the II), and the parallels are therefore not objectionable. — *3) Six-four chords cannot appear in succession (unlike the 6ths), because of the weakness of the successive chord-fifths in bass.

138. These three connections of the tonic 6-4 chord constitute the basis upon which the movements of **all second inversions** are regulated. Hence the following deductions are applicable to second inversions in general:

RULE I. Six-four chords can neither enter nor progress with a *skip in the bass voice,* excepting when a repetition. That is, the bass is either *stationary,* or is limited to *diatonic* (step-wise) progression, or leaps along its own chord-line.

RULE II. Six-four chords must be connected with *triads or 6ths;* not with other 6-4 chords.

RULE III. In six-four chords, the **bass tone** (the chord-fifth) is almost invariably doubled. See also par. 121, Rule III.

139. One exception to Rule I, above, is applicable to the *tonic* 6-4 chord only, in the major mode, namely: A leap in bass from the II to the I_2, when the latter is *accented.* Thus:

LESSON 17.

A. Write out the following chord-progressions in at least four major keys, in 4-part harmony: V–I_2–V; I–I_2–I_1; IV | $\hat{I}_2$–V; VI–I_2–I_1; IV_1–I_2–VI; II_1 | $\hat{I}_2$–V; II | $\hat{I}_2$–V.

B. Play all the above chords (excepting the last one), in the corresponding minor keys.

C. Construct 4-measure phrases in G minor, A minor, F-sharp minor, and B-flat minor, (3–4 measure) with the following chords: I | V–I–V | I–I–I | IV–I–V | I ||, substituting I_2 for I at option. D. Construct 4-measure phrases in F and D major (4–4 measure) with the following chords: I | IV_1–I–II_1–I–V | VI–IV–I–V | VI–I–I–I | I–V–I ||, substituting I_2 for I where desirable *or necessary.*

CHAPTER XVIII.

OTHER SIX-FOUR CHORDS. MELODIES.

140. The next 6-4 chord in order of importance and frequency is that of the **subdominant** (IV_2). Its treatment is as follows:

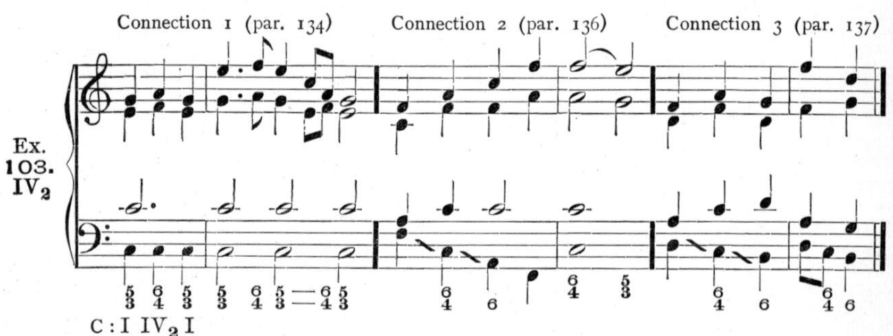

141. The **dominant** 6-4 chord (V_2), though a principal chord, is one of the weakest and least common of second inversions. Unlike the I_2 and IV_2, which appear equally well accented or unaccented, the V_2 is usually *unaccented*. It is limited chiefly to the *diatonic* progression (scale-line in bass). For example:

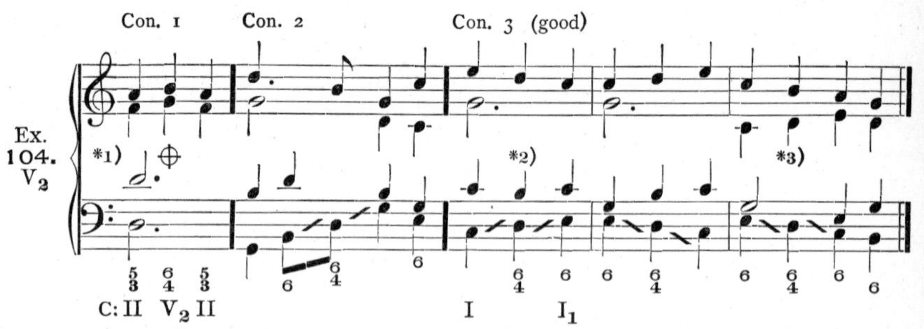

*1) Wrong, for obvious melodic and harmonic reasons. — *2) The 6-4 chord stands, as *passing* chord, between a triad and its first inversion. This is always effective, when possible. It is seen (with the I_2) in Ex. 101, group 5. — *3) The 6-4 stands, as *passing* chord, between two chords of the 6th; also good, but less frequent than the preceding.

142. The subordinate 6-4 chords are rare. The best one is, probably, the II_2, which is connected as follows:

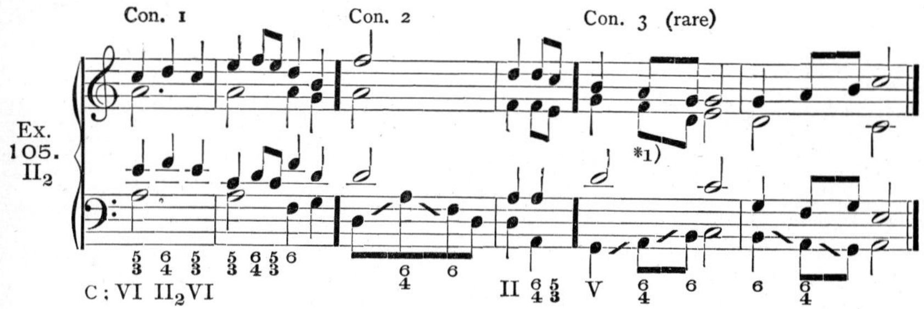

*1) See Ex. 104, note *2).

143. The VI₂ is fairly good, especially as *passing* chord. Review par. 122, and note that while the first inversion of the VI is very rare, the second inversion may be used effectively. For example:

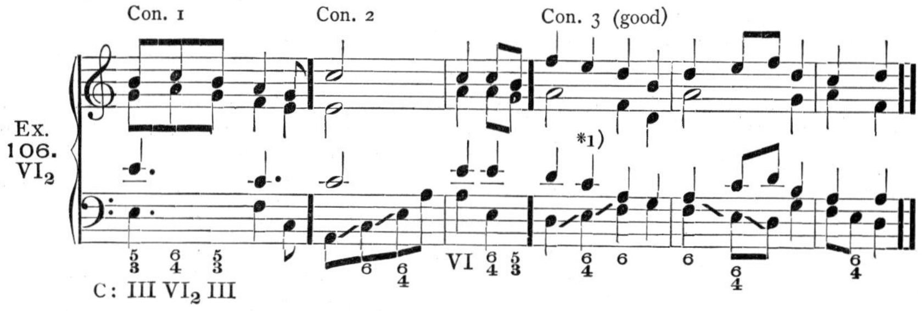

*1) See Ex. 104, note *2).

144. The III₂ is extremely rare; it may be used only as *passing* chord, after the triad I. Thus:

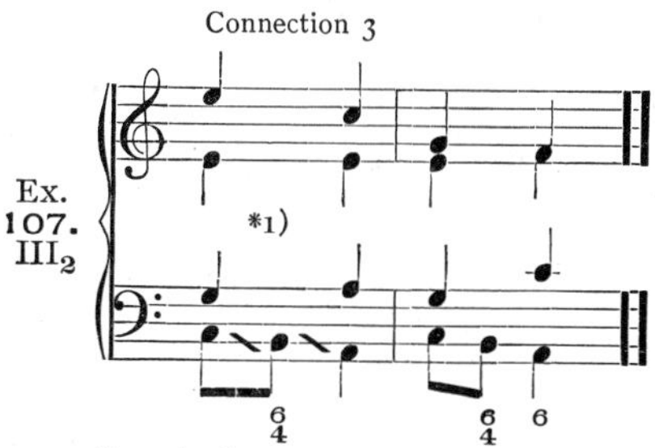

*1) The 6–4 chord passes diatonically *downward from a triad;* this connection is generally made in a single beat, and it will be noticed that the *root* of the triad is not *doubled* — in order not to interfere with the bass tone of the 6–4. See also Ex. 101, group 6; Ex. 103, last measure; Ex. 106, last measure.

145. The above examples refer to the major mode. But they are valid for minor also, *excepting where the* II *or* III *occur, and where the 6th and 7th steps appear in succession;* these are limited to major.

For instance, Ex. 103, connection 3 — doubtful in minor, because the II is not inverted; Ex. 104, last measure — steps 7–6 in soprano; Ex. 105, connection 3 — steps 6–7, 7–6, in soprano and bass; Exs. 106 and 107 are good only in major.

146. When a six-four chord occupies an *accented beat*, it evinces a strong inclination to progress into the triad of the *same bass tone*. Thus:

Ex. 108.

*1)
C: I 6/4 5/3 6/4 6 IV 6/4 5/3 VI 6/4 5/3 II 6/4 5/3

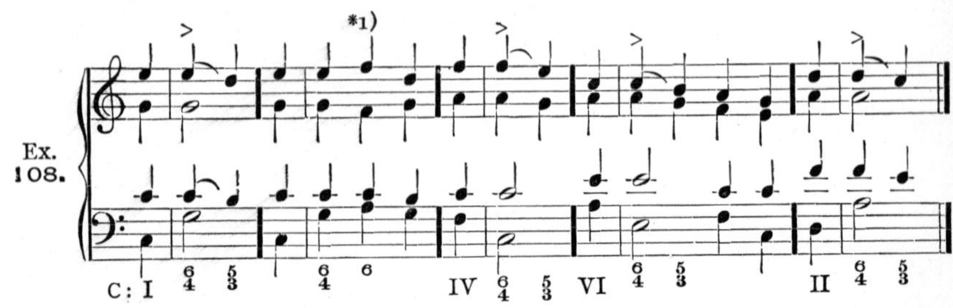

*1) This IV_1 sounds like an *interposed* chord which only defers the natural progression I_2–V.

LESSON 18.

A. Re-harmonize, with triads and both inversions, Lesson 10, Nos. 1, 2, 3, 5, 16.— Lesson 11, Nos. 1, 6, 12.— Lesson 13, Nos. 1, 5, 6.— Lesson 16, Nos. 2, 4. *First review par. 138*, especially Rule 111.

B. Harmonize the following:

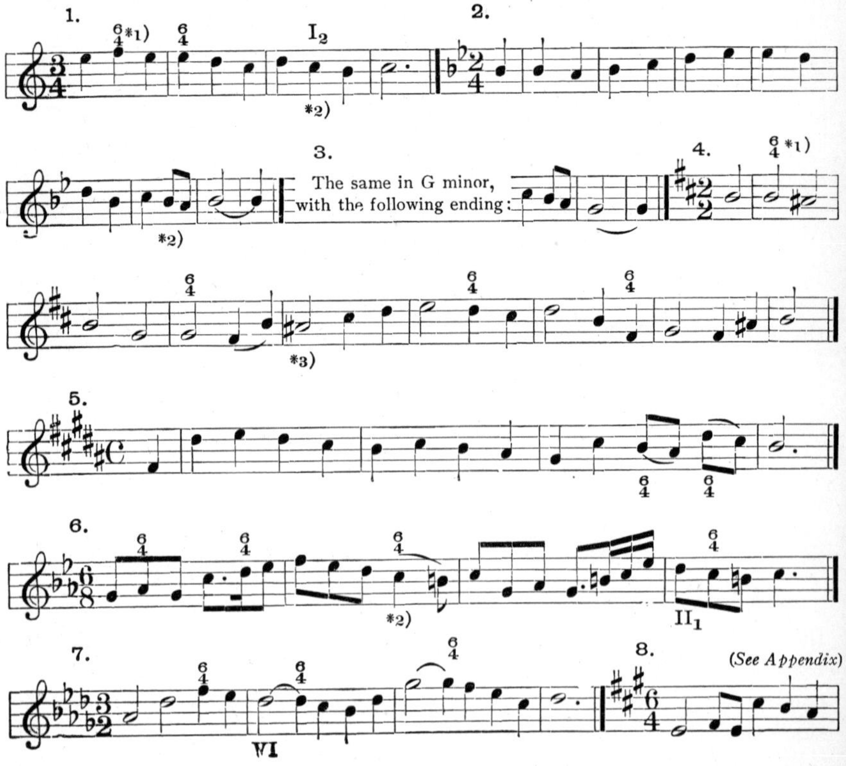

1.
6/4 *1)
6/4
I2
*2)
2.
3.
*2)
The same in G minor,
with the following ending:
4.
6/4 *1)
6/4
6/4
6/4
*3)
5.
6/4
6/4
6.
6/4
6/4
6/4
*2)
6/4
II1
7.
6/4
6/4
6/4
VI
8.
(See Appendix)

*1) These figures indicate that a 6–4 chord *may* be used. But this is wholly optional; the student *may ignore all these figures*, and harmonize the melody according to his own judgment and preference. — *2) Par. 135. — *3) The semicadence. — *4) Par. 127.

DIVISION TWO.

DISCORD-HARMONIES.

INTRODUCTORY.

147. The possibility of extending the 3-tone fundamental harmonies, by the addition of another (higher) third, was demonstrated in par. 26, which review. The 4-tone chords thus obtained are designated "**chords of the seventh,**" because the new interval (which distinguishes its chord from the consonant triad in extent, harmonic effect, and obligations) is a **seventh:**

148. The 7th is a *dissonant* interval (par. 23), and its adoption transforms the concord into a *Discord;* the pure and simple triad, an independent primary chord, into a restless and dependent harmonic body. The general conditions associated with a discord are given in par. 27, which review. Besides the latter, the following special obligations must be observed:

149. Rule I.

A chord-seventh must progress diatonically downward. This is called its "resolution."

Rule II. The interval of a 7th should not be followed by an 8th, as the succession 7-8 (or 8-7) is usually quite as objectionable as 8-8.

Rule III. A chord-seventh need not, and should not, be *doubled.*

For illustration:

*1) In the chord g-b-d-f, the tone *f* is the *chord-seventh,* and it is therefore *this tone* to which the rules apply. — *2) Called "Unequal octaves."

DISCORD-CLASSES.

150. Any step of the scale — excepting the leading-tone — may become the root of a *triad,* as has been seen (par. 31). But **only four of the seven steps may be the legitimate root of a discord.** These are found, and at the same time classified, in conformity with the law of tone-relation, in degrees of the perfect fifth, above the tonic. Thus:

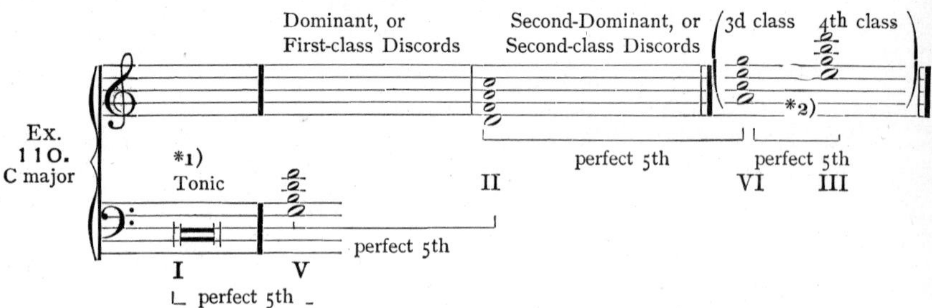

*1) It might be supposed that the *tonic*-discords would be the First, and best, class; but it must be considered that the tonic would inevitably forfeit its independence, and the attribute of repose peculiarly essential to it as "Tonic," the instant it became alloyed with a dissonance. Hence the tonic harmony is exclusively consonant, and for that reason the **First-class** discords must be sought beyond the tonic, namely, upon the **dominant.** (When another 3d is added to the tonic triad, above or below, it ceases to be a tonic-harmony and becomes a Third-class discord.) — *2) The 3d and 4th discord-classes are extremely rare, and scarcely maintain any appreciable connection with their key.

CHAPTER XIX.

THE CHORD OF THE DOMINANT-SEVENTH.

151. The **chord of the seventh upon the dominant** is obtained by adding one higher third to the dominant triad.

a) In keeping with par. 69, Rule III, its natural inclination is toward the *tonic* harmonies. Therefore it resolves into the I (or inversion), and into the VI (triad-form only).

b) The resolution of the dominant-seventh chord into the I is called **normal.** The resolution into the VI is called **deceptive** (comp. Ex. 80, note *3).

c) The form and general treatment of the chord are *identical in major and minor* (comp. par. 90, 92).

d) In the progression V^7–I, when both are *fundamental*, the fifth of either of the two chords is usually omitted, and the root doubled.

For illustration:

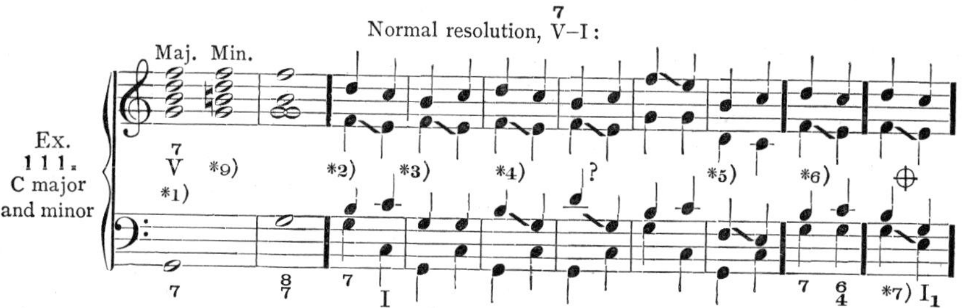

*1) Marked thus: V^7: and called "**Five-seven.**" — *2) Here the chord-fifth (*d*) appears in the V^7, but is omitted in the following I (*g*). See par. 151*d*. — *3) The chord-fifth is omitted in the V^7 and retained in the I. — *4) Both fifths may be obtained, if the leading-tone has a right thus to descend to *g* (Ex. 48, note *2). The next measure is doubtful, though possible. — *5) The seventh may lie in any part. — *6) The V^7 may resolve into the tonic 6–4 chord, with stationary bass. — *7) The resolution into the I_1 is, however, impossible, because of the unequal octaves (par. 149, Rule II). — *8) In the deceptive resolution, neither chord-fifth is omitted. — *9) All these examples are equally good *in minor; the chord-seventh descends either a half-step* (*in major*), *or a whole step* (*in minor*).

152. The manner in which the seventh of the dominant chord is *introduced* is almost entirely optional. The following modes are, however, distinguished:

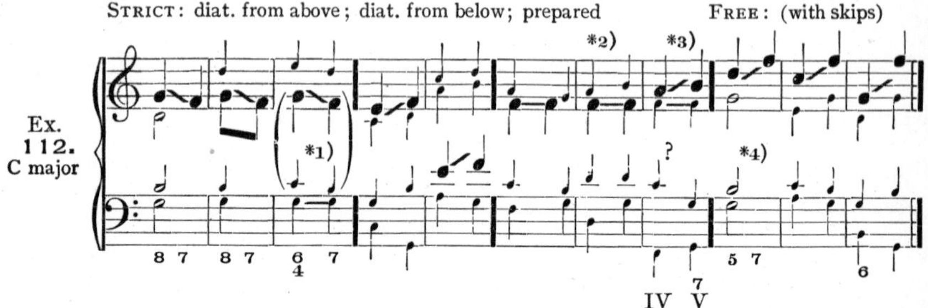

*1) Here parallel 5ths occur, between alto and tenor; they are admissible because one of the 5ths (*b-f*) is not *perfect*. Comp. Ex. 101, note *2). — *2) Comp. Ex. 68, note *4). — *3) Comp. Ex. 51, note *1). This connection, with the V^7, is a trifle better than with the triad V. — *4) A wide leap to the seventh is best made from *below*. Comp. Ex. 34*c*.

LESSON 19.

A. Write out the V^7 in every major and minor key, with its two resolutions (V^7–I and V^7–VI), in ordinary 4-part harmony. — B. Find and play these chords at the pianoforte in the usual manner, without notes. — C. Write out the following *cadence-formulæ*, in a number of different keys (major or minor), measure and rhythm optional:

$\text{I–V–}\overset{7}{\text{V}}$ | I || $\text{IV–I}_2\text{–}\overset{7}{\text{V}}$ | I || $\overset{8}{\text{II}}\text{–VI–}\overset{7}{\text{V}}$ | I || $\overset{5}{\text{III}}\text{–IV–}\overset{7}{\text{V}}$ | I || $\text{VI–II}_1\text{–}\overset{7}{\text{V}}$ | I || $\overset{7}{\text{V}}\text{–VI–IV}_1\text{–}\overset{7}{\text{V}}$ | I ||

CHAPTER XX.

DOMINANT-SEVENTH, AND ITS INVERSIONS.

153. The principle of inversion is applied to 4-tone chords as well as to triads, and is effected in the same manner, namely, by placing the third, fifth or seventh in the bass part, instead of the root. Review pars. 117, 118.

154. The effect of inversion upon chords of the seventh is as follows:

a) When the bass assumes the **third**, the chord stands in **first inversion** (as usual); the root and seventh lie above the bass tone in the intervals of a 6th and a 5th, wherefore the designation "**Chord of the six-five**" is adopted.

b) When the bass has the **fifth**, the chord stands in **second inversion**; the root and seventh lie respectively a 4th and 3d above the bass tone, giving rise to the designation "**Chord of the four-three.**"

c) When the bass has the **seventh**, the chord stands in **third inversion**; the root lies above the bass tone in the interval of a 2d, hence the designation "**Chord of the second.**" For illustration:

Fund. chord (*g-b-d-f*) First **inv.** (*b-d-f-g*) Second **inv.** (*d-f-g-b*) Third **inv.** (*f-g-b-d*)

*1) The complete figuring (including the note *d* also) would be, $\frac{6}{\frac{5}{3}}$; but it is only necessary to indicate the *root and seventh*, as these define both the *name and quality* of the chord. These two tones (in this case *f-g*) are contiguous, and therefore easily distinguishable. In the first inversion they are at the *top*, in the second inversion in the *middle*, and in the third inversion at the *bottom* of the chord-form; thus:

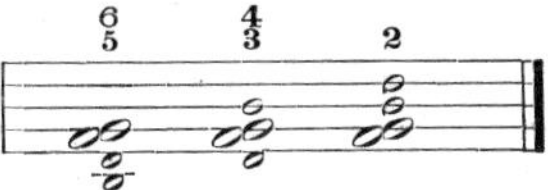

155. These various forms of the dominant-seventh chord are extremely important in harmony, and though differing apparently but little in effect, they possess, respectively, marked *individual* characteristics, which are of significance to the discriminating composer. Their treatment is governed as follows:

Rule I. The chord-seventh resolves as before, *diatonically downward.*

Rule II. In the inversions, *no interval should be omitted.*

Rule III. The inversions of the V^7 are limited **almost exclusively to the normal resolution** (into I or I_1); that is, only the V^7 *itself* can pass into the VI.

Rule IV. The treatment is identical in major and minor.

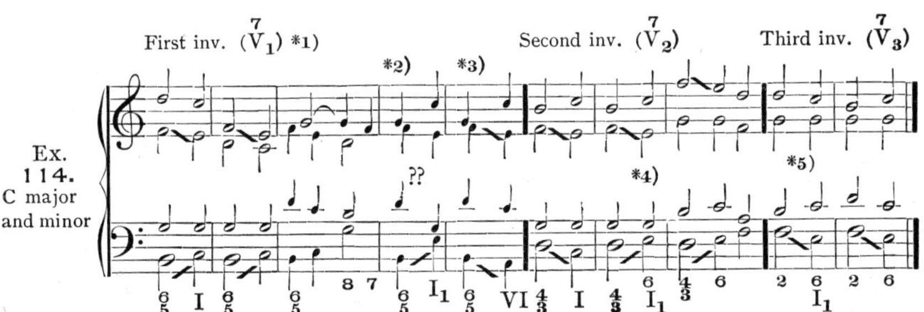

*1) $\overset{7}{V_1}$—spoken **"Five-seven-one."** — *2) An awkward skip from the leading-tone (in bass). — *3) The Deceptive resolution of the *first inversion* of the V^7, into the VI, is possible in *major only*, and very rare. The parallel 5ths which must result (in this case they are in alto and bass) are not inadmissible, because one of them (*b-f*) is not a *perfect* 5th. — *4) The second inversion of the V^7 may resolve into either the I or I_1. In the latter case, the third of the I must be doubled. — *5) The third inversion can resolve *only* into the I_1, on account of the seventh in bass.

156. The introduction of the inversions corresponds to that of the V^7 itself. For illustration (comp. Ex. 112):

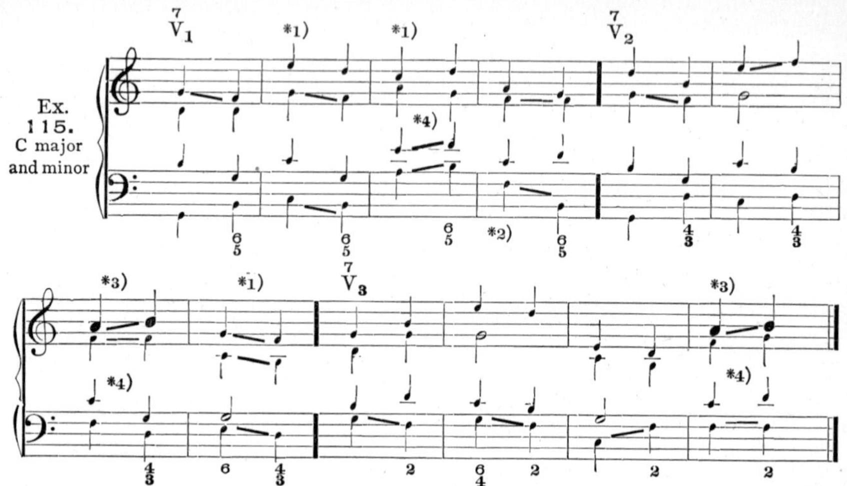

*1) In each of these cases parallel 5ths occur; they are all allowable, because one of the 5ths (*b-f*) is not *perfect.* — *2) Ex. 34, *a.* — *3) Ex. 112, note *3). — *4) Major only.

LESSON 20.

A. Write out the following chords, in 4-part harmony as usual; the soprano optional: (G major and minor) I–$\overset{7}{V}_1$–I; (F major and minor) I_1–$\overset{7}{V}_1$–I; (D major and minor) IV–$\overset{7}{V}_1$–I; (B-flat major) VI–$\overset{7}{V}_1$–I ; I–$\overset{7}{V}_1$–VI ; (A major and minor) I–$\overset{7}{V}_2$–I_1 ; (E-flat major and minor) I_1–$\overset{7}{V}_2$–I ; (E major and minor) IV–$\overset{7}{V}_2$–I ; II_1–$\overset{7}{V}_2$–I_1; (A-flat major) V–$\overset{7}{V}_3$–I_1; (B major and minor) I_2–$\overset{7}{V}_3$–I_1; (F-sharp major and minor) I–$\overset{7}{V}_3$–I_1; (D-flat major) IV–$\overset{7}{V}_3$–I_1; (G-flat major) II_1–$\overset{7}{V}_3$–I_1.

B. Find and play these chords at the pianoforte in the usual manner.

CHAPTER XXI.

DOMINANT-SEVENTH AND INVERSIONS. MELODIES.

157. In applying the dom.-seventh chord and its inversions to the harmonization of melody, the following facts must be recalled:

a) **First:** that the $\overset{7}{V}$ is simply an extended form of the dominant *triad;* therefore it harmonizes the 5th, 7th and 2d steps of the scale, as substitute for the V. For illustration:

Compare these two versions carefully; note that the chord basis is exactly the same, but the seventh is simply added, in each case, to the dominant triad. This is not always feasible, or necessary; but generally so.

b) **Second:** that the $\overset{7}{V}$ contains, besides the tones of the dom. triad, the additional *chord-seventh*, which is the *fourth step of the scale.* Therefore the 4th step may be harmonized, not only by the *subdominant* chords IV and II as heretofore, but also by the *dom.-seventh* chord. The choice is determined chiefly by the *direction* in which the 4th step progresses; it is only when it *descends diatonically* that the $\overset{7}{V}$ can be employed for this step. In other words, steps 4-3 are favorable for the $\overset{7}{V}$ and I (or VI). The inversion depends upon the melodic movement of the bass; the *third* inversion is impossible, because of the chord-seventh in the soprano. For illustration:

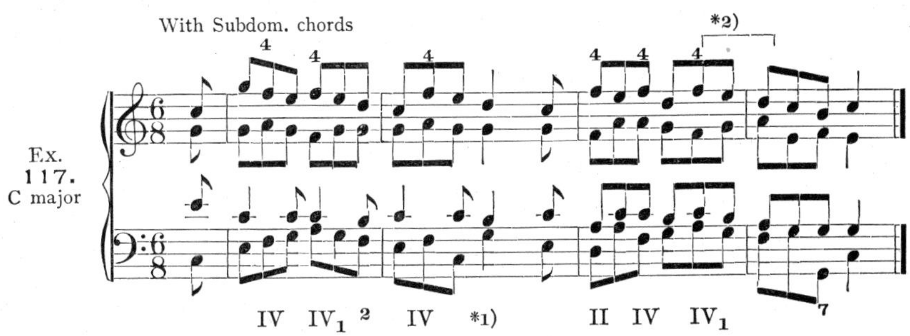

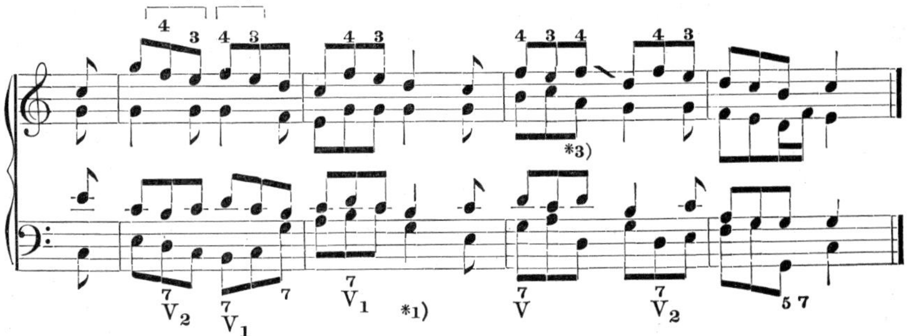

*1) It is not advisable to use a dom.-*seventh* at the semicadence; the dom. *concord* (i.e., the triad) is preferable for this point of repose, because less active. — *2) A line of 6ths (Ex. 89). — *3) Here, the 4th step in the melody must be harmonized with II or IV, because it *leaps* downward to *d*.

LESSON 21.

A. Harmonize the following melodies, with the $\overset{7}{V}$ and its inversions; and with reference to this summarized table:

*1) This mark indicates the semicadence. See Ex. 117, note *1). — *2) At each of these rests, the bass begins on the first beat (as whole note), and the three upper parts follow on the second beat.

B. Re-harmonize Lesson 10, Nos. 2, 7, 11, 16. — Lesson 13, Nos. 4, 9. — Lesson 16, Nos. 2, 8. — Lesson 18, Nos. 2, 5, 7.

LESSON 22.

*1) One chord, or two, at option. — *2) One bass tone (*e-flat*) for both of these notes. Comp. Ex. 93, note *2). — *3) The slurs indicate, as usual, that the chord remains the same. The lower parts may change, or may be simply *held;* the latter is preferable, almost regardless of duplications, as such active melodic figures should be harmonized as quietly as possible. — *4) At each repeated tone throughout this melody the *bass note* must be changed.

CHAPTER XXII.

DOM.-SEVENTH. LICENCES OF CHORD-REPETITION.

158. When the chord of the dom.-seventh is **repeated,** the following liberties may be taken with the chord-seventh:

a) During the repetition of the $\overset{7}{\text{V}}$, *the seventh may pass* **downward** to *any other interval of the chord.* This is possible in any part, and is equivalent **to resolution.**

*1) The seventh disappears; $\overset{7}{\text{V}}$ becomes V — another form of the *same chord.* — *2) Here the seventh reappears, in another part. — *3) Carefully note the manner of *figuring the bass*. These figures should indicate all the essential tones, and, generally, the manner in which they *move*.

b) Much more rarely, the seventh may pass **upward**, when the chord is repeated, but only in an *inner part*, as a rule.

If the seventh passes upward, *in soprano or in bass*, it should immediately *turn back*, if possible into the resolving-tone.

*1) Better, because the seventh, after ascending, *returns to the resolving-tone.* — *2) The seventh resolves where it last appears. — *3) In the *outer* parts, the resolving-tone must follow immediately, as here. — *4) This is wrong, because both parts aim for the resolving-tone, and make unequal octaves. — *5) The ascending seventh, *in bass especially,* **must** return to the resolving-tone.

LESSON 23.

*1) One bass note, at each of these slurs. — *2) A different bass note for each repeated tone, throughout this melody. — *3) The lower parts as quiet as possible. A single bass tone is possible, though not imperative. An occasional irregular duplication is freely permissible — even that of the chord-seventh and leading-tone — when the melody thus "breaks" the chord.

LESSON 24.

Construct 4-measure phrases with the following chords, in duple and triple measure alternately, and in at least 4 alternate major and minor keys; the *rhythm*, the *chord-form* and the *inversions* (bass) *of every V* optional, as usual. See directions, Lesson 14 C.

I-V-V-V-I-V-I-IV-II_1-V-V-V-V-I.

CHAPTER XXIII.

OTHER LICENCES. THE STATIONARY RESOLUTION. ASCENDING RESOLUTION.

159. Besides the above licences, naturally attendant upon chord-repetition, there are two others of a more irregular nature, namely, the **stationary seventh**, and the **ascending resolution**.

160. The chord-seventh may be *held* (in the same part) while the $\overset{7}{V}$ progresses into either of the **subdominant** chords (IV or II). The harmonic progressions $\overset{7}{V}$–IV, and $\overset{7}{V}$–II, are exceptions to par. 69, Rule III; but they are rendered feasible by the connecting-link which the stationary seventh provides. Being "irregular," however, they produce the best impression, as a rule, when followed by a *return to the dominant harmony.*

RULE. The chord-seventh, during this change of harmony, *must remain undisturbed in the same voice;* and it must not be *doubled.* For example:

*1) After the irregular progression $\overset{7}{V}$–IV, the $\overset{7}{V}$ returns. — *2) The stationary 7th is possible in any part, but rare in bass. — *3) Here the stationary 7th is followed by a tonic chord; but the V soon after reappears. — *4) The *f* in bass doubles the stationary 7th in soprano. This always disturbs and mars the characteristic effect of the progression. See the Rule, above. — *5) In this progression the chord-seventh must remain in the same part.

161. A singular, but not uncommon, exception to the strict rule of resolution occurs when *the seventh ascends, diatonically, in parallel thirds with the bass.* For illustration:

*1) The parallel 5ths, in soprano and alto, are not perfect. — *2) Here the bass does not run in thirds with the ascending seventh. This licence is limited to the *second inversion* of the $\overset{7}{V}$ (fifth in bass).

LESSON 25.

A. Write out the following chords (in 4-part harmony, as usual) with uniform quarter-notes:

(Major) $\overset{7}{V}$–IV_1–$\overset{7}{V_1}$–V | $\overset{\frown}{I}$. — (Minor) $\overset{7}{V_1}$–IV_2–$\overset{7}{V_2}$–I_1. — (Major) $\overset{7}{V_1}$–II_2–$\overset{7}{V}$ | IV_1–I_2–$\overset{7}{V_3}$ | $\overset{\frown}{I_1}$. — (Minor) $\overset{7}{V_3}$–IV–$\overset{7}{V_3}$–$\overset{7}{V_1}$ | $\overset{\frown}{I}$. — (Major) $\overset{7}{V_2}$–II–$\overset{7}{V_1}$ | IV_2–I. — (Minor) $\overset{7}{V}$–IV_1–I_2–$\overset{7}{V_3}$ | $\overset{\frown}{I_1}$. — (Major) $\overset{7}{V_1}$–$\overset{7}{V}$ | II_2–VI. — (Minor) I–$\overset{7}{V_3}$–$\overset{7}{V_2}$ | IV_2–I.

B. Harmonize the following melodies:

*1) At each bracket, throughout this exercise, the *stationary resolution* is to be applied (par. 160, Rule). — *2) Three bass notes to this *e*. — *3) The ascending resolution (par. 161). — *4) Two bass notes. — *5) This melody is in the *tenor*. Add the other three parts, according to the same principles.

C. Construct a number of original phrases and periods.

CHAPTER XXIV.

THE INCOMPLETE DOM.-SEVENTH.

162. A chord is called "Incomplete" when its **root** is omitted.

This omission occurs, occasionally, in the chord of the dom.-seventh, and **the** result is a **triad upon the leading-tone.**

See Ex. 19, note *2). For illustration:

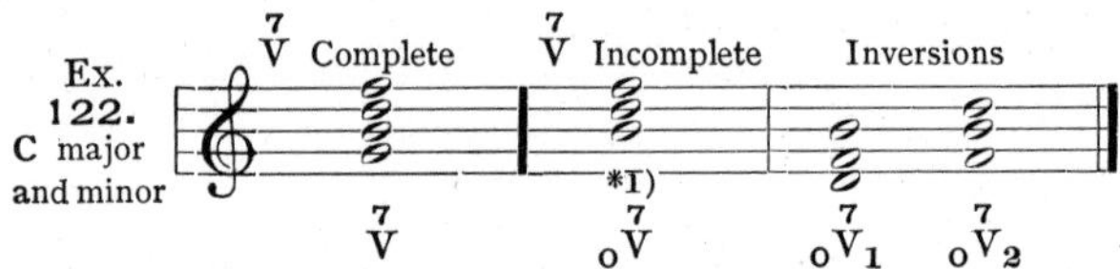

*1) Leading-tone triad (sometimes called the VII). The o denotes the Incomplete form.

163. The proofs that the leading-tone triad is simply an *Incomplete dominant-seventh* chord consist in the facts that it contains the most characteristic feature of all dominant harmonies, namely, the leading-tone; and that its harmonic movements coincide in every respect with those of the Complete $\overset{7}{V}$.

164. The $_{o}\overset{7}{V}$ is a diminished triad (because its fifth is diminished); therefore, like the II of the minor mode, it requires *inversion* to become available. Comp. Lesson 16, note *2).

The best form of this and all other diminished triads is the 1st inversion (chord of the 6th).

The 2d inversion, and the triad-form, are both possible, but very rare.

165. RULE I. The $_{o}\overset{7}{V}$ is alike in major and minor, both in form and general treatment. Its progressions correspond exactly to those of the $\overset{7}{V}$ itself.

RULE II. Any interval may be doubled, excepting the leading-tone.

RULE III. The dissonance (dim. 5th) **generally** *descends*, but may freely **ascend,** especially when doubled. For illustration:

***1) Triad-form:** rare. — *2) First inversion. This is far the best form, almost always; **namely, as** chord of the 6th, with the *leading-tone in the soprano.* Either *d* or *f* may be **doubled.** — *3) The dim. 5th (*f*) is doubled; comp. par. 56*a;* one ascends and the other descends. — *4) Comp. Ex. 68, note *4). — *5) Comp. Ex. 77*a*. — *6) The 2d inversion; treated like any other 6-4 chord. — *7) A succession of 6-4 chords, contrary to par. 138, Rule II. This is always permitted when one of the 6-4 chords is a *Discord*, as here. — *8) Also applicable to minor, excepting where the 6th and 7th steps are melodically connected — as in measures 5, 6, 7, 8.

166. The Incomplete $\overset{7}{V}$, and the II in minor, are the only two legitimate diminished triads in harmony.

To what has already been said about the II in minor, the following may be added:

a) The best form is the **first inversion.** The second inversion is also available; but the triad is very rare. See, again, Lesson 16, note *2).

b) Either the root or the third may be doubled.

c) The diminished 5th resolves *downward.*

d) The best progressions are: II_1–V; II_1–$\overset{7}{V}$; II_1–I_1; II_1–I_2. For example:

*1) Comp. Ex. 123, note *7).

LESSON 26.

A. Write out the ${}_{o}\overset{7}{V}$ of every major key (with its inversions), and note the Relative minor key in which it is the II, thus:

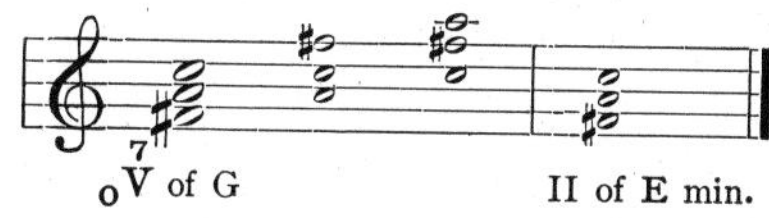

B. Find and play these chords at the keyboard.

LESSON 27.

Harmonize the following melodies, using the ${}_{o}\overset{7}{V}$ (*at option*) at each *:

*1) Review Ex. 123, note *2), and observe that *the leading-tone in soprano may*, **under all circumstances,** *be harmonized as chord of the 6th* ($_0\overset{7}{\text{V}}$). This is, of course, not obligatory — for the Incomplete $\overset{7}{\text{V}}$ is, at best, a comparatively rare chord. — *2) Observe how serviceable this chord of the 6th is, when the melody has the irregular succession 6–7, or 7–6. This is amply shown in Ex. 123. — *3) One bass tone. — *4) Successive 6ths (par. 127). — *5) Par. 161.

CHAPTER XXV.

CHORD OF THE DOMINANT-NINTH. MAJOR.

167. According to par. 26, chords of the seventh may further be extended from 4 to 5 tones. In the latter case they are termed **"chords of the ninth,"** because the new and distinctive interval is a ninth from the root.

168. A five-tone chord may be erected upon each of the four fundamental steps (V, II, VI, III) as defined in Ex. 110 (which review, with context), and they are classified accordingly, that of the *dominant* belonging to the First class.

169. The **chord of the ninth upon the dominant** is obtained, then, by adding one higher third to the dom.-seventh. This demonstration of the origin of the uppermost interval is significant, as it determines the correct *location of the ninth,* in relation to its root. For illustration: in the 5-tone chord

obtained by superposing one more third (over the 4 tones *g-b-d-f*), the tone *a* is removed from the root (*g*) by a distance *exceeding an octave;* the *a* immediately above the root

has no legitimate place in this chord. Hence the distinction which must here be made between a second and a ninth (see Ex. 6, note *3).

170. Like all dom. chords, the dom.-ninth tends toward the tonic harmony. The details of its treatment are as follows:

RULE I. The chord-ninth may never lie less than 9 tones above the root. **In major, the ninth of the dom. is rarely placed in any other voice than the soprano.**

RULE II. The ninth resolves *diatonically downward,* like the seventh.

RULE III. In the **Complete** chord, the root is generally given to the bass; and the 5th (*never the 3d, nor the 7th*) is omitted. For example:

*1) The "Five-nine." — *2) Ninth in soprano (Rule I). — *3) The ninth *below the leading-tone* is never legitimate. In this case, *a* must be differently analyzed; see later. — *4) See Rule I. — *5) The seventh is omitted (Rule III). — *6) The third omitted. — *7) Possible; but see Rule I. — *8) The ninth may be resolved alone.

THE INCOMPLETE DOM.-NINTH.

171. In the 5-tone chords the root is much more likely to be omitted than in those of four tones. In fact, it is more common to omit the root than the fifth; therefore

The dom.-ninth generally appears in its Incomplete form, as chord of the seventh on the leading-tone.

a) The root is omitted ($_{0}\overset{9}{V}$).

b) The bass takes either the third, fifth or seventh — *never the ninth.*

c) In major, the ninth is usually given to the soprano, but is possible in an inner part, *if not placed below the leading-tone* (Ex. 125, note *3).

d) In the Incomplete chord, no interval may be doubled, and, consequently, no omissions are possible.

e) The resolution corresponds to that of the Complete chord. For example:

*1) Ninth in soprano. — *2) Ninth in bass. — *3) These parallel 5ths are extremely tempting, and demand especial vigilance. The best remedy is to *double the third of the resolving I* (as seen in the preceding measure). Thus: $_{0}\overset{9}{V}$ — $\overset{3}{\overset{3}{I}}$. — *4) Ninth in alto. This is good, though rare. The ninth lies *above* the leading-tone. — *5) See Ex. 125, note *3). — *6) Ninth resolved alone.

172. The licences in the resolution of the $\overset{9}{V}$ and $_{0}\overset{9}{V}$ correspond in general to those of the $\overset{7}{V}$ (par. 158, 160, which review). Namely: During *repetition* the 7th and 9th may leap downward; and the dissonances may be held, during the progression into the IV. For example:

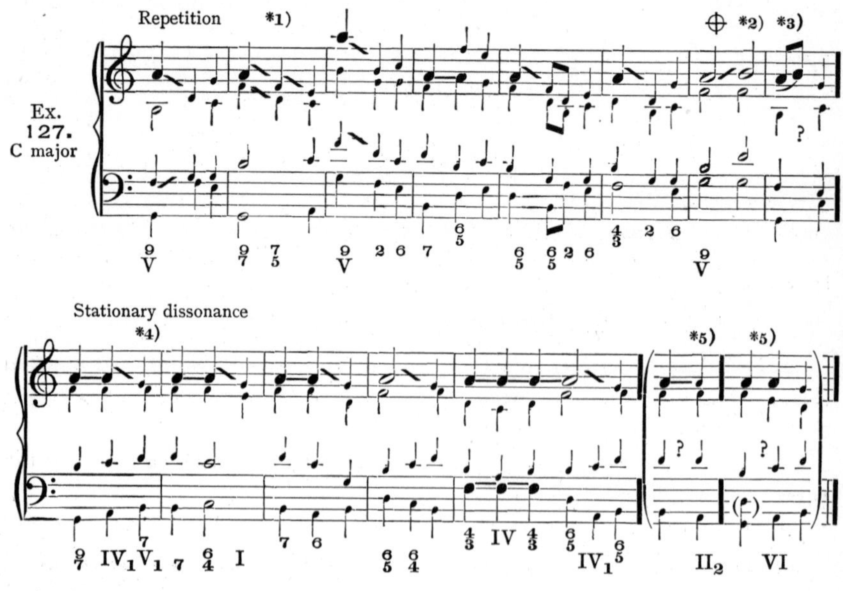

*1) When the 9th progresses thus into the 7th, the resolution of the latter suffices for both. In the next measure the 9th leaps down to the leading-tone. — *2) The 6th step (*a*), as 9th of the dominant, should not progress *upward* (into *b*), for obvious reasons. — *3) In such rapid succession, this may be justifiable. — *4) A dominant chord; comp. Ex. 120, note *1). The next measure, $\overset{9}{V}$-IV-I, is, however, also possible. — *5) These transitions into II or VI are doubtful.

LESSON 28.

A. Write out the $\overset{9}{V}$, and ${}_{0}\overset{9}{V}$ (with inversions), in every major key, followed by a resolution into the tonic harmony.

B. Find and play these chords at the keyboard.

C. Harmonize the following major melodies, with reference to this summarized Table:

*1) According to the rules, and the above Table, the $\overset{9}{V}$ and ${}_{0}\overset{9}{V}$ *in major* are limited almost exclusively to those points in the melody where the *sixth step* occurs (descending). — *2) One bass note through each slur. — *3) Two bass notes. — *4) A different bass tone at each repeated note.

CHAPTER XXVI.

CHORD OF THE DOM.-NINTH. MINOR.

173. The ninth of the dominant chord, being the *6th step* of the scale, undergoes modification in the minor mode (par. 87). Therefore, the dom.-ninth is the first dominant chord *which differs in major and minor*. Comp. par. 90; par. 151 *c*. Thus:

Ex. 128.

C: $\overset{9}{\mathrm{V}}$ in major $\overset{9}{\mathrm{V}}$ in minor

174. The transformation of the 9th from a major to a minor interval does not alter, but rather confirms, its obligations, and facilitates its treatment in many respects.

The rules given in par. 170 (which carefully review) are also valid for the minor dom.-ninth, with one exception, namely:

The ninth of the minor chord may lie in either inner part, quite as well as in the soprano.

But the 9th is not possible in bass. And, as usual, it lies never less than nine tones from the root (in the Complete form). For illustration:

COMPLETE $\overset{9}{\mathrm{V}}$. (Compare Ex. 125.)

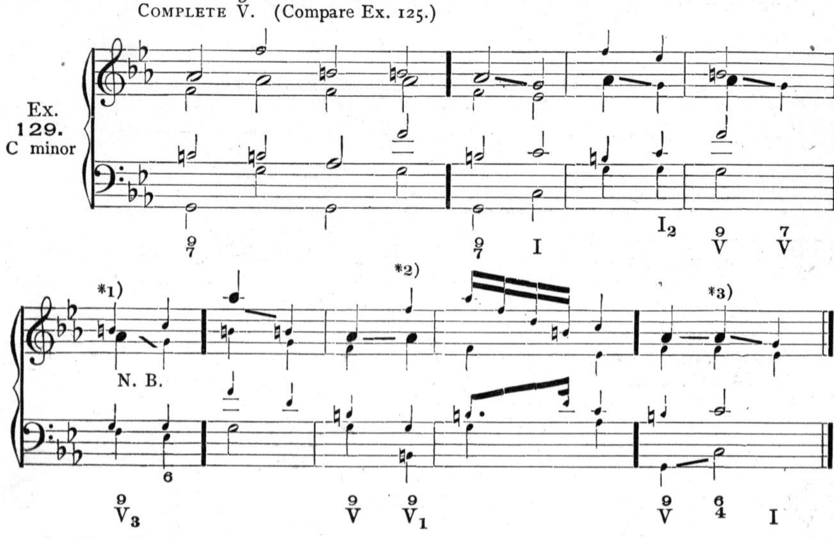

*1) The third inversion of the *Complete* dom.-ninth (i.e., 7th in bass). Extraordinary as this chord looks (and sounds), it is nevertheless perfectly correct. — *2) The first inversion of the Compl. V^9. These unusual forms are somewhat more easily obtained in minor than in major. — *3) Stationary dissonances. Here, a 6-4 chord is exceptionally introduced with a leap in bass. It resembles Ex. 102.

THE CHORD OF THE DIMINISHED SEVENTH.

175. The difference between the major and minor chords of the dom.-ninth is most marked, and most significant, in the **Incomplete form,** which, here again, is by far the most common.

176. The Incomplete dom.-ninth, or the chord of the seventh on the leading-tone, in the minor mode, is a chord of the diminished seventh.

It bears this name because it is the only legitimate chord which contains the peculiar interval of a dim. 7th. It is one of the most frequent and important forms of the dominant harmony, distinguished alike for its great tonal beauty, and its almost incredible flexibility.

177. The treatment of the chord of the dim. 7th coincides with that of the Compl. V^9. The 9th (i.e., the 7th from the leading-tone) may lie **in** *any voice, either above or below the leading-tone* (but it should be avoided in the *bass* voice, as much as possible); and it resolves diatonically downward. For illustration:

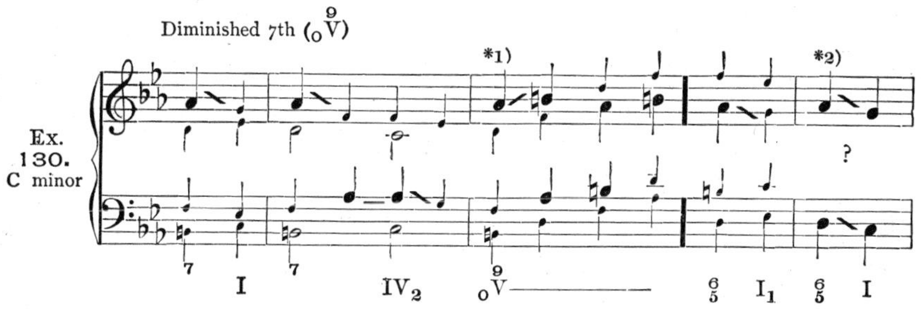

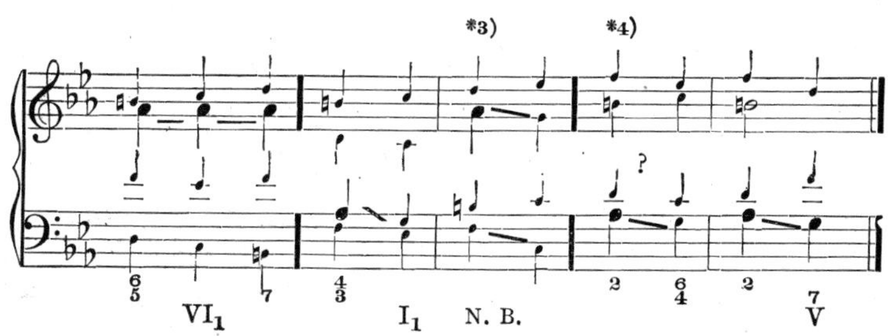

*1) The false melodic progression from the 6th step to the 7th, in minor, is here *justified by chord-repetition.* — *2) Even in minor, where one of the 5ths is imperfect, these parallels should be avoided. Comp. Ex. 126, note *3). — *3) The *f* in bass is actually the 7th of the chord, wherefore its best progression is *diatonically* downward. But comp. Ex. 123, measure 7 (alto). — *4) The original 9th in bass is objectionable, because it gives a very weak chord-form. It is best in repetitions.

Additional illustration, for analysis :

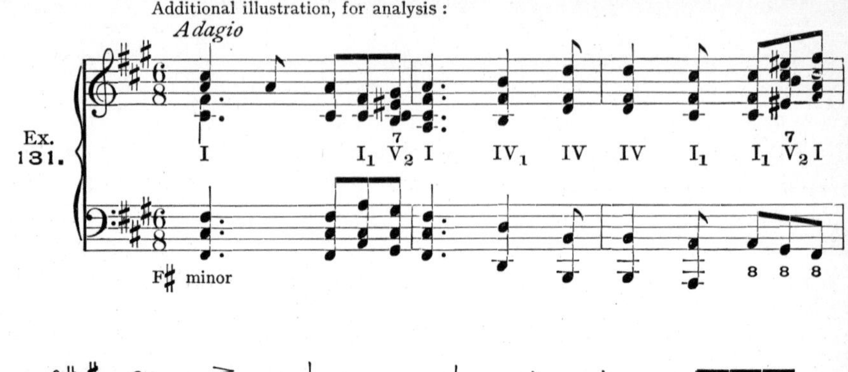

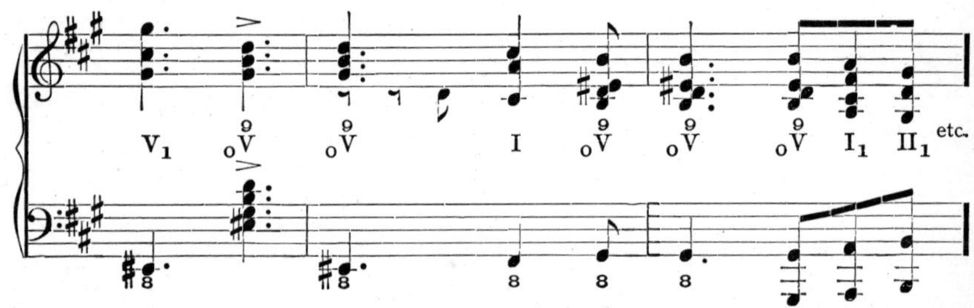

LESSON 29.

A. Write out the $\overset{9}{V}$ Complete in every minor key. — B. Write out the chord of the Dim.-7th, and its inversions, in every minor key. — C. Find and play these chords at the pianoforte, without notes.

LESSON 30.

A. Re-harmonize, chiefly with the dim.-7th chord, Lesson 11, Nos. 1, 5, 6, 7, 10. — Without reference to any directions there given: Lesson 16, Nos. 5, 10. — Lesson 18, Nos. 4, 6, 10. — Lesson 21, Nos. 4, 5. — Lesson 22, Nos. 3, 4.

B. Harmonize the following, using the V^9, occasionally Complete, *but chiefly Incomplete.* **A dom.-ninth chord (or dim.-7th) is possible, but not obligatory, at each *:**

*1) Two bass notes. — *2) Lower voices may be held through the measure. — *3) Lower voices [notation]; and the same in the next measure.

CHAPTER XXVII.

UNFIGURED BASSES.

178. In adding the three upper parts to an *unfigured bass*, the same general rules must be observed as in adding three lower voices to a given *melody*. The two processes, though inverse, are nearly identical. The following table (which compare carefully with that given in Lesson 28) will therefore suffice:

Ex. 132. C major and minor

Steps:	1	2	2	3	3	4	4	5	6	6	7
	I IV_2	II Maj. (II Min.) V_2	7 V V^7 $_0V^7$ $_0V^9$	I_1 (III)	I_1	IV II_1	V^7 V^7 $_0V^7$ $_0V^9$	V V^7 V^9 I_2	VI IV_1	VI IV_1 ($_0V^9$) (II_2)	V V^7 V^9 $_0V$ ($_0V^7$)

179. Besides which, however, the following generalities must be recalled and borne in mind: The bass note is not as likely to be the *chord-fifth* as it is to be the root, third or seventh. The leading-tone is not likely to be a "root apparent" (see par. 164), as $_0V^7$. And *in minor*, neither the 2d nor 3d steps are likely to be roots.

In all minor basses, the Incomplete dom.-ninth (chord of the dim.-7th) is to be used *very freely*.

LESSON 31.

Add soprano (and then alto and tenor) to the following basses.

*1) All stems down. — *2) Basses 1, 2, 3, 7, in *minor* also. — *3) Two melody-notes (at option). — *4) When step 2 is followed by step 1, as here, it is far more likely to be a *dominant* chord, than the II. — *5) All minor basses in at least two ways. — *6) One melody-note to each slur.

LESSON 32.

*1) Three melody-notes. — *2) In two ways. — *3) Also in *minor*. — *4) The three upper parts together on the G-staff. Pay strict attention to the slurs; *one melody-note to each slur*.

CHAPTER XXVIII.

CHORD OF THE DIMINISHED-SEVENTH, CONTINUED.

180. In working out this lesson, all in the **minor mode,** the student will put the broadest possible construction upon the term "Dom.", and determine at his own discretion the **form** (V, V^7, $_{o}V^7$, V^9, or $_{o}V^9$), and the **inversion** (bass note), of each dominant chord, giving preference, however, to the *chord of the dim.-seventh.* The **rhythm** (arrangement and repetition of the given chords in the measure and beat) is also quite optional. The following example will serve as a model:

Given the chords (minor mode):

I | Dom. | I–IV | I_2–Dom. | I ||

Solution:

Ex. 133.

LESSON 33.

A. Construct two phrases (at least), in different *minor* keys, with each of the following chord-series. The required number of beats (or of melody-tones) will be obtained by *chord-repetition*. Study the above model closely, and review the directions given in Lesson 14C:

($\frac{4}{4}$ and $\frac{6}{8}$) I–Dom.–I | Dom.–VI–Dom. | I–Dom.–I–II_1 | Dom.–I ||

(₵ and $\frac{3}{8}$) I–IV | Dom.–IV–Dom. | I–II–Dom. | I ||

($\frac{4}{4}$ and $\frac{3}{2}$) I | Dom. | I–II_1 | I_2–Dom. | I ||

B. Construct two (or more) periods, in *minor*, with the following chords, using the **dim.-seventh** at each *; everything else optional:

($\frac{3}{4}$ and $\frac{4}{8}$) I–*–I | *–IV–V | I–*–I | $\overset{\frown}{V}$ | *–IV–* | * *–I | II_1–I_2–V | I ||

Some experiments may be made with these chord-series in *major* also. In this case the dim.-seventh will not appear, although the $_0V^9$ (with the limitations of par. 171) will be available.

C. Construct a number of *original* 4-measure phrases (both major and minor), following the above process.

CHAPTER XXIX.

SECOND-CLASS DISCORDS.

181. The fundamental tone of the Second discord-class must be sought one perfect 5th higher than the dominant, or **two perfect 5ths above the tonic;** it is therefore the **second step of the scale.** Review Ex. 110, and context. The Second class comprises the same number and forms of chords as the dominant class, namely: The triad; the chord of the seventh, Complete and Incomplete; and the chord of the ninth, Complete and Incomplete. Thus:

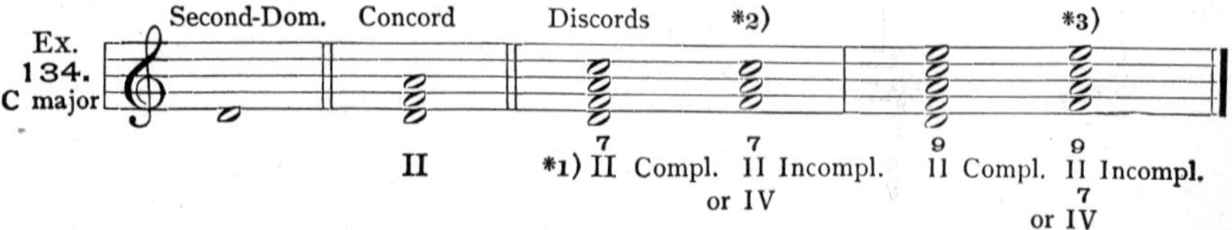

*1) "**Two-seven.**" — *2) The II^7 without its root proves to be the subdominant triad (the IV). See next paragraph. — *3) Called "**Four-seven,**" instead of $_{o}II^9$, because of its relation to the IV, the name of which is established.

182. It is now necessary to revert to Ex. 19. note *1), and par. 96 (which see), and elucidate the apparent contradictions which are presented by the subdominant or Second-class body of chords. About the *discords* of this Class there is no uncertainty, but the *concords* (II and IV), as has been seen, do not, in practice, preserve their actual theoretical co-relations with full emphasis. From the above example it is theoretically apparent that the **triad II** is the principal representative of the "subdominant" harmony, while the IV is only an Incomplete form of the II^7. This confirms the theory that no chord-root can be accepted upon any perfect 5th **below** the keynote. Practically considered, preference is likely to be given to the IV, because of its *direct* perfect-fifth relation to the tonic. The degree of prominence which either of these two equally important chords assumes, depends upon the accidental emphasis given to the tones *d* or *f* respectively. The following table illustrates this (in C major), and demonstrates the coincidence of the subdominant with the Second-class chords, in the tones *f-a-c*:

Third rank — Second-Dom. (7th) . . . . *d–f–a–c.*
5th
Second rank — Dominant . . . . *g–b–d.*
5th
☞ FIRST RANK — **Tonic** . . . . *C–E–G.*
5th
(Third rank ?) — Subdominant . . . . *f–a–c.*

One significant deduction for the student is, that *the Second-dominant and Subdominant chords bear the same relation to the dominant harmonies, that the dominant does to the tonic.* Therefore the term "Second-dominant" is peculiarly indicative, and preferable to "Subdominant."

183. The distinctive external characteristic of fundamental Second-class chords is their *minor third* — in C major the tone *f* instead of *f-sharp:*

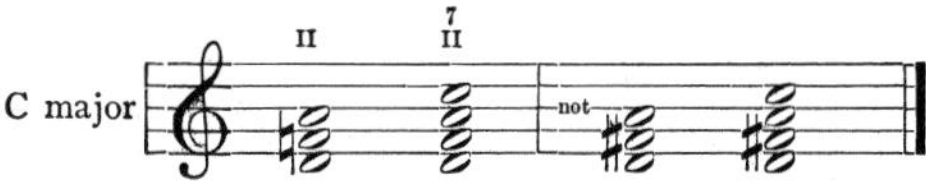

This interval distinguishes them from the dominant or First-class chords, whose *major third*, being the leading-tone, is their most significant feature.

THE CHORD OF THE SEVENTH ON THE SECOND STEP.

184. The chord of the 7th upon the second step, the II^7, and its inversions, resolve most naturally into the preceding chord-class, namely:

Into the dominant chords, whereby the chord-seventh descends diatonically, as usual.

*1) *A-natural* in major, and *a-flat* in minor. — *2) These first five measures illustrate the resolution of the II⁷ into *each of the five dominant chord-forms.* — *3) The *second* inversion of the II⁷ is best *in minor.* Otherwise no distinction is made between the two modes.

185. The $\overset{7}{\text{II}}$ and its inversions, like the dominant discords, are also entitled to the *licences of chord-repetition* (review par. 158); and those involving the *stationary seventh* (review par. 160).

For the progressions with stationary seventh (into the tonic chords I or VI) the Second-class discords all evince great preference.

Ex. 136. C major and minor.

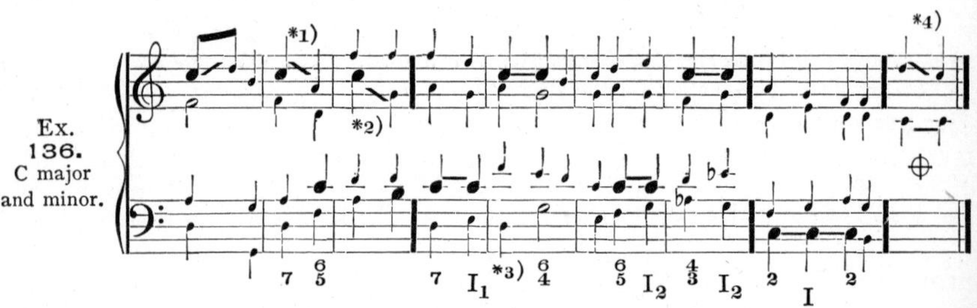

*1) A curious example of parallel 5ths (perfect) in both pairs of upper and lower parts. They are *justified by chord-repetition.* — *2) It is not unusual for the 7th of the II⁷ to *leap downward,* thus, to the dominant, to avoid doubling the leading-tone, when the latter is in bass. Here it is the *tonic* — a tone whose importance gives it certain privileges. — *3) Comp. Ex. 102. — *4) Wrong, like Ex. 120, note *4), which see.

186. The *introduction* of the dissonances in Second-class chords demands closer attention and more restriction than in dominant chords. Review Ex. 112, and limit the seventh of the II⁷ to *strict* introduction, as much as possible. Thus:

Ex. 137. C major and minor.

*1) In the II^7 itself (root in bass) the *chord-fifth may be omitted*, and very frequently is. In the inversions, however, there are, as usual, no omissions. — *2) These 5ths are wrong in *major* only; in *minor* they are not perfect. Comp. Ex. 101, note *2). In passing from I into II^7 it is usually necessary to omit the fifth of the latter, especially in major.

187. Especially unique is the introduction of these chords after **dominant harmonies,** thus: V^7–II^7, V^9–II^7, etc. This is merely another version of par. 160 (which review), and involves the following rules:

a) The 7th (or 9th) of the dominant chord remains stationary.

b) After the Second-class chord, a dominant chord must return, in some form or other.

*1) These first 2 measures are applicable to major *and minor*. But the others demand modification, as usual, wherever the 6th and 7th steps are melodically connected. — *2) Two stationary 7ths in succession are objectionable.

Further illustration:

LESSON 34.

Write out the following chord-successions in different keys, in 4-part harmony, with uniform quarter-notes. All inversions are optional, unless specified. Resolve all sevenths properly. See Ex. 137, notes *1) and *2):

(Major) I–II^7–V^7–VI. — (Minor) VI–II^7_1–V^7_3–I_1. — (Major) I_1–II^7_1–I_2–V^7. — (Minor) I–II^7_2–${}_0\text{V}^9$–V^7_2–I. — (Major) I–II^7_1–VI_2–II^7–${}_0\text{V}^7$–I. — (Minor) I–IV_2–II^7_3–V_1–V^7_3–IV–${}_0\text{V}^9$–${}_0\text{V}^9$–I.— (Major) I^8–V^7_2–II^7–V^7_2–II^7_3–${}_0\text{V}^9$–V^7–I. — (Minor) I–V^7–II^7_2–V^7–V^7_3–II^7_1–${}_0\text{V}^9$–I_1–II^7–I_1. —

LESSON 35.

A. Re-harmonize Lesson 10, Nos. 1, 2, 3, 8.—Lesson 11, Nos. 1, 4, 6.—Lesson 13, Nos. 2, 5.—Lesson 18, Nos. 2, 4.—Lesson 21, Nos. 1, 2.—Lesson 27, No. 6.

N.B. The II^7 is possible (not obligatory) at those steps where either the IV or II would be used.

B. Harmonize the following melodies. Some form of the II^7 is *possible* at each * :

CHAPTER XXX.

OTHER SECOND-CLASS DISCORDS.

188. The 5-tone chord upon the second step (second-dominant) is extremely rare in its Complete form, but is available and not uncommon **without its root,** as **chord of the seventh on the fourth step** (IV^7, or Incomplete II^9—compare Ex. 134, note *3).

The treatment of the IV^7 corresponds in every essential particular to that of the II^7, but is more rigorous. Licences of introduction and resolution are almost entirely precluded. Review par. 184, 185 and 187. The seventh descends, as usual, or remains stationary; and there are no omissions. Thus:

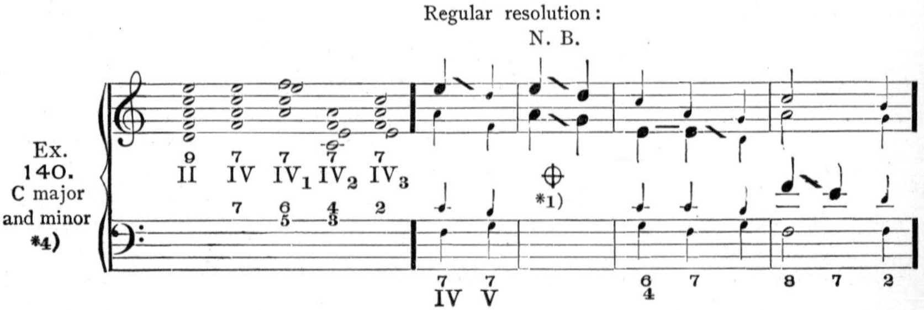

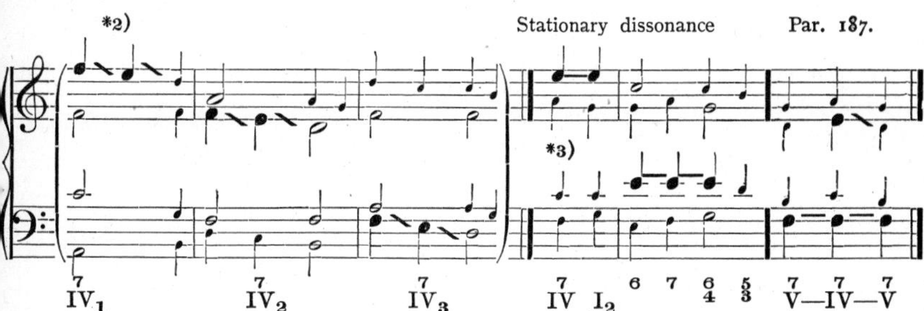

*1) The IV⁷ rarely resolves into the *triad-form* of the dominant, on account of these 5ths, which disappear when the *dominant-seventh or ninth* follows. — *2) The inverted forms of the IV⁷ are rarely used. — *3) The resolution into the tonic, with stationary seventh, is very frequent and effective, and removes the danger of parallel 5ths. — *4) In minor, *e-flat* and *a-flat*.

THE THIRD AND FOURTH DISCORD-CLASSES.

189. Of these extremely rare chords, the best is the seventh upon the 6th step — VI⁷. Its connections are as follows:

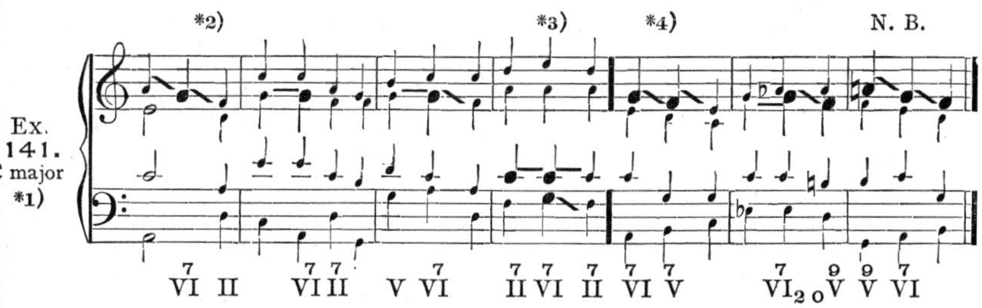

*1) Principally in major; possible in minor only where the melodic connection of the 6th and 7th steps can be avoided. — *2) Third-class chords resolve "regularly" into those of the Second class (II, II⁷, etc.). — *3) Analogous to par. 187. — *4) An "irregular" (but very common) resolution, into *dominant* chords.

SEQUENCES.

190. All the rest of these remote Discords are least objectionable, because most comprehensible, when used in **sequence-relations** with better chords. Review paragraphs 128, 129, and 130, with their examples. The possibilities here are more numerous than in the former lessons, because the sum of chord-forms and inversions is much greater. But, as stated in par. 130, sequences are *far less common in minor than in major.* All questions of quality or admissibility must be left to the ear. A few random examples will suffice:

Further illustration:

*1) When the tempo is so rapid, successive beats, of similar harmonic import, blend; therefore these chords are defined by grouping both beats (represented by each bass figure) together. — *2) The figure in ♪-notes continues throughout, as in the first and last measures. The pupil is to play it in its correct form.

THE AUGMENTED TRIAD.

191. One unusual chord, of the Fourth discord-class, claims special mention, namely: **the triad upon the third step,** in the **minor mode.** It is an *augmented triad* (par. 111*b*), and is treated thus:

FIGURED BASSES.

192. The student is now sufficiently familiar with the figures placed below the bass tones, to work out an exercise from a figured bass. The figures indicate the *shape* of the chord; that is, *the intervals which accompany the given bass tone,* reckoned upward from the latter. The most important aim is to secure a good *soprano melody.* The following fairly elaborate model should be carefully studied:

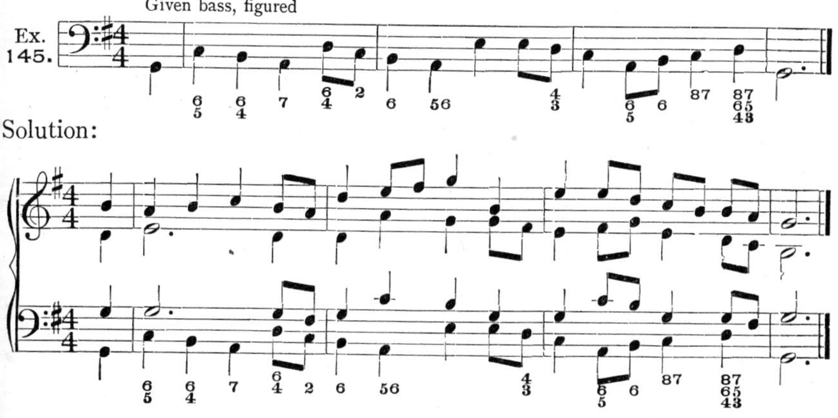

LESSON 36.

A. Harmonize the following melodies. A Second-class discord ($\overset{7}{\text{II}}$ or $\overset{7}{\text{IV}}$) is *possible* at each * :

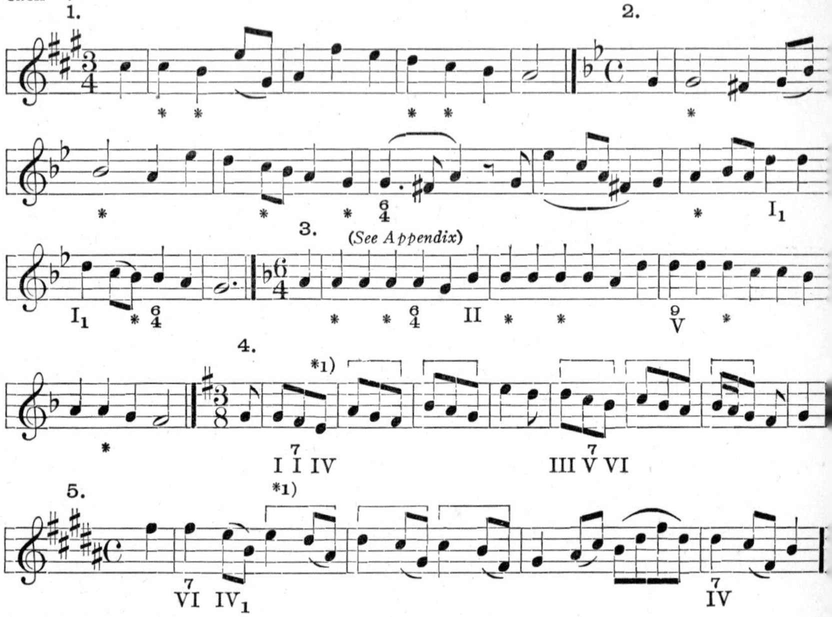

1.
2.
3.
(See Appendix)
4.
*1)
5.
*1)

*1) The brackets indicate sequences.

B. Work out, and analyze, the following figured basses:

1.
3*1)
2.
3.
*2)
4.
5.
6.

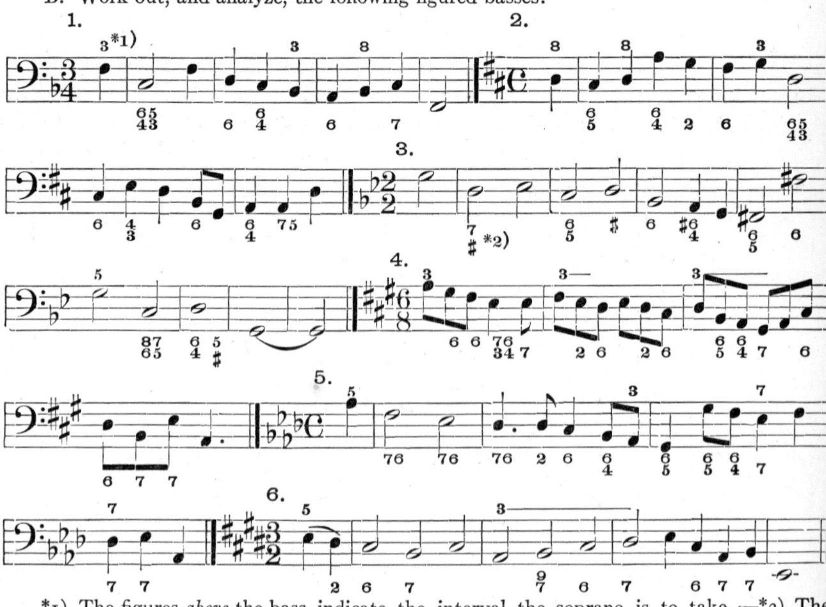

*1) The figures *above* the bass indicate the interval the soprano is to take. —*2) The sharp is a necessary reminder of the accidental before the leading-tone, in minor.

DIVISION THREE.

KEY-RELATIONS AND ASSOCIATIONS. MODULATION.

CHAPTER XXXI.

THE SYSTEM OF KEYS AND MODES.

193. The relation of key to key is precisely the same as that of tone to tone, and is measured by the interval of the perfect fifth (**harmonic degree,** par. 8). Keynotes which lie a fifth apart have *adjacent signatures;* for example, *e-flat* (3 flats); *b-flat,* its upper perfect fifth (2 flats); *a-flat,* its lower fifth (4 flats).

As shown in Ex. 64, N. B., the *relative minor* of a major key has the *same signature* as the latter.

194. From this it appears that

The degree of relation between one key and another is indicated directly by their signatures.

The following circular arrangement of keynotes and signatures illustrates this clearly:

Ex. 146. *1)

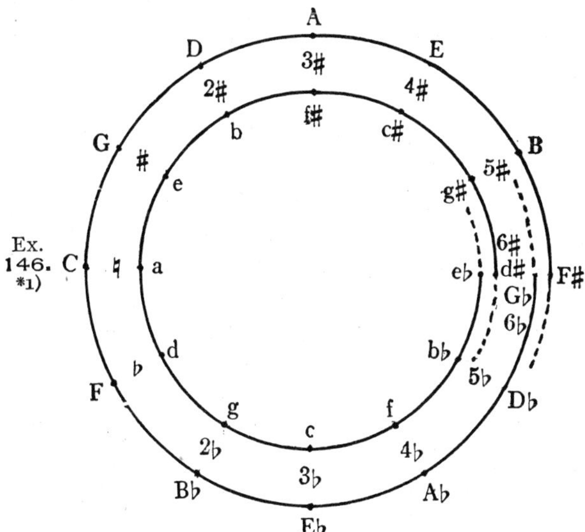

*1) The distance from point to point is a perfect 5th, or **harmonic degree,** along each line — major and minor. The outer circle represents the major keynotes, indicated by capital letters; the inner circle, minor keynotes, small letters. The difference between the size of the upper and lower arcs serves to illustrate the *actual* difference between *g-flat* and *f-sharp* (*e-flat* and *d-sharp*), but is intentionally exaggerated.

195. Each key is seen, in the above chart, to be surrounded by five other keys (major or minor). These are called the **attendant, or next-related, keys.** For example, from *C major* (natural signature):

1. The Relative key, *a minor* (same signature);
2. The Dominant key, *G major* (1-sharp signature);
3. The Relative of the Dominant key, *e minor* (1-sharp signature);
4. The Subdominant key, *F major* (1-flat signature);
5. The Relative of the Subdom. key, *d minor* (1-flat signature);

All the rest of the 24 major and minor keys are more or less *foreign* to the key of C. The so-called **remotely-related** keys will be defined later.

MODULATION.

196. Modulation is the act of *progressing from one key or mode into another*, or of exchanging one key for another.

197. The **process of modulation,** while subject in general to the foregoing rules of part-writing, is furthermore regulated by the following special rules:

RULE I. Modulations are limited ordinarily to the five next-related keys. A transition which extends *beyond the next signature* is called "extraneous," and is always subject to special conditions.

RULE II. The desired key is most easily and legitimately reached through one of its dominant (first-class) chords (V, V^7, ${}_oV^7$, V^9, or ${}_oV^9$ in any form).

RULE III. The key may also be entered through any **second-class** chord (II, II^7, IV, IV^7) in any form.

As a rule, it is not satisfactory to enter a key through any **tonic** chord; but there is one notable exception, namely: the **tonic 6–4 chord, when accented.** This is due to its intimate relation to the *dominant* harmony; comp. par. 135, and 146.

RULE IV. It is always best to close the original key upon one of its tonic chords (I or VI in the usual forms).

It is also possible to abandon a key at some other, non-tonic, chord, but often awkward, and always conditional. Hence the following fundamental modulatory formula:

198. Abandon the first key at one of its tonic chords, and enter the desired key through its dominant class; more rarely through its second class; or through the accented tonic six-four.

Illustration of these rules:

*1) The modulatory transition is effected by the connection of the two chords under the ⌐¬ ; the first one is the I_1 of the original key (C), which brings the latter to a sufficiently marked close, leaving no impediment to the change of key, or modulatory digression; the second of the two chords ushers in the desired key (G), through the agency of its dominant chord, which contains the *leading-tone.* — *2) It is evident that the rhythmic location of the modulatory chords (on heavy or light beats) is of comparatively little moment. — *3) The new key (G) is entered through one of its Second-class chords (the II); *this resolves into the dominant,* and therefore merely serves to protract the modulatory process. — *4) G is entered through its *accented tonic 6-4 chord.* — *5) *These examples are also valid for the modulation from C minor into G minor,* with the usual reservation (par. 92).

199. The last chord of one key may, in many cases, be at the same time the *first chord of the next key.* If this is the case — if this chord has its place and name in the coming key — the modulation is called **diatonic**. But if the last chord does not belong to the next key, one (or more) of its tones *must be inflected chromatically* (by an accidental). The modulation is then known as **chromatic.** For illustration:

Ex. 148.

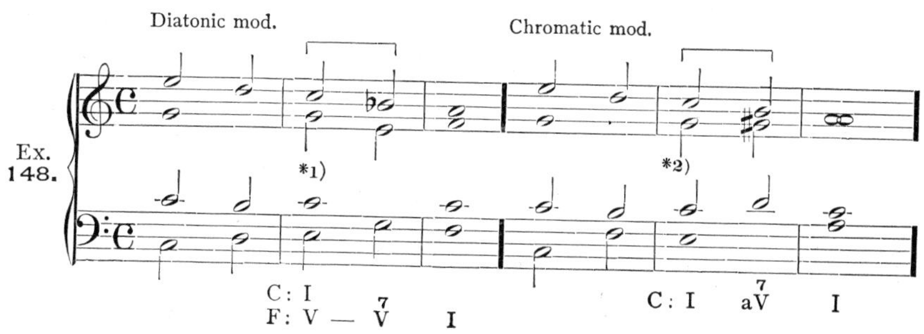

*1) This chord, the last one in C, is, at the same time, the V of the coming key — F. (In Ex. 147, the modulations are all diatonic. Analyze carefully, and note the double name of the last chord in C, in each case — as above.) — *2) Here, the last chord in C does not belong to the coming *a* minor, because of the *g;* therefore, this *g* must be inflected to *g-sharp.*

200. The rules of chromatic inflection are as follows:

a) As a rule, the chromatic change should be made in *one and the same part* (as above, in alto).

b) If, however, the two chromatic tones are not in the same part (causing the so-called "cross-relation"), it is simply necessary that *the first one of these tones should not skip.*

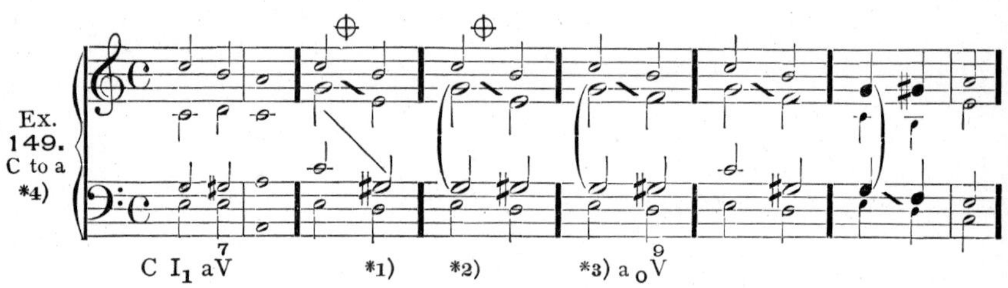

*1) The chromatic inflection (*g* — *g-sharp*) is divided between two different parts. — *2) The alto note *g* *skips* to *e*, while its duplicate in tenor is being chromatically inflected. *3) This measure, and the following ones, are correct, because the *g* progresses *diatonically* to *f* in one of the parts. — *4) That is, *C major* to *a minor.*

LESSON 37.

A. Name the 5 next-related keys of every major and minor key, mentally.

B. Write out the following chord-progressions, in ordinary 4-part harmony, as usual; each in several different ways; all chord-forms (inversions) optional:

G I–C $\overset{7}{V}$ *1) || **e I–a $\overset{7}{V}$** *1) || **F I–d V** || **d I–F $_0\overset{7}{V}$** || **A I–E $\overset{9}{V}$** || **f♯ I–c♯ $_0\overset{9}{V}$** || **A♭ I–c $\overset{7}{II}$–$\overset{7}{V}$** || **f I–E♭ $\overset{7}{II}$–$\overset{7}{V}$** || **D I–e $_0\overset{9}{V}$** || **E I–f♯ $\overset{7}{II}$–$\overset{7}{V}$** || **g♯ I–E $\overset{7}{V}$** || **b♭ I–G♭ $_0\overset{7}{V}$** || **c I** | **B♭ $\overset{>}{I_2}$–V** || **b I** | **f♯ $\overset{>}{I_2}$ $\overset{7}{V}$** ||.

*1) Capital letters represent major keys, small letters, minor keys. Resolve the last chord of each group into its I.

CHAPTER XXXII.

NEXT-RELATED MODULATIONS, COMPLETE.

201. A modulation is distinguished as **complete,** when the prospective key becomes the final aim of the digression, and is confirmed as such by a complete perfect cadence in the new key. Such transitions require, as a rule, a whole phrase or period.

LESSON 38.

Harmonize the following melodies, with a change of key at each * :

*1) This is the first chord of the new key; either a dom. chord, or a Second-class chord, may be used (par. 197, Rules II and III). Review par. 198.

LESSON 39.

A. Harmonize the following melodies, as in Lesson 38; each in at least two different ways:

*1) $\overset{7}{\text{II}}$. — *2) These two *a's* may be either I_2–$\overset{7}{\text{IV}}$, or $\overset{7}{\text{IV}}$–I_2 of the new key. — *3) $\overset{7}{\text{V}}$ or II^7.

B. And the following basses. Analyze the keys and chords:

C. Construct original 4-measure phrases, each with one complete *next-related* modulation.

CHAPTER XXXIII.

NEXT-RELATED MODULATIONS, TRANSIENT.

202. A modulation is distinguished as **transient** when the new key occurs *in the course* of a phrase or period, and is followed either by the original key again, or by some other next-related key. Transient modulations are frequently very brief, extending through only a few beats, sometimes including only two chords, but *not less than two*. Because:

203. A modulation is never consummated until the new dominant chord has been resolved into (and confirmed by) its tonic harmony; no key can be unmistakably represented by less than these two chords, V–I (or V–VI), in some form or other.

The modulatory process is the same as in complete transitions. For illustration:

204. Transient modulations often assume the form of *sequences*, whereby, as usual, certain irregularities are tolerated. For example:

MENDELSSOHN. Op. 7

Ex. 151.

*1) The meaning of this *c-natural* is explained in par. 207, No. 1.

LESSON 40.

Harmonize the following melodies, introducing transient modulations as indicated (at each *):

*1) The sequences define the keys.

LESSON 41.

Harmonize the following unfigured bases, with transient modulations at each *:

*1) Two melody-notes. — *2) One melody-note to *each slur*. The three upper parts together on the G-staff.

CHAPTER XXXIV.

ALTERED CHORDS IN MAJOR.

205. Altered chords are such as contain one or more tones *foreign to the scale in which they appear.* They represent the most fugitive grade of key-association; or, more strictly, they are only *incipient* modulations, not consummated by regular resolution *into the key to which they legitimately belong according to their notation.* From which it is to be inferred that an Altered chord is distinguished from the legitimate chords *by the manner in which it progresses.*

206. An altered chord is always followed by some chord which unmistakably characterizes and confirms the prevailing key, i.e., usually by the I; sometimes by a Dom.-Discord; rarely by any other chord.

For illustration:

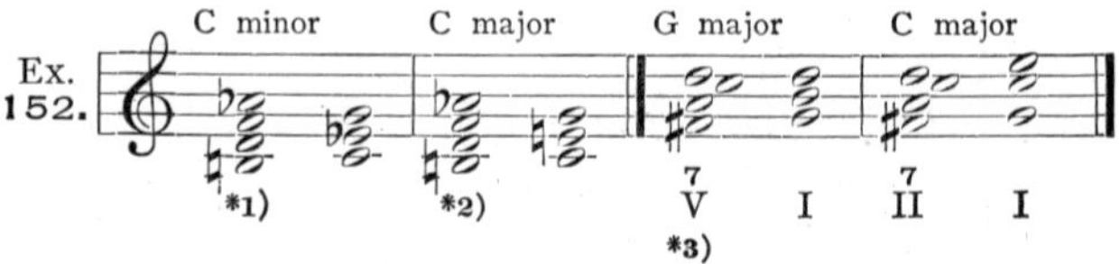

*1) This is the legitimate Incomplete $\overset{9}{\text{V}}$ (chord of the dim. 7th) of *c* minor, and is confirmed as *c*-minor chord by its resolution into the I of that mode (*c*–**e-flat**-*g*). — *2) Here the very same chord progresses (resolves) into the I of **C major** (*c*–**e-natural**-*g*), thus identifying itself as a C-major chord, in which the 6th scale-step, *a*, has been *casually altered (lowered) to a-flat.* — *3) This chord appears to be the dom.-seventh of *G* major, and is confirmed as such, by resolving into the *G-major* I; the *f-sharp* is indispensable. In the next measure its appearance (notation) is *not* confirmed in this manner, but, progressing into the I of *C-major*, it proves to have been a *C-major* chord, *Altered;* the *f-sharp* (4th step raised) in this case is arbitrary, and optional. The other examples are demonstrated similarly. Compare par. 203, and observe that

the identity of a chord depends upon what it does (i.e., upon its progression).

207. The most frequent alterations **in major** are:

1. The **lowered 6th scale-step,** in **all** chords which contain that step;
2. The **raised 2d step,** in the **dominant triad;**
3. The **raised 4th step,** in all **Second-class** chords (Ex. 134);
4. The **raised 2d and 4th steps together,** in the II^7.

For illustration:

Ex. 153. C major

*1) The chord of the dim. 7th can thus be used *in major* as well as in minor. Comp. par. 176, last clause. — *2) A very exceptional, but not uncommon, resolution. — *3) Observe the manner in which the alteration is indicated in the chord-name. The inversions are not marked.

208. Other alterations are possible, but *far less usual.* Namely:

1. The *raised 1st step* (in the I or VI^7, *always* resolving into the *dom.-7th*).
2. The *raised 1st and 6th steps* together (only in the VI^7, followed by the V^7).

For example:

Ex. 154. C major

Raised tonic
*1)
Raised 1st and 6th steps
I♯
V7
VI♯7
V7
d min.
VI♯♯7
V7
*2)

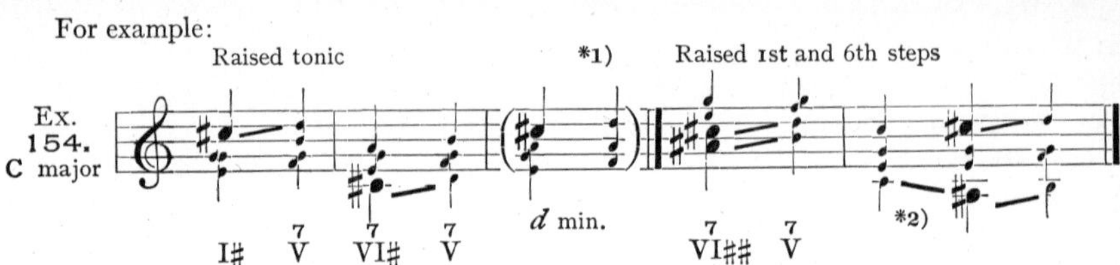

1) *Not* thus, into the II of C, as this would corroborate the preceding chord as a *legitimate* dom.-7th chord in *d minor*. — *2) In connection with altered chords, such unusual interval-progressions as *c–a♯*, etc., are permissible.

Additional illustrations:

Ex. 155.

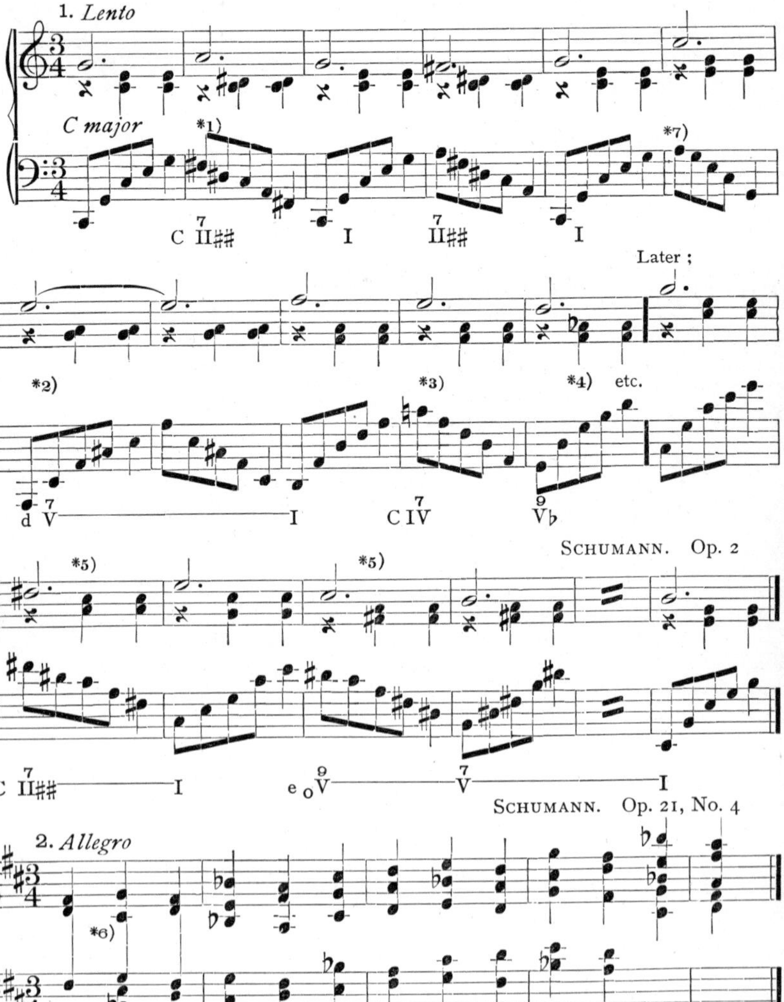

1. Lento
C major
*1)
*7)
C II♯♯7
I
II♯♯7
I
Later ;
*2)
*3)
*4) etc.
d V7
I
C IV7
V♭9
SCHUMANN. Op. 2
*5)
*5)
C II♯♯7
I
e oV9
V7
I
SCHUMANN. Op. 21, No. 4
2. Allegro
*6)
D major

*1) The altered II^7 of C major (raised 2d and 4th steps); repeated two measures later. — *2) Here a transient modulation is made into *d* minor; — *3) and here C major is re-entered, through its IV^7. — *4) The lowered 6th step of C major. — *5) *5) The comparison of these two measures illustrates the distinction between an altered and a legitimate chord. At first, the *d♯–f♯–a–c* is an altered II^7 of C, because it resolves into the I of that key; two measures later, *the same chord* proves to be the legitimate dim.-7th of *e* minor, because it progresses into the V^7 (and then into the I) of the latter. — *6) The dim.-7th chord in the *major mode*, on every alternate beat. See Ex. 153, note *1). — *7) This *a* is an embellishing neighboring-note. See later. — See also: **Chopin,** Mazurka 34, measures 53–68 (raised 4th step).

209. The treatment of altered chords is very simple, not differing materially from that of the corresponding unaltered chords. *Raised notes resolve diatonically upward* (with very rare exceptions, as in Ex. 153, note *2); *lowered notes always downward.* Altered tones should not be doubled.

Observe smooth voice-progression. Review par. 200.

LESSON 42.

Harmonize the following melodies, *each in two ways,* with an altered chord at each *:

*1) Ex. 153, note *2). — *2) Par. 208; resolution into the dominant-*seventh.*

CHAPTER XXXV.

ALTERED CHORDS IN MINOR.

210. Review, carefully, par. 88. The alterations in minor are defined on the basis of the **harmonic minor scale.** Their most obvious purpose in harmony consists in obviating the awkward interval-progression between the 6th and 7th steps of the harmonic scale (par. 92), by substituting a melodious succession which gives rise to the **melodic** minor scale.

211. For this purpose,

> **The 6th step is raised in the ascending scale, and the 7th step is lowered in the descending scale.**

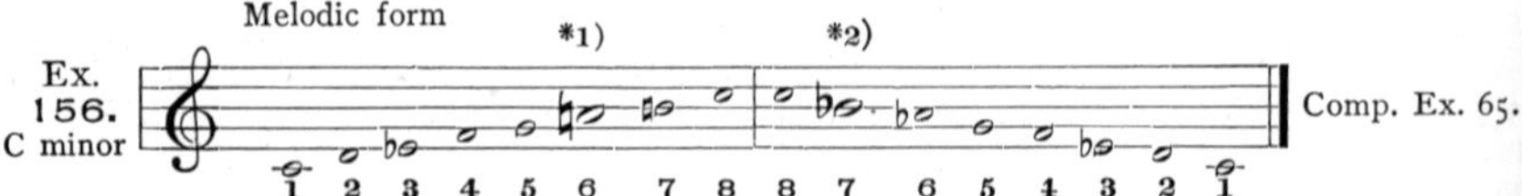

*1) By raising the 6th step from *a*♭ to *a*♮, the awkward interval of an augmented second (between steps 6 and 7) is reduced to a simple, melodious, major second. This is the *only reason* why the alteration is made. It is done only in the *ascending* scale, which thereby assumes the *original major form* (at those steps). — *2) The same change from an augmented second to a major second is made, in *descending*, by lowering the 7th step from *b*♮ to *b*♭. This descending form of the melodic minor scale exactly agrees with the adopted *signature* (par. 91).

212. The external proportions of these various minor scales may be systematized without confusion as follows:

1. The first five tones, from tonic to dominant, are *the same in all the forms of minor*, and contain the *lowered (minor) third step*.

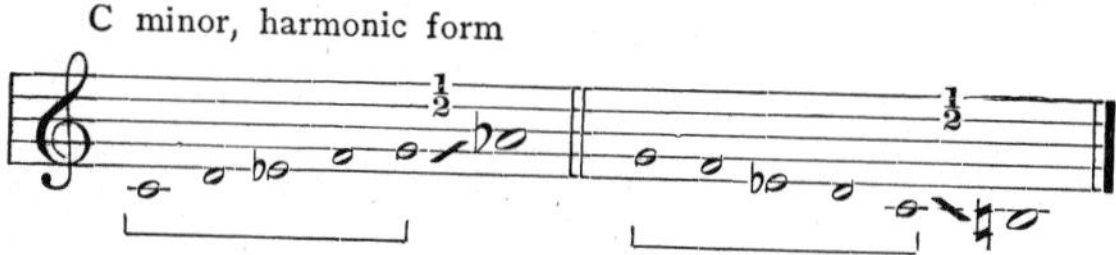

2. In the melodic scales, the *upper* series of tones, between dominant and upper tonic, consists of "whole step, whole step, half-step" in *both* directions; thus:

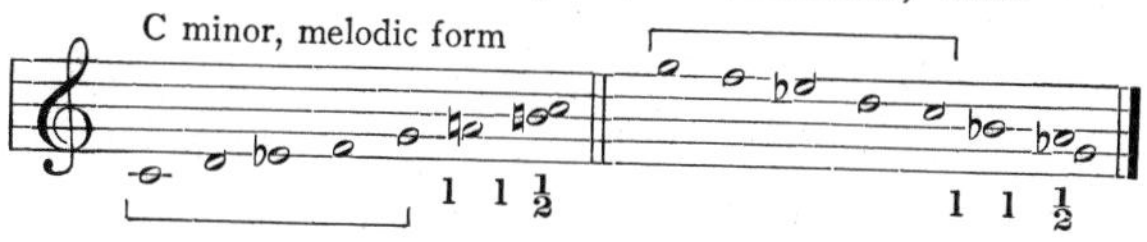

213. From this the important deduction is made, that the **third scale-step** is the only distinctive tone between the major form and the various minor forms; it is major in major, and minor in minor.

214. The **raised 6th step** is applied and treated as follows:

*1) The progression of these chords is defined by the resolution of their altered step; not rigidly by par. 206. Here, *dominant chords must follow.* — *2) The resolution of this 7th (*c* in alto) corresponds in this case to Ex. 121. — *3) The *a*♮ in soprano is followed by *a*♭ in tenor. See par. 200 *b*.

215. The **raised 4th step** often accompanies the raised 6th step, in **Second-class chords.** In this case only the 4th step requires the ascending resolution; the 6th step may rise or fall. For illustration:

*1) See Ex. 136, note *2). — *2) Resolution into the I; stationary dissonances. — *3) Analogous to Ex. 153, note *2); rare. — *4) Comp. Ex. 157, note *3). — *5) The resolution into the *triad* V resembles a modulation. The dominant *discords*, or the I, are more genuine. Comp. par. 206.

216. The **lowered 7th step** is applied and treated thus:

*1) Comp. Ex. 157, note *1). — *2) Compare Ex. 77. — *3) The lowered 7th step is rarely employed in *dominant* chords; especially so in the *discords* of the dominant.

217. Aside from these alterations, which are identified with the melodic minor mode, there is one other very common alteration, namely, the **lowered 2d step,** which occurs in the *1st inversion of the* II (more rarely in the II itself). For illustration:

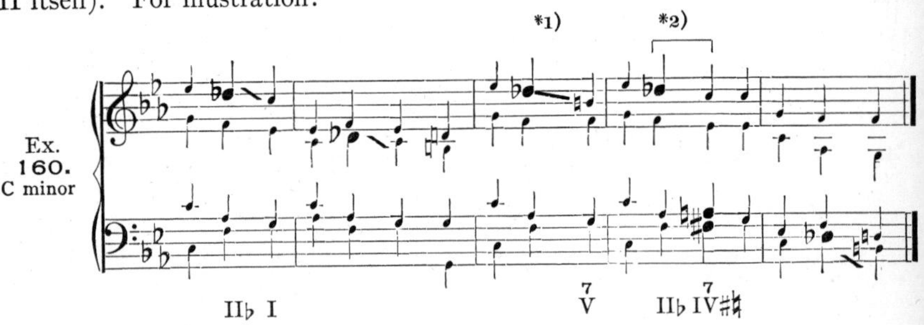

*1) See Ex. 154, note *2). — *2) Two different altered chords in succession; observe that they both belong to the Second-dominant class, so the progression is practically chord-repetition.

Additional illustrations:

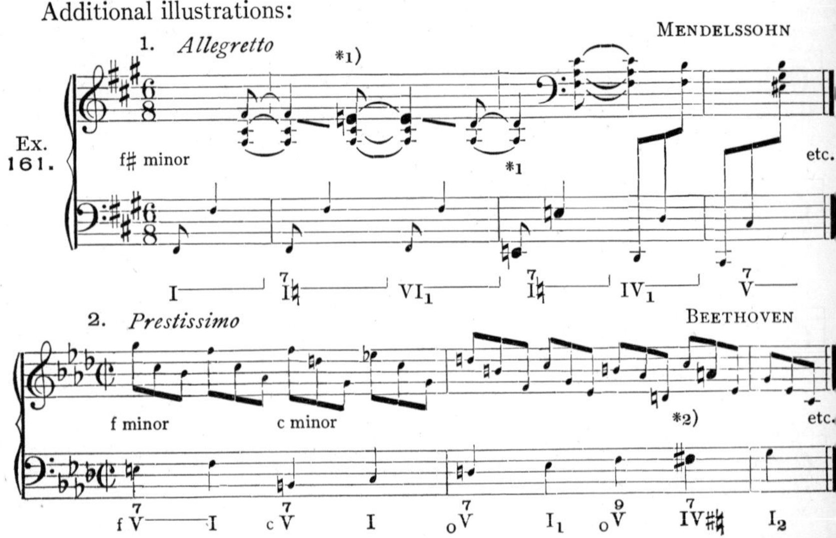

*1) Lowered 7th step. — *2) Raised 6th and 4th steps. — *3) Raised 6th step. — *4) Lowered 2d step. — *5) Embellishing (neighboring) notes.

LESSON 43.

Harmonize the following minor melodies and basses, introducing altered chords at each * (in some cases definite, in others optional); and modulating as indicated:

*1) One bass note for the beat. — *2) Like Ex. 160, note *2). — *3) These irregular key-relations (contrary to par. 197, Rule I) are justified by the sequences. — *4) The three upper parts on the G-staff. One melody-note to each slur, strictly.

CHAPTER XXXVI.

MIXED CHORDS IN MAJOR AND MINOR.

218. Mixed chords, usually called **chords of the augmented sixth** (because they all contain that peculiar interval), have an illegitimate or deformed shape, resulting from the more or less unnatural association of steps which are peculiar to different scales. They are very effective, frequent, and easy to manipulate. Besides the rules in par. 206, 209 (which review), which apply literally to the mixed chords, also, it must be observed, that

The interval of an augmented 6th is rarely inverted; and mixed chords usually resolve into the tonic chords.

219. Mixed chords in **major** are obtained, first, by *raising the 2d step* of the scale, in *dominant discords;* second, by *lowering the 6th step* in conjunction with the *raised 4th* (or *raised 4th* and *2d*) steps, in *Second-class* chords.

Third, and very rarely, by *lowering the 2d step* in the dominant seventh.
Mixed chords of the dominant class:

Mixed chords of the Second class:

*1) The augm. 6th arises from the association of *d*♯ (the raised step) with *f*♮ (the 7th of the dominant chord). — *2) Here the augm. 6th is inverted to a dim. 3d (*d*♯–*f*♮) which sounds ambiguous, and even disagreeable. — *3) The augm. 6th arises from associating *d*♭ with the leading-tone *b*. — *4) The augm. 6th (*a*♭–*f*♯) is here again inverted (to a dim. 3d, *f*♯–*a*♭). — *5) When the augm. 6th is inverted *beyond the octave* (i.e., as dim. *tenth*) the effect is much less objectionable. — *6) The *d*♯ in these chords is quite frequently written *e*♭, erroneously. The latter could appear only as distinctive tone of the *minor mode* (see par. 213).

220. Mixed chords in **minor** are limited to the **Second class** (II–II⁷–IV–IV⁷), and are obtained by *raising the 4th scale-step,* while the 6th step remains minor. For example:

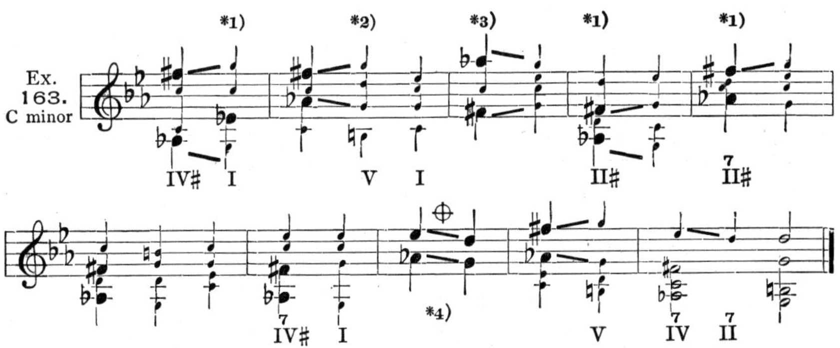

*1) The identity of these chords in *C major* on one hand, or in *C minor* on the other, depends, as usual, upon the *resolution,* — here solely upon the tones *e-flat*, as above, or *e-natural*, as in Ex. 162, measure 6. See par. 206, and 213. — *2) For the reasons given in note *1), the progression into the *dominant* (instead of the tonic) chord is indefinite; the I must immediately follow, at all events. — *3) The augm. 6th (*a*♭–*f*♯) is here inverted, as dim. 10th. Comp. Ex. 162, note *5). — *4) These perfect 5ths are so seductive, that unusual caution must be observed in using the mixed IV⁷; the only reliable safeguard is the resolution into a *tonic* chord. See Ex. 140, note *1). In the following measure, the 5ths are inverted (as 4ths); and the last measure shows still another method of avoiding them — by resolving the 7th (*e*♭) alone, into the II⁷.

Additional illustrations:

Ex. 164.

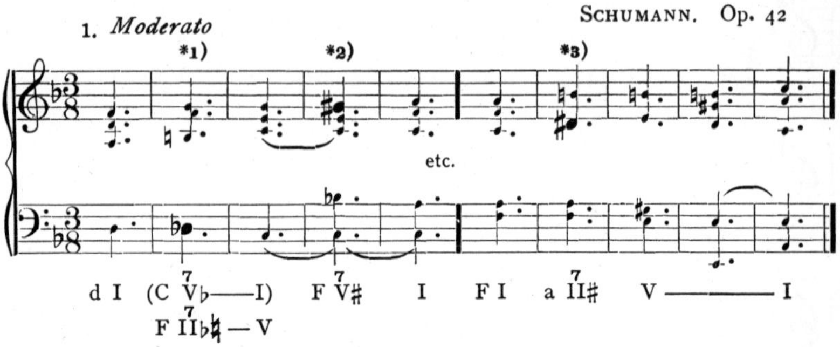

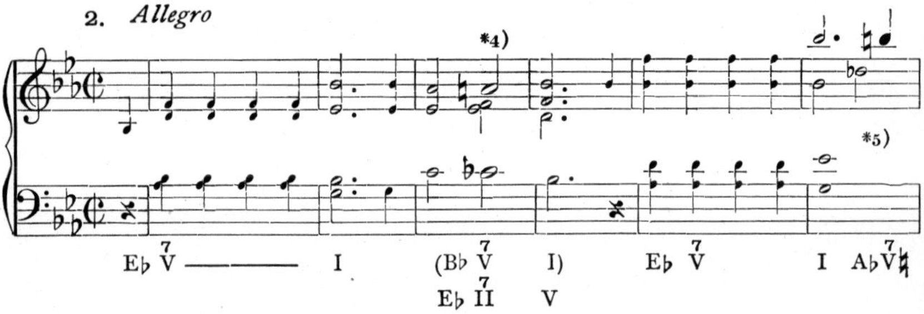

1. *Moderato* SCHUMANN. Op. 42

*1) *2) *3)

etc.

d I (C V^{7}♭—I) F V^{7}♯ I F I a II^{7}♯ V——I

F II^{7}♭♮ — V

2. *Allegro*

*4) *5)

E♭ V^{7} —— I (B♭ V^{7} I) E♭ V^{7} I A♭V^{7}♮

E♭ II^{7} V

BEETHOVEN

3. *Allegretto* MENDELSSOHN

*6) *6)

I E♭ V^{7} I E I A V^{7}♯—I E II^{7}♯♯—I A V^{7}♯—I

*1) Possibly the lowered second step of *C* major, but more likely a lowered 6th and raised 4th step of *F* major. — *2) Raised second step. — *3) Raised 4th step. — *4) This, like note *1), may be analyzed either way, but *E-flat* major is far the most plausible, because the lowered second step in major is very rare. — *5) Mixed dom.-7th of *A-flat* major. — *6) Here the modulations are both effected through altered steps.

LESSON 44.

A. Harmonize the following melodies and basses, with altered or mixed chords (as marked Al. and M.), and modulating as indicated:

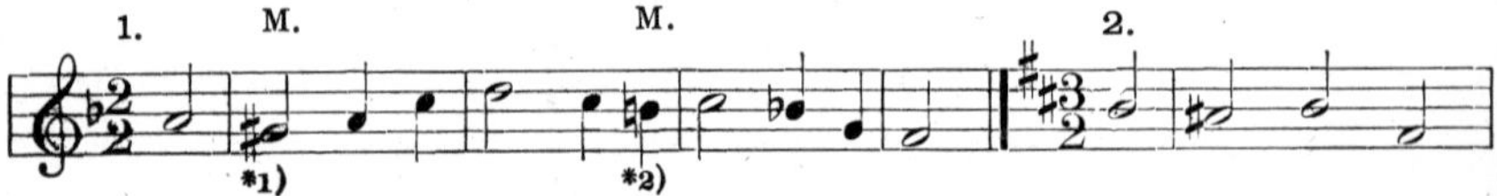

*1) The raised second step in soprano is most suggestive of a mixed *dominant* chord. — *2) The raised 4th step *must* be in some *Second-class* chord. — *3) The mixed chords in minor are exclusively Second class (par. 220). — *4) Begin with the *high* third in soprano. — *5) These last two chords, which follow the perfect-cadence chord, constitute a *Plagal cadence*.

B. Experiment with original 4-measure phrases.

CHAPTER XXXVII.

EXTRANEOUS MODULATION, INDIRECT.

221. Extraneous modulations are such as extend *beyond* the next-related keys, in any direction. Compare par. 197, Rule I. The remote key is usually reached indirectly, by modulating *through the next-related keys which intervene*, i.e., from signature to signature in the direction of the desired key — **whereby either the major or minor mode of the intermediate signatures may be taken.**

For illustration: from *C* major (or *a* minor) to *A-flat* major (or *f* minor), the following *signatures* will be involved: ♮—♭—2♭—3♭—4♭ (see Ex. 146). The modulation may therefore represent any of the following lines of keys:

C (a)—F—B♭—E♭—A♭ (f) (Capital letters, major;
" " —d—g —c " " small letters, minor)
" " —F—g —E♭— " "
" " —d—B♭—c — " "
" " —F—B♭—c — " "
" " —d—g —E♭— " "

Or: from *B*♭ (or *g*) to *A* (or *f*♯), through the signatures 2♭—1♭—♮—1♯—2♯—3♯. Or: from *D*♭ (or *b*♭) to *E* (or *c*♯) thus: 5♭—6♭=6♯—5♯—4♯.

LESSON 45.

Harmonize the following melodies (Nos. 2 and 4 in several ways), modulating at each *: N.B. Use the *dim.-7th* chord very freely — *in both modes* (Ex. 153, note *1).

LESSON 46.

Harmonize the following melodies, each in at least two ways, with a modulation at each * (major or minor):

*1) Where the key is not specified, the student can easily define it.

LESSON 47.

Harmonize the following basses, each in at least two ways, with a modulation at each * (major or minor):

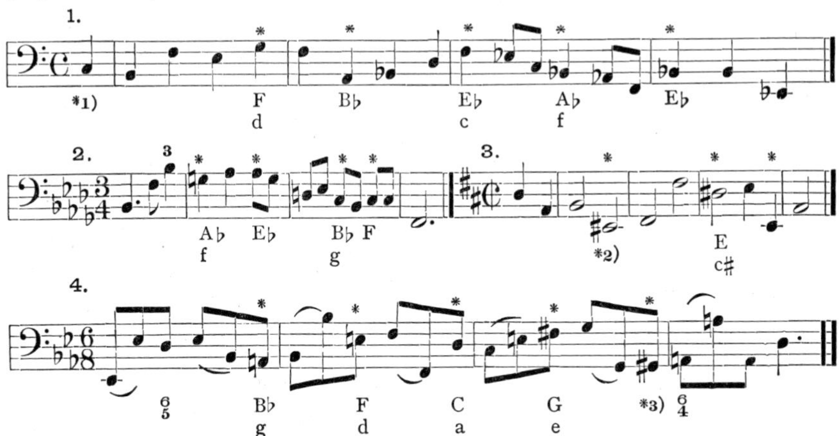

*1) Use the dim.-7th chord freely, especially in minor. — *2) Lesson 46, note *1). — *3) Raised 4th step of D major.

CHAPTER XXXVIII.

DIRECT EXTRANEOUS MODULATION. THE STRIDE.

222. Under certain favorable circumstances a remote key may be reached *directly;* that is, without passing through the intervening signatures.

223. The first and best of these cases is a direct transition of four degrees (or signatures), for which the author has adopted the term "**modulatory stride,**" and which is defined as follows:

The "stride" is a perfect fifth downward from any major keynote, and upward from any minor keynote, with a change of mode.

For example: from *C major* down to *f minor;* or from *c minor* up to *G major.* The Stride-relation is therefore represented in both directions by any perfect 5th, *the upper tone of which is a major tonic, and the lower tone a minor tonic.*

Ex. 165.

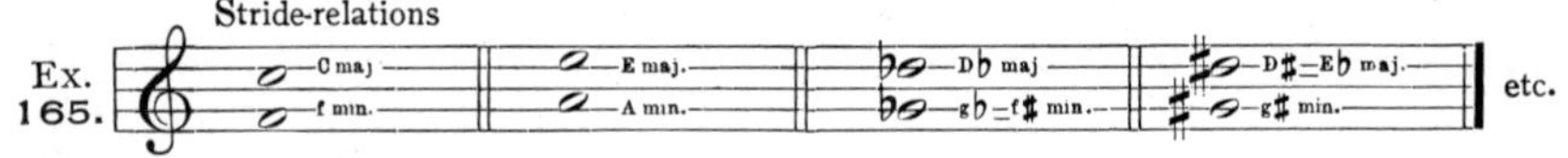

224. Upon reflection it will become apparent that the remote transition called the Stride results simply from an *exchange of mode* (minor for the expected major, and vice versa); without the change of mode it would be an ordinary dominant or subdominant modulation, respectively. That is, the Stride from *C major* is *f* **minor** instead of *F major;* and from *g minor* it is *D* **major** instead of *d minor.*

Confusion can however be avoided only by mechanically observing the formula in par. 223.

The Stride-modulation is made in the usual manner, according to par. 198. For example:

Ex. 166.

*1) With *f-natural* (instead of *f-sharp*) it would be the next-related key, *d minor*. That *f-sharp* should however be preferred to *f-natural*, in the vicinity of *g minor*, is very obvious, and affords the best demonstration of the practically close intimacy of the Stride-relation, notwithstanding the actual difference of four degrees in the key-signatures (*g minor* — *D major*).

LESSON 48.

A. Indicate the Stride-relation (by keynotes) from every major and every minor key.
B. Harmonize the following melodies and basses, introducing the modulatory Stride at each *:

1. * * 6/4

2. * * 6/4

3. * A maj. V * 6/4

4. * c min. * 6/4

5. * A♭ maj. * A maj. * 6/4 *1)

6. (*See Appendix*) * V * e min. * Al. *2) I

7. 3 3 *3) 7 6 6/♮5 ♭3 ♮6/♭5 ♯6/4 6/♮5 ♭3 7/♭5 7/♯3 6/5 ♯3 6 6/♮5

*1) The Stride from *A*♭ major is *d*♭ minor, or its equivalent, *c*♯ minor, which is more convenient. — *2) When the last chord of a key is, as here, the *dominant* chord of the coming key, the latter may enter at once — apparently through its tonic. — *3) The basses must be thoroughly analyzed.

CHAPTER XXXIX.

DIRECT EXTRANEOUS MODULATION. THE OPPOSITE MODE.

225. The next best direct transition to a remote key is the **change of mode** (from major to minor, or vice versa) upon the **same tonic;** for instance, from *C* to *c*, or *d* to *D*, or *G-flat* to *f-sharp*, etc. Although this transition into the **opposite mode** actually effects a *change of location* in the modulatory circle (equal to 3 degrees —*C* — *c*), it is hardly to be regarded as a modulation in the strict sense of the term; for it is only a modification of one and the same tone-family or key, as was demonstrated in par. 86 and 89, which review.

226. The possibility of thus changing the mode of any keynote is traceable to **the coincidence of the dominant chords** (V, V^7, $_oV^7$, V^9 altered and $_oV^9$ altered) in the two modes. (See par. 90; 151 *c;* 165, Rule I; Ex. 153, note *1):

By reason of which any dominant chord may be resolved at option either into the major or minor tonic chord of the corresponding key.

See Ex. 111, note *9). The resolution into *major* is, however, always the more natural. For example:

Ex. 167.

*1) The tone upon which this exchange of mode devolves is the mediant (third step) of the key; in this case *e*♮ for *C* major, and *e*♭ for *c* minor. See par. 213.

227. Any dominant chord, then, which enters from major (i.e., as major-key dom.) may resolve into the corresponding minor tonic (by substituting the minor mediant for the expected major mediant); or, inversely, a dominant chord which enters from minor, may resolve into the corresponding major tonic; thus effecting an *exchange of mode.* This may be done at any point in a phrase, and is subject only to such conditions and limitations as are patent to a cultivated ear.

228. The coincidence of the dominant chords in major and minor is frequently utilized as a means of reaching other remote keys directly, *by substituting the Opposite mode* for what would otherwise be a *next-related* key. This is always the case with the Stride (see par. 224); and also with such examples as the following:

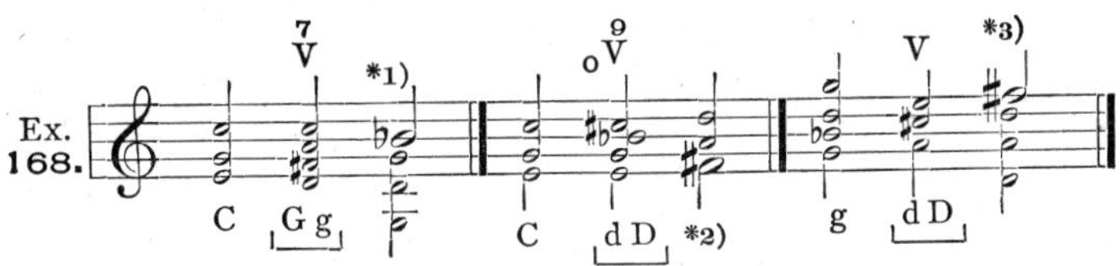

*1) With *b♮* it would be *G major*, a *next-related* key of the *C* major which precedes. Substituting the minor mediant *b♭* makes the modulation remote. — *2) With *f♮* it would be the next-related key, *d-minor;* with *f♯* it is a remote modulation. — *3) The Stride.

229. Further, the exchange of mode may also be accomplished by the simple *chromatic inflection of the mediant itself* (Ex. 169 *a*);

Or, perhaps best of all, through altered chords with the *lowered 6th step* (Ex. 169*b*):

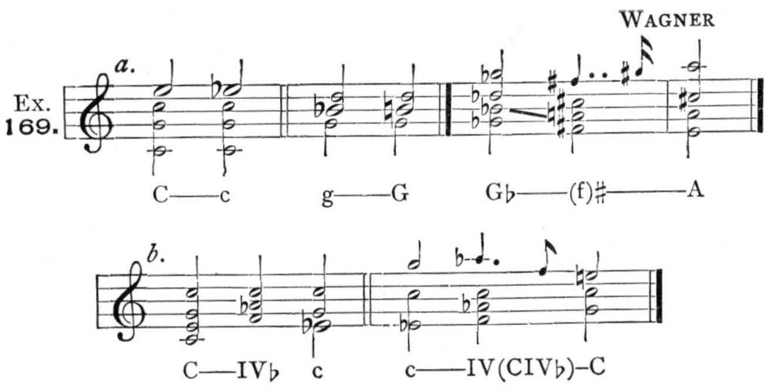

Additional illustrations:

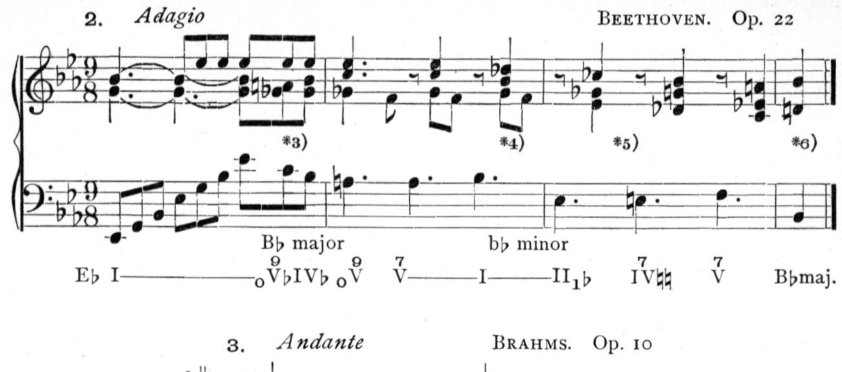

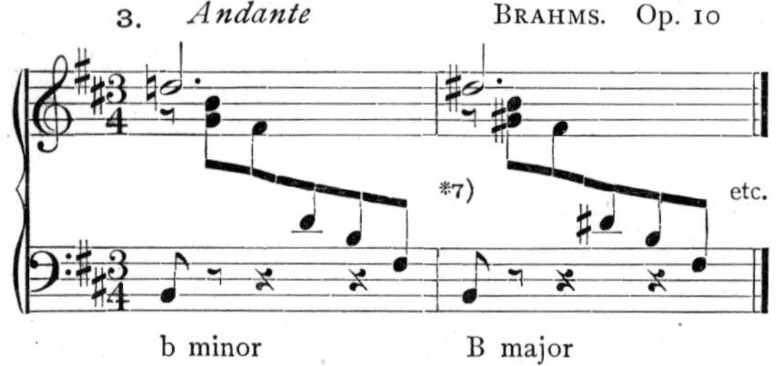

*1) The dom. triad of *a minor*, resolving into *A major*. — *2) A direct chromatic transition from major to minor. — *3) The *g-flat* is the lowered 6th step of the *next-related* key, *B-flat major*. — *4) The dominant chords of *B-flat major* resolve here into *b-flat minor*. — *5) See Ex. 160, note *2). — *6) *B-flat major* here finally asserts itself. — *7) Direct chromatic transition from *b minor* to *B major*.

LESSON 49.

Harmonize the following melodies and basses, introducing the Opposite mode at each *:

*1) At each †, the foregoing dominant chord is resolved into the opposite mode of the *expected* (next-related) key. — *2) Lesson 48, note *2). — *3) This is the Stride (*G–c*), simply because minor is substituted for the expected major. — *4) The cross-relation (see par. 200*b*) is often unavoidable in *sequences*, as here; but, as usual, the sequence justifies it. — *5) The signature is omitted here, and in No. 5, because the notation, during such extensive modulation, is more convenient with accidentals. — *6) Analyze the basses thoroughly.

CHAPTER XL.

SEQUENCE AND CADENCE MODULATIONS.

230. In all the foregoing modulations, both next-related and extraneous, the fundamental rule given in par. 198 has been strictly observed. But more abrupt and irregular modes of transition are possible, under favorable circumstances. The most auspicious conditions are afforded by the momentary *breaks or interruptions* which occur between **sequences,** or at (i.e., after) **cadences** of any kind. Hence:

231. Upon passing into a sequence, or into a new phrase, or distinct member of a phrase, an abrupt transition may be made into the desired key (whether related or not) without necessarily interposing the usual dom. (or second-dom.) modulatory chord.

For example:

*1) The transition is made abruptly from the I of the old key, *into the I of the new* (comp. par. 197, Rule III, second clause). There is no common tone connecting the keys (see par. 232), but the sequences are so close and coherent that the connecting-link may be dispensed with. — *2) This modulation is made in the regular way, but the keys are not related. — *3) Here there is a *succession of tonic chords*, and one single chord must suffice to represent a key. Comp. par. 203. It is all accounted for by the sequence. — *4) The old key is abandoned at its dom.-7th (comp. par. 197, Rule IV). The connecting-link into the first sequence (which is a very close one) is the tone c× = d (leading-tone becoming a tonic).

232. The limitations for such abrupt modulations are: That there shall be a reasonable degree of coherency between the keys; and, as a general though not strict rule, that at least *one tone* be sustained from the old key into the new one, as connecting-link. Of these "pivotal" modulatory tones the best are

the tonic, the mediant, or the dominant of the old key,

which may be exchanged at option for either the dominant, the mediant, the tonic, or the *leading-tone* (perhaps the 4th or 6th steps, as seventh or ninth of the dominant chords) of the new key.

Illustrations of abrupt cadence-modulations, and "pivotal" modulations:

2. Allegro
BRAHMS
*2)
etc.
D I — V — ‖ C I — II# I II## I
3. Vivace
HUMMEL
*3)
etc.
D I A V — I — ‖ C I V I V
4. Lento
*4)
A♭ V — I — V — I — ‖
come sopra. . . . . . .
C I — F V — I —
SCHUMANN
5. Idem.
*5)
etc.
*6)
V — I — ‖ D I — a I2 — V — B♭ I —

*1) Cadence (semi-) in *a* minor, followed by the abrupt announcement of the *f*-minor I. The connecting-link is c-c (mediant becoming dominant). — *2) Dom. semicadence in D, followed by the I of C. Connecting-link e-e (2d step becoming a mediant). — *3) Tonic cadence; connecting-link e-e (dominant becoming mediant). — *4) Transient tonic cadence; connecting-link c-c (mediant becoming tonic). — *5) Connecting-link a-a (mediant becoming dominant). — *6) Dom. semicadence in *a* minor, followed by the I of *B-flat* major. There is no common tone; this is a typical *cadence*-modulation. — See also Ex. 201, No. 2, a typical *sequence*-modulation.

LESSON 50.

Harmonize the following melodies and basses, with abrupt modulations as indicated:

*1) The bass begins on the first beat; the three upper parts follow on the second. — *2) Like note *1) throughout. — *3) This irregular rhythmic form of the perfect cadence (unaccented) is not unusual, and is justified here by its agreement with the semicadence. — *4) Plagal ending. Comp. Lesson 44, note *5). — *5) The three upper parts on the G-staff. One melody-note to each slur.

CHAPTER XLI.

SPECIAL APPLICATION OF THE DIMINISHED-7TH CHORD, IN BOTH MODES.

233. The most efficient and attractive form of the entire dominant chord-class, and the most flexible chord in the whole range of harmony, is the **chord of the diminished 7th.** It is very frequently employed for the purpose of modulation, and, on account of the unlimited facility of its connections, it serves as a transitional medium between *any keys, regardless of mode,* and almost entirely irrespective of the ordinary consideration of key-relation.

234. The following points must be borne in mind:

a. The chord of the dim. 7th is the Incomplete form of the dom. ninth, and is found upon the *leading-tone of the minor mode* (par. 176).

b. Though legitimately a *minor-mode* chord, the dim.-7th is equally available (as altered chord) in the *major* mode; i.e., it may resolve indifferently, either into the minor or major I. Ex. 153, note *1).

c. **A dim.-7th may be introduced, in some form or other, after the tonic chords (I or VI) of any other major or minor key.**

The choice of inversion will depend upon the form and location of the preceding chord.

d. The *notation* of the dim.-7th must conform to the **new key** (into which it resolves). See the table made in Lesson 29, B. Whatever chromatic inflections appear, must be effected according to the rules in par. 200, which see. For illustration:

Ex. 173.

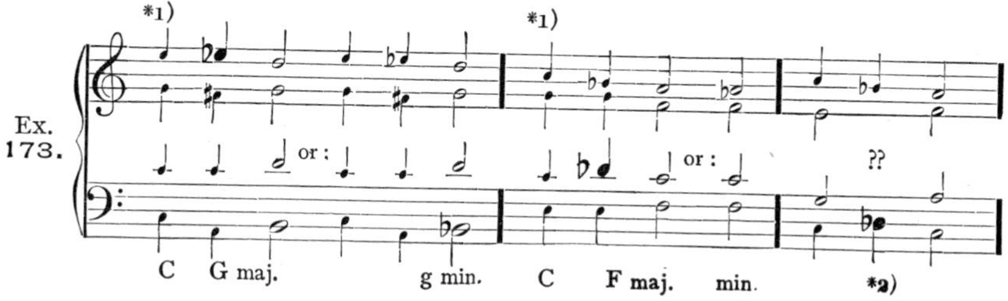

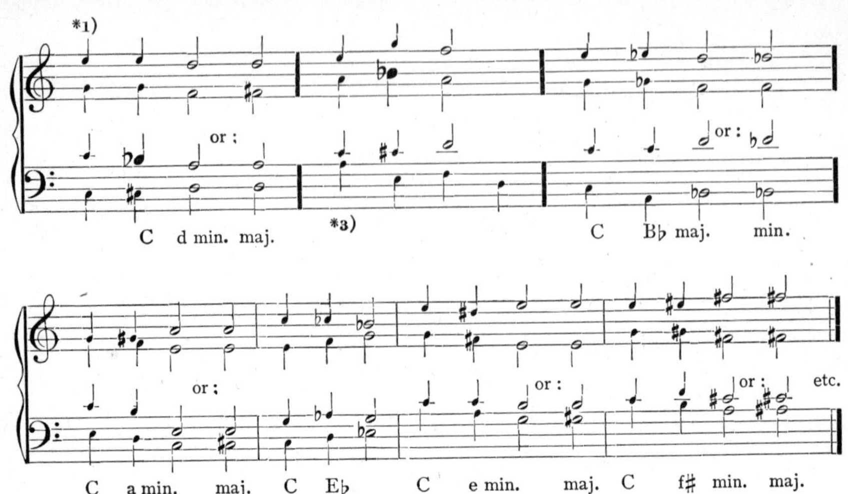

*1) With *e-flat*, instead of *e*, the first chord will represent the I of *c minor* also. —*2) Avoid that form of the dim.-7th in which the 7th (the original 9th) lies in the bass. See Ex. 130, note *4). — *3) In this example the VI of C major is used. It represents, at the same time, the I of *a minor*.

LESSON 51.

A. Connect the I of every major and minor key, with the dim.-7th of C major (and minor), in the manner of Ex. 173. — B. Connect the I of G major with the dim.-7th of every other major (and minor) key, as in Ex. 173. All inversions optional.

LESSON 52.

Harmonize the following melodies and basses, introducing a dim.-7th (*choice optional*) at each *:

*1) The dim.-7th of *d* minor, *D major*, or *F major*, at option. — *2) The dim.-7th of *C major*, *c minor*, or *E-flat major*, at option. — *3) The choice here is limited to *c-sharp minor*, in view of the approaching cadence in that key. — *4) The choice here is limited to *D major* or *d minor*, in view of the following slur. — *5) Place the three accompanying parts together upon the bass staff, and use one chord to each slur, strictly. The choice of key is rendered evident by the slurs. — *6) The three upper parts *rest* on the 1st beat of each measure, excepting the cadence, and enter together on the 2d beat. Thus: 𝄽 ♩ ♩ | — together on the G-staff, throughout.

CHAPTER XLII.

CONSECUTIVE DOMINANT CHORDS.

235. The most notable exception to the fundamental law of dominant chord-progression given in par. 69 (Rule III), is encountered when the dominant chord, instead of resolving into the tonic harmonies of its own key, **digresses into another dominant chord** (of some other key). This irregular but by no means infrequent progression may be demonstrated on the ground that the obligations of the first dominant chord are simply *transferred* to a chord of exactly similar obligations in another key. And the connection is moreover usually effected by means of one or more *chromatic* inflections, which is the smoothest of all modes of melodic progression, and justifies every irregularity.

236. The **chromatic inflection** is directly opposed to the diatonic progression, and consists, as has already been seen, in simply *raising or lowering* a certain letter or scale-step by an accidental, without effecting an actual progression from one letter or step into another. It does not conform to the line of the diatonic scale, but is *oblique* to the latter. It is an abrupt digression from the natural order of tones, and its effect is therefore to *cancel the key instantly and completely*. No resolution, and no diatonic chord-progression of any kind, within the same key, can include any chromatic inflection (only excepting the possible chromatic introduction of **altered tones**). Consequently, the chromatic inflection (*unless incidental to an altered or mixed chord*) invariably executes a change of key, as abrupt as it is inevitable, and usually so quietly and smoothly that this species of melodic succession, i.e., "Chromatics," is properly regarded as the most powerful and seductive factor in **modula-**

tion. The fundamental principle of chord-analysis, that "the identity of a chord depends upon its progression" (Ex. 152, note *3), is also canceled by every chromatic inflection, which, as stated above, instantly severs the connection of the chord with its key. From this, the peculiarity, but at the same time the extreme importance of the chromatic inflection, and the frequency of its employment, especially in modern composition, may be inferred. A great number of curious chord-progressions may be and are effected through the agency of chromatics, which elude all rational demonstration, and can be accounted for in no better way than as a manifestation of seductive chromatic agency. Therefore, the chromatic inflection must be accepted as one of the chief excuses for the peculiar harmonic connection of which this chapter treats, namely, **the direct succession of different dominant chords.**

237. This principle of chromatic Dominant succession is to be applied in the most general and comprehensive sense; i.e., the dominant chords of one key **in any form** (V, V^7, $_{o}V^7$, V^9 or $_{o}V^9$) can progress into **any form** of the dominant of another key (V, V^7, $_{o}V^7$, V^9 or $_{o}V^9$), *either major or minor.*

This sweeping rule is tenable in theory, but in practice it is limited. By far the best and most common successions are those in which **the third of the first dom.-chord is chromatically lowered, or its root chromatically raised.** See Ex. 174, measure 1 (lowered third), and measure 2 (raised root).

238. The new dominant chord may resolve properly into its tonic, or it may be followed again by another dominant chord. When the series of dominant chords is thus protracted, either the soprano or the bass is likely to progress in *continuous chromatic descent or ascent* (Ex. 174, B).

239. Rule I. The *seventh* of each dominant discord should be correctly resolved (diatonically downward), *if possible.*

Rule II. The chromatic progression should be approached, if possible, in the corresponding direction. Review par. 200, and par. 60.

*1) May also be *c minor.* — *2) May also be *any other form* of the dom. harmony of C (V, $_{0}V^{7}$, V^{9}, $_{0}V^{9}$). — *3) May be *any other* dom. chord of F. — *4) May also be *f minor*. Note that in this succession the third of the first dom.-chord is lowered chromatically (*b* to *b*♭). See also measures 5, 6; and B, measure 1. — *5) *5) In both of these cases there is no chromatic inflection involved. — *6) Here the seventh of the dom. chord remains stationary. — *7) The substitution of the *diminished*-7th ($_{0}V^{9}$) for the dom.-7th, is an effective means of facilitating all such awkward successions as these. — *8) *8) In both of these cases the 7th is obliged to ascend. See par. 239, Rule I. Therefore the connections are somewhat objectionable. — *9) See par. 238; and par. 239, Rule II. The identity (i.e., the keys) of each of these chords can be determined only by conjecture. Comp. par. 203; and par. 236. — *10) The *notation* of the diminished-7th, in chrom. succession, cannot be definitely regulated, because the keys represented are only conjectural. In descending succession *flats*, and in ascending succession *sharps*, are apt to prevail. — *11) Comp. par. 200*b*.

Additional illustrations :

LESSON 53.

A. Connect the following chords, in 4-part harmony, inversion (bass) optional:

A maj. $\overset{7}{V}$—D $\overset{7}{V}$ *1) ; E♭ $\overset{7}{V}$—c $\overset{7}{V}$; D $\overset{9}{V}$—F $\overset{7}{V}$; f $_{o}\overset{9}{V}$—D♭ $\overset{7}{V}$; E $\overset{7}{V}$—C $\overset{7}{V}$; B♭ $\overset{7}{V}$—A♭ $_{o}\overset{7}{V}$;
G $\overset{9}{V}$—A $\overset{7}{V}$; B $\overset{7}{V}$—f♯ $_{o}\overset{9}{V}$; g $_{o}\overset{9}{V}$—d $_{o}\overset{9}{V}$—a $_{o}\overset{9}{V}$—e $_{o}\overset{9}{V}$; c♯ $_{o}\overset{9}{V}$—f♯ $_{o}\overset{9}{V}$—b $_{o}\overset{9}{V}$—e $_{o}\overset{9}{V}$.

B. Find and play these successions at the keyboard, the bass alone in the left hand.

C. Harmonize the following melodies, with successive dom. chords, as indicated at each * (inversion optional):

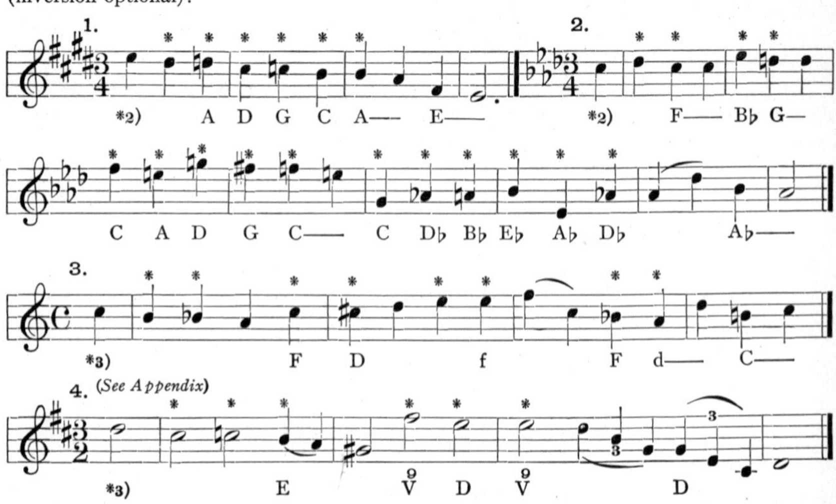

*1) Resolve the last chord, in each case, into its tonic. — *2) The V^7 at each * in these melodies. — *3) Either V, V^7, or $_0V^7$ at each *. — *4) A dim.-7th at each *.

CHAPTER XLIII.

ENHARMONIC TREATMENT OF THE CHORDS OF THE DIMINISHED-7TH AND DOMINANT-7TH.

240. The **enharmonic change** (or exchange) is obtained by inflecting the next higher or lower letter so that it **agrees in sound** with the original tone. Thus, the tone *g-flat* is "enharmonically identical" (in musical practice) with *f-sharp*, and either of these two tones may be enharmonically exchanged for the other. The enharmonic equivalent of *b* is *c-flat;* of *f*, *e-sharp;* of *d* there are two enharmonic equivalents, *c-double-sharp* and *e-double-flat;* and so on. Review Ex. 146, with its note.

241. The enharmonic exchange involves an inevitable change of key, or modulation, as the two enharmonic equivalents cannot belong to the same key.

242. This modulatory factor is most commonly applied in the **chords of the diminished-7th,** which admit of the enharmonic exchange to a very remarkable extent, and with that facility and flexibility which characterize every movement of these extraordinary chords.

243. The wonderful ambiguity of the dim.-7th is owing chiefly to the peculiarity of its structure, consisting, as it does, of *equal contiguous intervals* (of three half-steps each), which divide the 12-tone chromatic octave into four equal parts. This is best seen and understood at the keyboard. Thus:

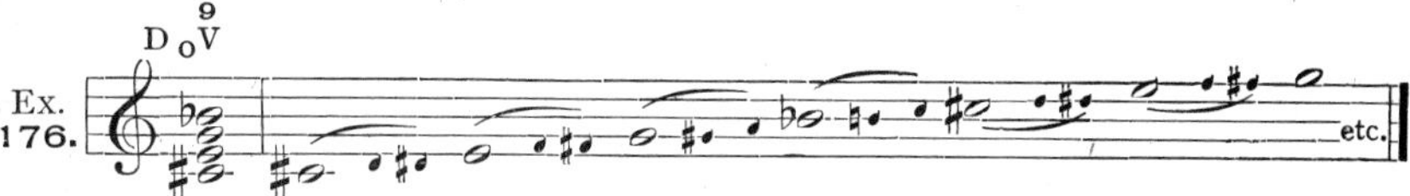

In consequence of this uniformity of structure, there is no external mark of recognition by means of which the various forms or inversions of the diminished-7th chord might be distinguished **in sound** from each other. The four forms (inversions) of the above chord:

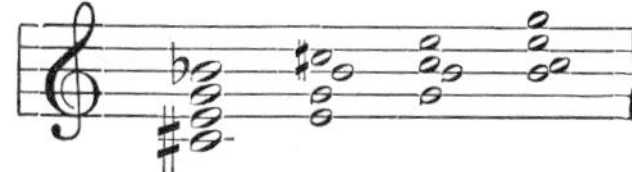

all present the selfsame *external form, upon the keyboard, and are not distinguishable from each other* as chords of the 7, $^6_5$, $^4_3$ and 2, respectively; because the actual difference in the size of the interval *b-flat* — *c-sharp* (augmented second), while recognizable on the paper, in the *notation* of the dim.-7th chord, disappears in the *sound* of the chords, on account of the enharmonic coincidence of the augm. second with the minor third.

244. As the different inversions of the dim.-7th chord can therefore not be distinguished from each other in sound, it follows that the identity of the *separate intervals* is not distinctly definable, or recognizable by ear. That is, it is impossible to determine, by ear, *which of the four tones is the leading-tone,* which the original *9th,* which the *7th,* etc. Hence,

each tone of the dim.-7th chord may be assumed in turn to be a leading-tone, whereby it will represent in each case a different key, and will be subject to a corresponding alteration of notation.

As the alteration in notation does not alter the *sound* of the interval or chord, it will simply be an enharmonic exchange.

For example, adopting the dim.-7th chord of b minor:

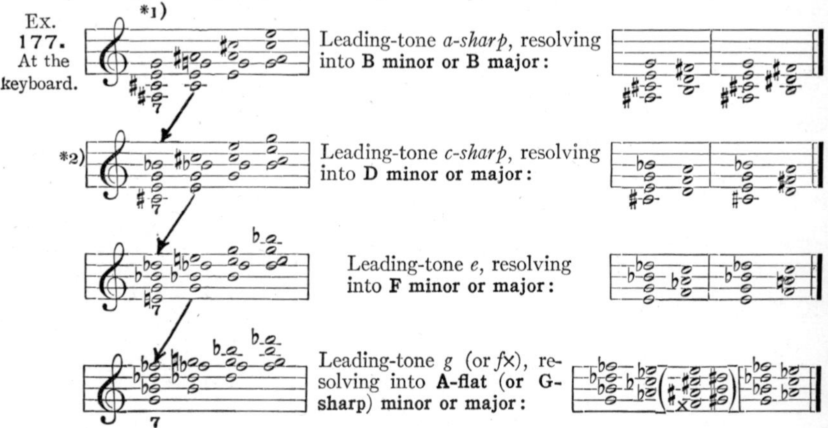

*1) The form and notation of each chord of the dim.-7th is defined by the formula given in par. 176 (which see); namely: it must constitute a *chord of the seventh upon the leading-tone* of each key, respectively, and correspond in notation to the minor scale of its key. — *2) Here the $\frac{6}{5}$-form of the original chord ($_{0}V^{9}$ in *b minor*) on *c-sharp,* is transformed into a chord of the 7th on the tone *c-sharp,* whereby an *enharmonic change from a-sharp to b-flat* is involved. The selfsame procedure gives rise to the other two enharmonic exchanges which follow.

245. The same system of enharmonic exchange is applied with similar results to the *other two* chords of the dim.-7th, which lie respectively a half-step above and below the one upon *a-sharp* (manipulated in Ex. 177). For illustration:

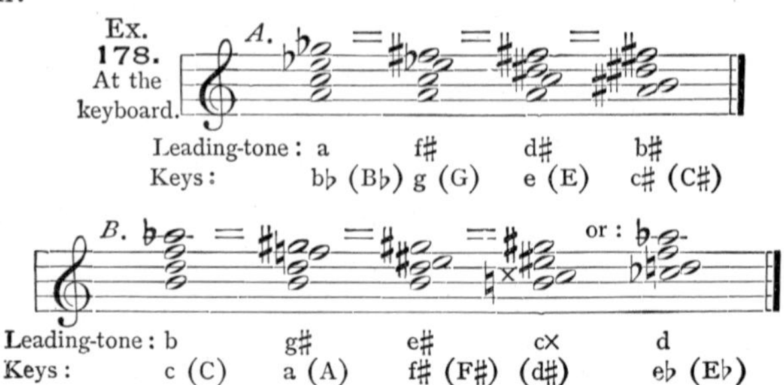

246. The application of these exchanges in enharmonic modulations is made as follows: The chord of the dim.-7th is introduced in its own key (i.e., in the notation corresponding to its scale, — but in minor or major, indifferently), and, upon repetition, or during a series of repetitions, the *notation* is altered, according to the given tables, to agree with that of the desired key. For example:

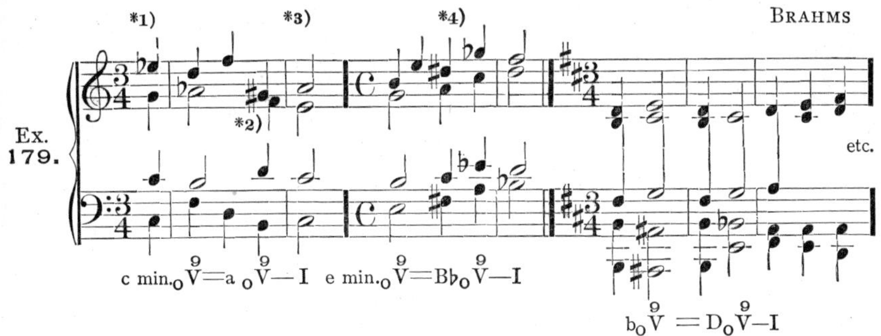

*1) Or C major. — *2) *A-flat* is enharmonically exchanged for *g-sharp*. And, as is here shown, the exchange need not be made in the same part. — *3) Or A major. — *4) The enharmonic coincidence of the chords (practically chord-repetition) renders all peculiar melodic progressions, as here in soprano, excusable.

ENHARMONIC TRANSFORMATION OF THE DOMINANT-7TH.

247. The chord of the dom.-7th is identical *in sound* with a mixed Second-class chord of the *minor and major keys upon the tonic immediately* (i.e., a half-step) *below the original tonic*. By means of this enharmonic exchange, a modulation may be made, in other words, into the *next lower key* (the *leading-tone becoming a tonic*). For example, from C (or *c*) to B (or *b*); from B (or *b*) to A♯ = B♭ (or *b*♭). Thus:

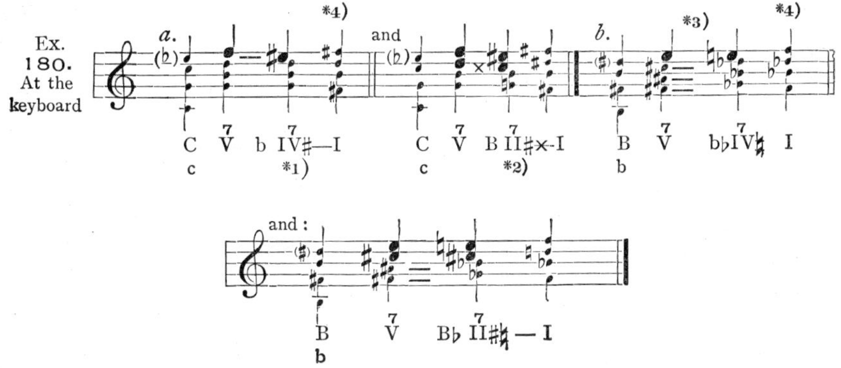

*1) Raised 4th step in *minor* (IV⁷). — *2) Raised 4th and 2d, and lowered 6th steps, in *major* (II⁷). — *3) Generally, the 7th, or the 7th and 5th, of the dominant chord are enharmonically changed (see the first measures); but here, owing to the unusual location (or signatures) of the keys (B major progressing into *a-sharp* minor), the 7th remains, and the *lower* intervals are changed. — *4) The resolution into the I is the more legitimate progression, because these are mixed chords. *But the progression into the dominant chord is more common, in practice;* in which case, the parallel 5ths must be guarded against (usually by omitting the 7th of the mixed IV⁷ — reducing it to the IV). See Ex. 163, note *2), note *4); and Ex. 181, measure 4.

Additional illustrations:

LESSON 54.

A. Harmonize the following melodies, introducing a chord of the dim.-7th at each *, with enharmonic exchange at the following *, as indicated by the key, and according to Exs. 177 and 178:

*1) The three lower parts together on the bass staff.

B. Transform the dom. 7th-chord of *every key*, enharmonically, in exactly the manner shown in Ex. 180.

C. Harmonize the following melodies, with an enharmonic change at each *, according to Ex. 180:

SUPPLEMENTARY EXERCISE.

Harmonize each of the following fragments, *in as many keys as may be found to contain the notes*, either as legitimate or as altered steps:

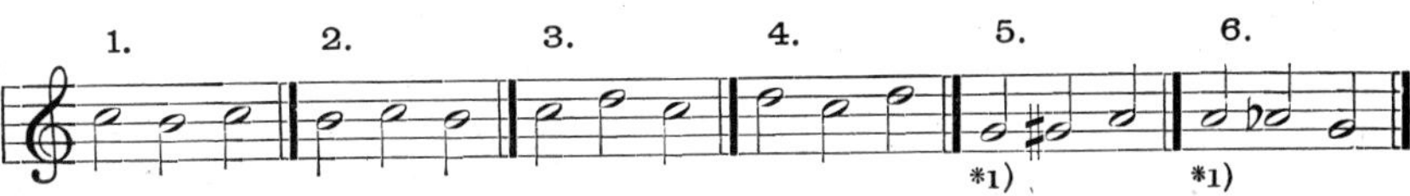

*1) An excellent *general* rule for chromatic successions is, to harmonize the first tone with some (almost any) *3-tone chord*, and the second tone with some *dominant* harmony.

DIVISION FOUR.

INHARMONIC TONES.

INTRODUCTORY.

248. A chord, as a cluster of accordant tones, is defined in par. 28 as the combination of 3, 4 or 5 tones in *thirds*, or in inverted forms reducible to thirds. The simultaneous association of *more than five* different tones; or the association of even 3 tones in any other interval-relations than those embraced in the definition; or, in a word,

> **the addition of any tone which is foreign to the legitimate (harmonic) chord-structure, results in a so-called inharmonic discord.**

For illustration:

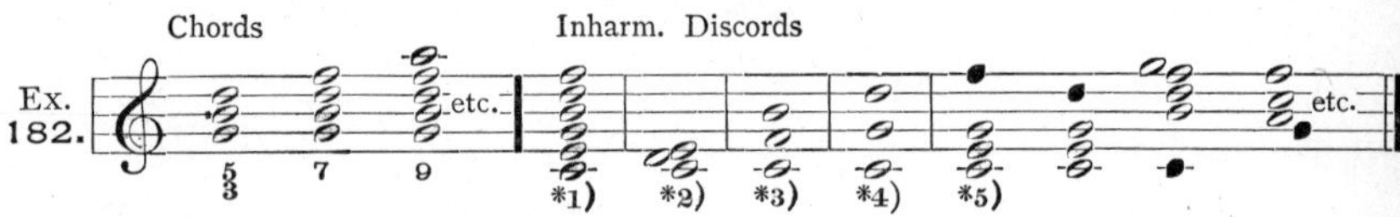

*1) *Six* different tones can not accord. — *2) Association of two seconds (*c-d* and *d-e*). — *3) Association of two 4ths. — *4) Two 5ths. — *5) These four harmonic bodies would be rendered inharmonic by the addition of the false tones (marked ●), which are foreign to their legitimate chord-form. Review par. 24–28.

249. The tone which is foreign to the chord is called the *inharmonic dissonance*, and it is invariably

> **either the upper or lower diatonic neighbor of one of the legitimate chord-intervals.**

It is evident that the identity of an inharmonic dissonance can not be determined until the identity of the *chord* with which it is associated has been clearly established. For example, in the combination *c-g-d* (Ex. 182, note *4), the *d* will be inharmonic if the chord can be proven to be the triad of C (*c-e-g*); but if it prove to be the triad of G (*g-b-d*) then the *c* is the foreign tone. *The identity of the chord will depend, as usual, upon its relations to the adjacent chords, particularly to the one which follows.*

250. There are four varieties of the inharmonic dissonance, distinguished from each other by the manner in which they enter or progress, namely, the **organ-point,** the **suspension,** the **anticipation** and the **neighboring** (or **embellishing**) **tone.**

CHAPTER XLIV.

THE ORGAN-POINT.

251. The natural preëminence of the tonic of a scale renders it admissible *to prolong* (*or sustain*) *that tone*, for a reasonable length of time, *while the other parts continue their harmonic progression*, almost or quite irrespective of the sustained tone.

252. The tone thus held or reiterated during a series of chord-progressions is called an **organ-point,** and it will almost inevitably become inharmonic from time to time (i.e., at those points where the other voices progress into a chord to which it is foreign). If the sustained tone is the tonic of its key, it is called a **tonic** Organ-point.

253. Organ-points appear most naturally and most frequently in the **bass voice,** but are possible, especially when more brief, in tenor, alto, or even soprano.

RULE I. The Organ-point should *begin, and also end, as an harmonic interval;* i.e., it should not make a progression during any chord to which it is foreign.

RULE II. It should not be associated with chord-progressions (or modulations) which render it too obstinately dissonant, or protract its inharmonic condition past 3 or 4 consecutive beats, as a rule.

Rule III. The other voices may progress freely, and modulate transiently into any related keys, but must all move as smoothly as possible.

For illustration (tonic Organ-point in D major):

*1) It is natural that the *dominant* chords of the key should constitute the simplest means of making the tonic (as Organ-point) inharmonic. — *2)*2)*2) These measures illustrate different forms in which the Organ-point may be reiterated, instead of being simply held.— *3) The modulation into *f-sharp* minor, though a next-related key, is somewhat doubtful, on account of the harsh dissonance involved. — *4) On the contrary, the modulations into *g minor* (the Stride) and *d minor* (the Opposite mode) sound perfectly well, for obvious reasons. — *5) This dom. chord of *B-flat* is very harsh, because of its location on the accented beat. It is, however, admissible, because brief.

254. The **dominant,** which is barely less important than the tonic itself, may also be sustained or reiterated as Organ-point, upon the same conditions. For example:

Ex. 184. F major

*1) The dominant note (as Organ-point) becomes inharmonic upon association with *subdominant* (*Second-class*) chords. Comp. Ex. 183, note *1). — *2) Dominant Organ-point in the *soprano*, as duplication of the bass. — *3) The first 4 measures might also be *f minor.*

255. Occasionally both the tonic and the dominant are sustained *together*, as double Organ-point in the perfect 5th; usually in the lowest parts. This is called the Pastoral Organ-point. For example:

Ex. 185. C major

256. The other steps of the scale are not adapted to this mode of treatment, on account of their comparative inferiority. Still, isolated examples of Organ-points upon the **mediant** or the **subdominant** occur, especially in modern composition, which are justified by the simplicity of the attendant harmony and modulation. For illustration:

Ex. 186.

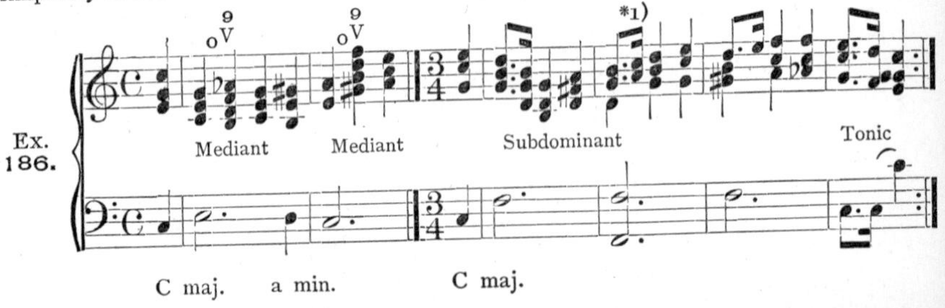

*1) The analysis of other inharmonic tones, like this brief *a* and *c*, will be shown later.

Additional illustrations:

Ex. 187.

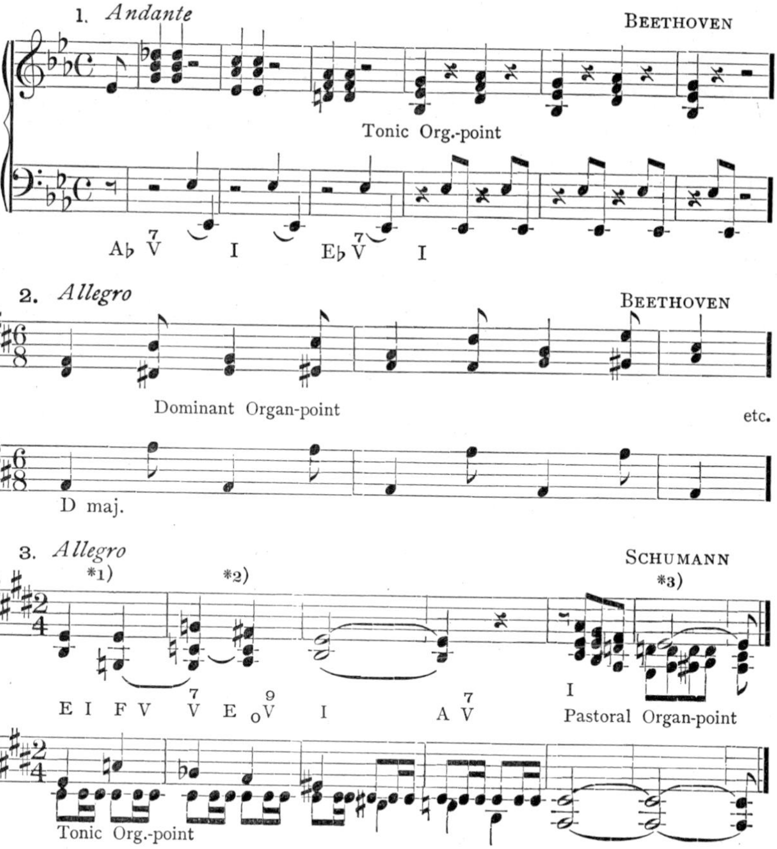
1. Andante
BEETHOVEN
Tonic Org.-point
A♭ V7 I E♭ V7 I
2. Allegro
BEETHOVEN
Dominant Organ-point
etc.
D maj.
3. Allegro
SCHUMANN
*1)
*2)
*3)
E I F V V7 E oV9 I A V7
I
Pastoral Organ-point
Tonic Org.-point

*1) In this curious modulation, the tonic (*e*) is transformed into a leading-tone (par. 232). — *2) Transition from one dominant chord into another (par. 235). — *3) See Ex. 186, note *1).

LESSON 55.

A. Take a number of the 4-measure phrases from Lessons 9 to 36, and add to them first a tonic, and then a dominant, Organ-point (in the lowermost, extra, part). The tonic may run through the whole phrase; but the dominant must begin upon some later accent. For example (Ex. 76):

Ex. 188.

Dom. Organ-point

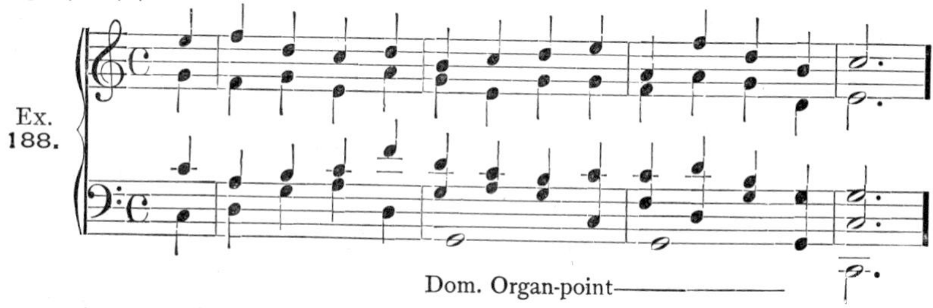

The most of these experiments may be made at the keyboard.

B. Complete the following periods, by harmonizing the melody with three parts — all on the G-staff:

*1) Plagal ending. Comp. Lesson 44, note *5). — *2) One inner voice will suffice, excepting at the two cadences, where the harmony should be fuller.

C. Construct a number of original phrases and periods, with Organ-points.

CHAPTER XLV.

THE SUSPENSION.

257. The suspension is a tone which becomes foreign, or inharmonic, by being held over from the preceding chord.

The tone which is thus sustained past the limits of its own chord, displaces or defers (literally "holds in suspense") the expected legitimate tone of the following chord, hence the appellation **Suspension.** The displaced tone is called the suspended tone, and it must obviously follow immediately, as *resolution of the Suspension.* The Suspension is the *Neighboring-note* (par. 249) of the tone which it defers.

258. For this reason, the prolongation of a tone as Suspension *can take place only in a voice which has a diatonic (stepwise) progression.* And unless the prolonged tone becomes *foreign* in the following chord, it will not produce the impression of suspension.

For illustration (given the chords tonic-dominant in C):

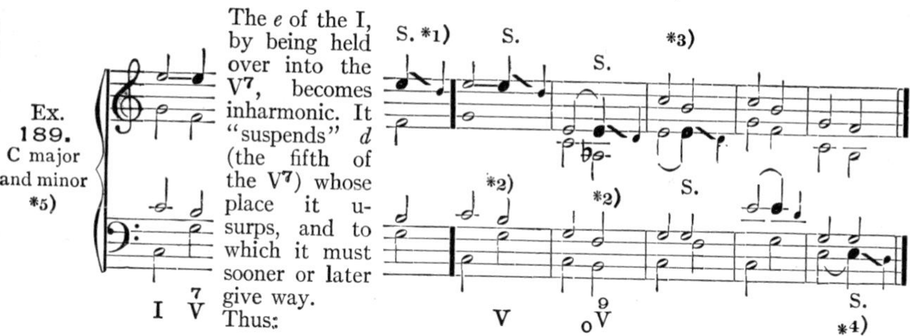

*1) *E* is the suspension, and *d* is the suspended or displaced tone; the Suspension is resolved (*stepwise*) by progressing into this *d*. — *2) *2) The *form* (or inversion) of the chords has no *essential* influence upon the Suspension. — *3) The same Suspension may occur in either inner part, nearly or quite as well as in soprano. — *4) In bass, Suspensions are somewhat rare. — *5) Play each example in *minor*, also.

259. In these same chords (I–V), the tone *c* may be held over, as Suspension of *b* (the third of the V or V7), to which it will diatonically descend, as resolution. Thus:

*1) Comp. Ex. 189 (note *2). The effect is substantially the same whether the dom.-seventh or the dom.-*triad* is employed.

260. If the tone *g* is held over from the I into the V or V^7, *it will not become inharmonic,* because it is the common tone. But if held over into the $_0$V^9 the *g* will be a Suspension. And the tone *e* can be sustained, as Suspension of *f* (the seventh of the V^7), in which case it will resolve diatonically *upward.*

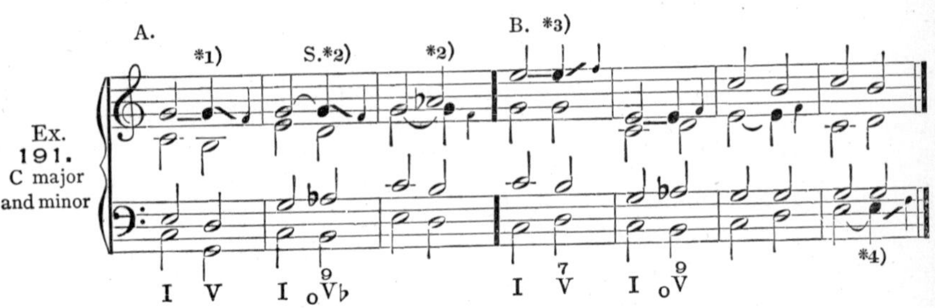

*1) G is the common tone between I and V, or V^7, and does not produce the effect of a Suspension. — *2) In connection with the dom.-*ninth,* however, the *g* becomes inharmonic. — *3) This Suspension, *e,* resolves *upward* into *f* (as well as downward into *d* — Ex. 189). — *4) Ex. 189, note *4).

261. The tones *c* and *e,* in this same chord-progression, may *both be sustained, as* **double suspension.** And, on the same principle, *triple* and even *quadruple* Suspensions are obtainable. For illustration:

*1) If the *c* and *e* are held over into the *triad* V (instead of the V^7 or V) they do not become inharmonic, and therefore do not create the distinct impression of a Double suspension, though virtually they are nothing else. Compare Ex. 108, numbers 1, 3, 4, 5. — *2) Triple suspension. — *3) Quadruple suspension.

262. Rule I. Any interval of any chord, in any voice which progresses diatonically (downward or upward), can be sustained (or repeated) during the change of chord, as Suspension. Compare par. 258.

Rule II. The Suspension usually appears on an **accented** beat of the measure; or, if not, it must always be at least *more accented than its resolution.* With this exception, the length (or accentuation) of the Suspension is optional.

RULE III. The Suspension and the suspended tone (its resolving-tone) should not, as a general principle, *appear simultaneously* in different voices. This, however, applies only to those cases in which the suspended tone is an *inferior step* of the scale, the duplication of which would be avoided in any case. For illustration:

*1) Suspension on the unaccented second beat, and resolved on the accented third beat. — *2) Palpably wrong to anticipate the resolution of the Suspension in soprano by the simultaneous *d* in alto. This example would be correct, however, if the Suspension (*e*) were to *ascend* into *f*. — *3) This is equivalent to a doubled leading-tone. — *4) Good, because the duplication involved is that of the *tonic* (*c*). — *5) If there is any doubt about the case, simply suspend the tone in *both parts* (as here the *e* in both soprano and tenor).

Additional illustrations:

LESSON 56.

Write out the following chord-progressions, in 4-part harmony, introducing a Suspension on the accented beat; at first a single Suspension in each adapted voice, successively; then Double, and Triple suspensions if practicable. The *rhythm*, and (unless indicated) the *inversions*, are optional:

G major: I | V^7 || D minor: I | $_0V^9$ || F major: V^7 | I || B minor: $_0V^9$ | I ||

E♭ major: V^9 | I || C♯ minor: V^7 | VI || A major: IV | I_2 || C minor: IV | V ||

D♭ major: II_1 | I_2 ||

LESSON 57.

A. Harmonize the following melodies and basses, with reference to the subjoined explanatory notes; modulate freely, as indicated, and at option:

*1) The first two melodies are taken from Lesson 10, as shown. Compare them with the unimbellished originals; *and make similar experiments* with other former melodies.— *2) Every note that is thus *repeated* (whether tied or struck) may be treated as Suspension, *by harmonizing the following tone* in its place (exactly as in Exs. 189 to 193). The original, simple, form of the third melody, before it was embellished by Suspensions, was thus:

*3) Susp. on the 1st and 4th beat of each measure. — *4) The *dot* is a Suspension. Comp. note *6). — *5) In this melody, Double suspensions may occasionally be used. — *6) Each dot is to be a Suspension, as if the notation were (s.) throughout. — *7) Suspension in alto. — *8) Susp. in tenor. — *9) Double suspensions in soprano and alto.

B. Construct Original phrases, with Suspensions.

CHAPTER XLVI.

IRREGULAR RESOLUTIONS OF THE SUSPENSION.

263. Simultaneously with the diatonic progression of the Suspension into its resolving-tone, *the other voices may make any smooth progression which does not interfere with the resolution* of the Suspension. This progression of the other parts, at the moment when the Suspension is resolving itself, may be limited to a simple alteration of the form or inversion of the *same* chord; or it may effect a change of chord, or even of key. For illustration:

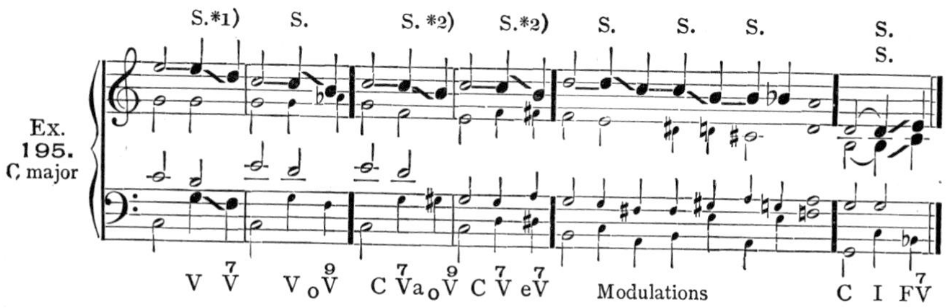

*1) While the Suspension (*e*) is resolving to *d*, the bass progresses in such a manner as to alter the dom.-*triad* to a dom.-*seventh;* in the next measure, to a dom.-*ninth.* — *2) During the resolution of the Suspension (*c*), a modulation is made.

264. Other licences of resolution, such as the *prolongation* of the Suspension — the *indirect resolution* (through an intermediate tone of the same chord) — and the *exchange* of Double suspensions, are possible, but of comparatively rare occurrence. For example:

*1) The Suspension (*c*) in soprano is prolonged for 3 beats, before its resolution into *b* takes place. — *2) All three Suspensions are prolonged, while the bass progresses. — *3) The Suspension (*d*) is resolved indirectly to *c*, through the lower *g*, which is a part of the same (resolving) chord. — *4) The Double suspension (*d* and *f*) changes voices.

LESSON 58.

Harmonize the following melodies, with reference to the subjoined explanatory notes:

*1) *Each repeated note*, whether tied or struck, is to be a Suspension, as in the preceding Lesson; i.e., the *following* tone is harmonized in its place. — *2) During the resolution of each Suspension, one or more of the other voices may progress, as in Ex. 195; i.e., the following tone may be harmonized independently. — *3) The second 16th-note is simply interposed, as in Ex. 196, note *3). — *4) Triple suspension.

CHAPTER XLVII.

IRREGULAR INTRODUCTION OF THE SUSPENSION.

265. A Suspension is not obliged to appear as *repetition or prolongation* of the preceding tone, in the same part, but may enter with any reasonable skip (best from below), as "unprepared" Suspension. As the Suspension must be an inharmonic tone which belongs to the foregoing chord, it is necessary to observe the following rule:

The original tone (the preparation of the Suspension) must either occur in some other voice, in the preceding chord, or must be *understood*, as possible interval of the latter. For example:

*1) The *e* in soprano, although it is not repeated, or tied over, from the preceding beat (as in Ex. 189), is a Suspension, referring to the foregoing *e* in alto. — *2) The *f* in soprano is a Suspension, because its preparation is *understood*, as possible seventh of the chord before. — *3) A possible 7th of the preceding II. — *4) The unprepared Suspension does not sound as well in an inner or lower voice, as in soprano. — *5) Play each example in minor also.

Additional illustrations:

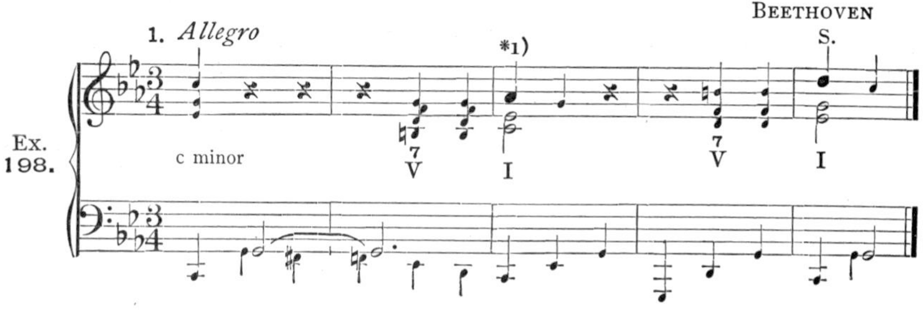

*1) The *a-flat* in soprano may be regarded as an understood ninth of the foregoing dominant chord. But it is more rational to analyze it as a Neighboring-note (of *g*), pure and simple. *All* unprepared Suspensions may be, and perhaps should be, analyzed as Appoggiaturas (par. 277). See, again, par. 249.

LESSON 59.

Harmonize the following melodies, with reference to the subjoined notes:

*1) The accented note becomes a Suspension by harmonizing the following note in its place, as usual. *But the preceding (unaccented) tone must be harmonized with some chord which contains, or might contain, the Suspension.* See par. 265. — *2) An additional (Double) Suspension, in alto or tenor, may in many places accompany the soprano Suspension. — *3) Triple Suspension.

CHAPTER XLVIII.

THE ANTICIPATION.

266. The **Anticipation** is a tone which appears in advance of the chord and beat to which it properly belongs. It may appear in any part, but always sounds most natural in the soprano. Though possible at any point in the course of a phrase, it is perhaps most effective *at the cadence.*

RULE. The Anticipation invariably appears on an **unaccented** beat, or unaccented fraction of its beat. *The more brief it is,* the less danger there will be of a misapprehension of the harmony and rhythm. Comp. par. 262, **Rule** 2.

For illustration (given the chords tonic-dominant in C):

Ex. 199. C major and minor

I

The b is inharmonic, or foreign, in the I. It "anticipates" the third of the V, into which it is immediately repeated. Thus:

Ant.
A.
A.
A.
*1)
I
7
V

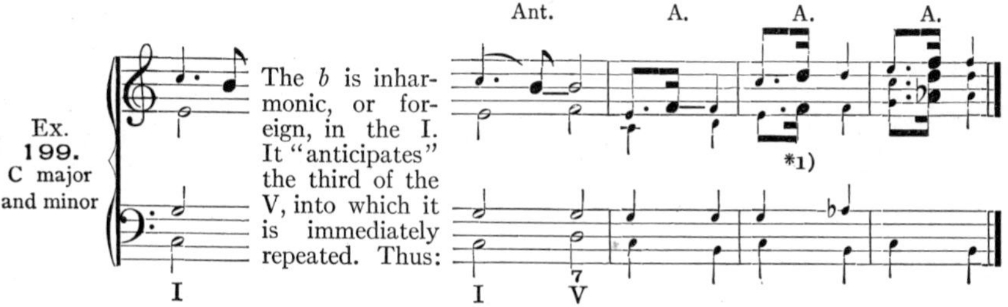

*1) Double anticipation. In the next measure, triple.

267. The Anticipation is usually, *but not necessarily*, an inharmonic (foreign) tone. Being in reality only a modification of the rhythm, its relations to the chord-progression are comparatively immaterial. It is even possible to anticipate the whole chord, in all of the voices. The violation of par. 39, which this occasions, is generally counteracted by making the anticipating chord very brief. For example:

Ex. 200.

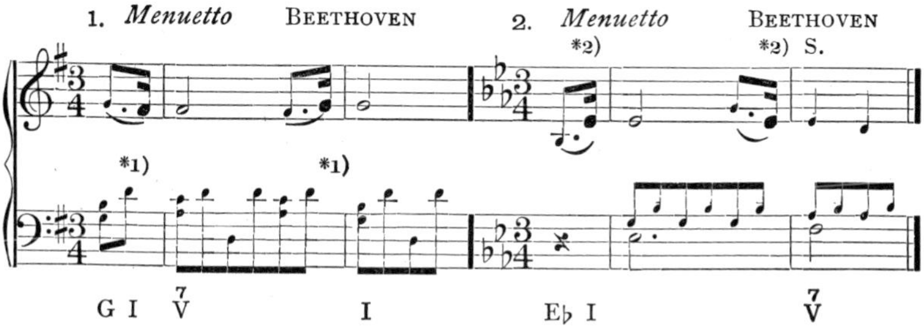

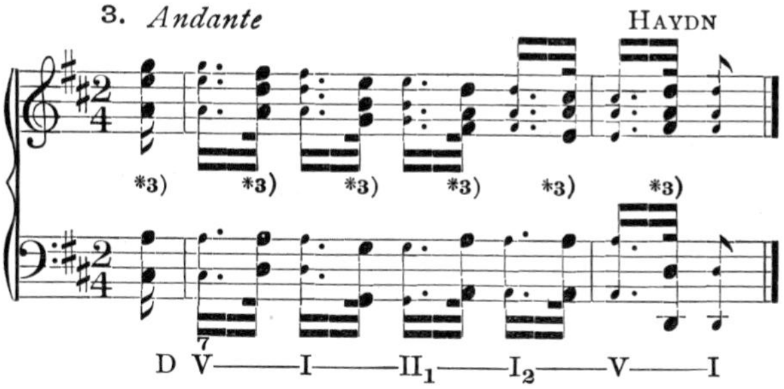

1. Menuetto
BEETHOVEN
2. Menuetto
BEETHOVEN
*2)
*2) S.
*1)
*1)
G I
7
V
I
E♭ I
7
V

3. Andante
HAYDN
*3)
*3)
*3)
*3)
*3)
*3)
D
7
V——I——II1——I2——V——I

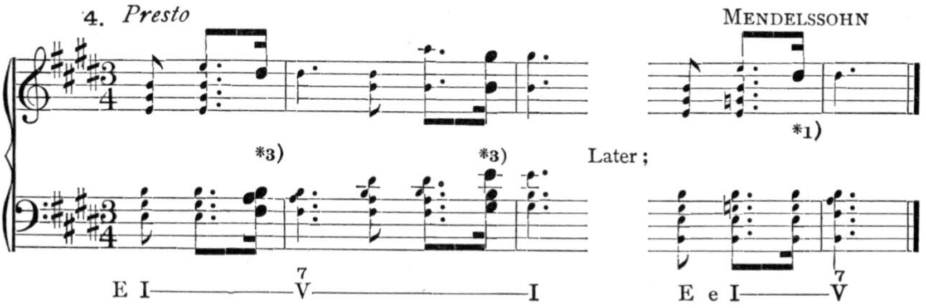

4. Presto
MENDELSSOHN
*3)
*3)
Later;
*1)
E I
7
V
I
E e I
7
V

*1) An inharmonic Anticipation, — foreign to the chord. — *2) An Anticipation which is *not* foreign to the chord in which it occurs; but nevertheless an "anticipation." — *3) Anticipation-*chords;* because they are too short to create the impression of true chords.

268. The free or **irregular** Anticipation is one which, *instead of remaining upon the note* which it anticipates, progresses into another tone, usually with a *skip downward.* The anticipated note should appear in some other voice, in the following chord, or it must be *understood,* as possible interval of the latter. See par. 265, Rule, of which this is exactly the reverse. For illustration:

Ex. 201.

1. HAYDN
2. *Andante* BRAHMS
3. BRAHMS
*1)
*1)
G I——$\overset{7}{V}$——VI
g♯ I $\overset{7}{V}$— I f♯ I $\overset{7}{V}$—I
$C_o\overset{9}{V}$—— I

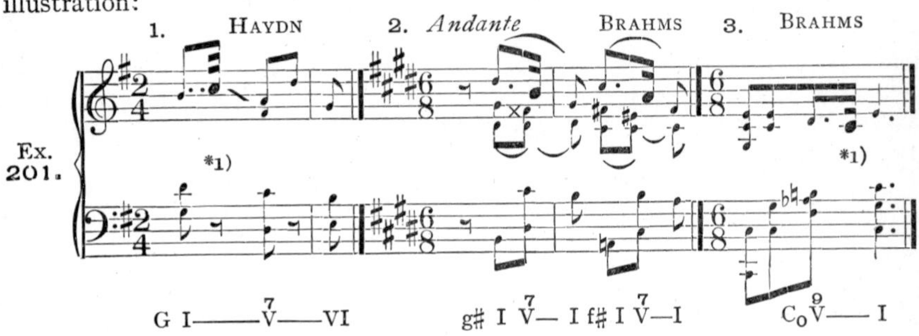

*1) The *c* in soprano is an Anticipation of *c* in the following chord (tenor). The irregularity consists in its progressing with a leap.

LESSON 60.

Harmonize the following melodies, with reference to the subjoined notes:

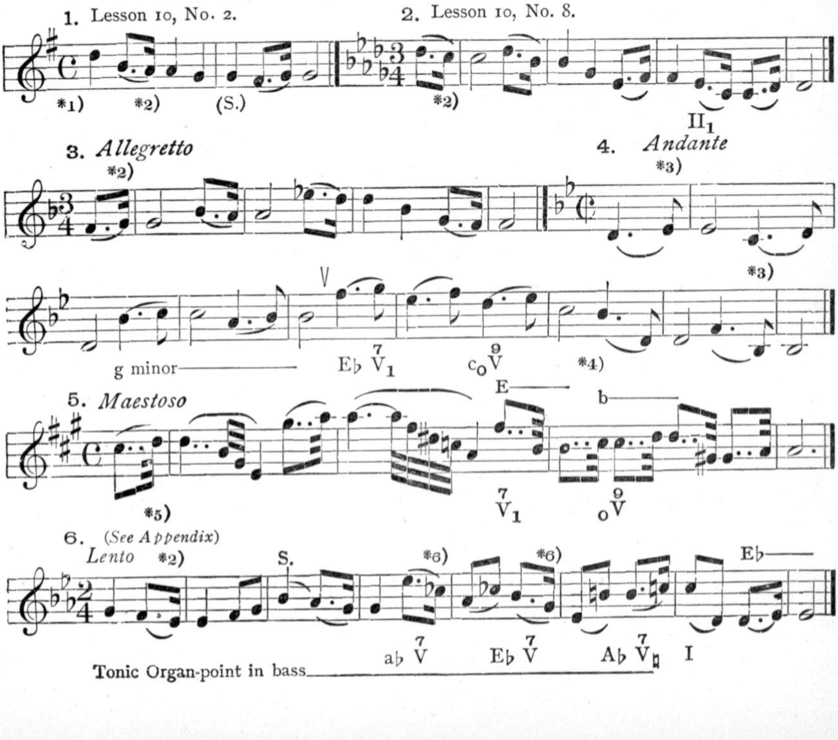
1. Lesson 10, No. 2.
*1) *2) (S.)
2. Lesson 10, No. 8.
*2)
II_1
3. *Allegretto*
*2)
4. *Andante*
*3)
*3)
g minor——
E♭ $\overset{7}{V_1}$
$c_o\overset{9}{V}$
*4)
5. *Maestoso*
E——
b——
*5)
$\overset{7}{V_1}$
$_o\overset{9}{V}$
6. (*See Appendix*)
Lento *2)
S.
*6) *6)
E♭——
a♭ $\overset{7}{V}$ E♭ $\overset{7}{V}$ A♭ $\overset{7}{V}$♮ I
Tonic Organ-point in bass

*1) The first two melodies are taken from Lesson 10, as shown. Compare them with the unembellished originals, and make similar experiments with other melodies. — *2) Each 16th-note is to be an Anticipation; that is, it is *not harmonized at all* (see Ex. 199). — *3) Each 8th-note an Anticipation, throughout. — *4) The altered IV of *B-flat*. — *5) Each single 32d-note an Anticipation. — *6) Irregular Anticipation (par. 268). — *7) Anticipation-*chord* (all four parts) at the end of each slur, throughout. — *8) Mixed IV^7 of *d* minor.

CHAPTER XLIX.

THE NEIGHBORING-NOTE.

269. As stated in par. 249, every inharmonic tone is the upper or lower diatonic *neighbor* of one of the legitimate chord-tones. The special designation **Neighboring-note** has been adopted by the author to indicate that simple form of melodic embellishment in which

either the upper or lower inharmonic neighbor alternates briefly with the principal (harmonic) tone.

Ex. 202.

*1) The Neighboring-note is everywhere indicated by o. The harmonic interval which it embellishes is called the principal tone.

270. This alternation of harmonic and adjacent inharmonic tones may be applied to *any* interval of *any* chord, and in *any voice*, subject only to the general conditions of rhythm. It gives rise to a number of different melodic groups, prominent among which are such conventional "grace-notes" as the Trill (long or short), the Mordent, the Turn, and other familiar Embellishments, but embracing also a great variety of special ornamental figures, whose importance and efficiency in enriching, adorning, and enlivening the primary harmonies can not be overestimated.

271. Rule I. The Neighboring-note enters from (i.e., follows) its own principal tone, and always **returns to the latter.**

Rule II. The *upper* Neighboring-note is generally used when the direction of the melody, into the next tone, is *downward;* and, inversely, the *lower* Neighbor when the direction is *upward*. In other words, the Neighboring-note should lie *opposite* the next essential melody-tone.

The *accented* Neighboring-note is more prominent, and sometimes more effective, than the unaccented one; otherwise the rhythmic location of a Neighboring-note (on or between the beats) is immaterial. (Comp. par. 275.)

Rule III. The upper Neighboring-note should *agree with the scale represented by the momentary chord* (more rarely, with that of the *next* beat).

The lower neighbor may also agree with the scale, but it is usually the **half-step.**

The leading-tone, however, is almost invariably embellished, both above and below, in accordance with its scale. For example:

*1) The Neighboring-note *d* must return to *e*, its principal tone. — *2) The *unprepared* Neighboring-note will be explained in a later chapter. — *3) The embellishing group may be thus extended by any leaps which conform to the chord. — *4) The *upper* Neighboring-note, before a *descending* progression. — *5) The lower Neighboring-note is possible, but less smooth in this connection. — *6) Whether the upper Neighboring-note is to be a whole step or half-step, depends upon the momentary key. — *7) These lower Neighboring-notes all agree with the scale (*B-flat* major, in this case). — *8) A half-step, contrary to the scale;

this is more common, and more graceful. — *9) The Neighboring-notes must *invariably* represent the next higher or lower *letter*. — *10) C major; but also valid for *c minor*, with *e-flat* and *a-flat*.

272. These embellishing tones may appear simultaneously in two or more parts, as *double* or *triple* Neighboring-notes; or even in all the parts, as *Neighboring-chord*. These and other forms are exhibited in the following example:

6. *Allegretto* — BEETHOVEN

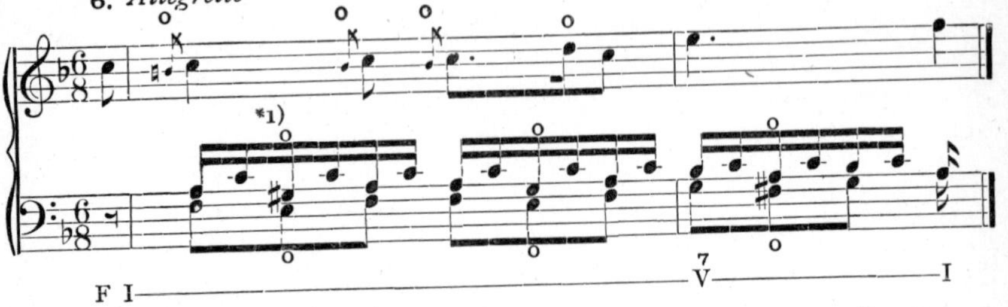
*1)
F I
7
V
I

7. *Andante* — BRAHMS

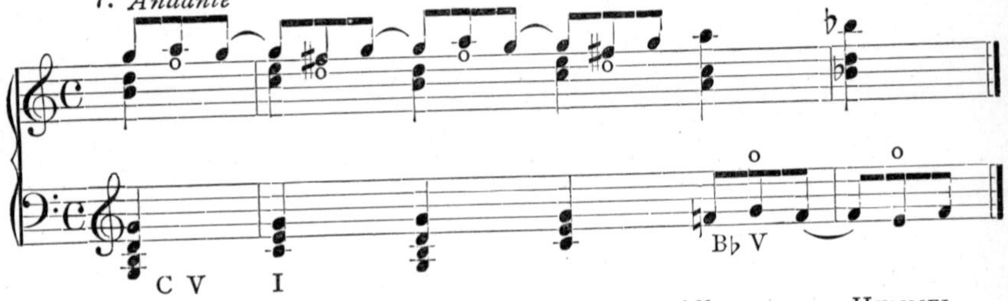
C V
I
B♭ V

8. *Allegro* — HUMMEL 9. *Allegro* — HUMMEL

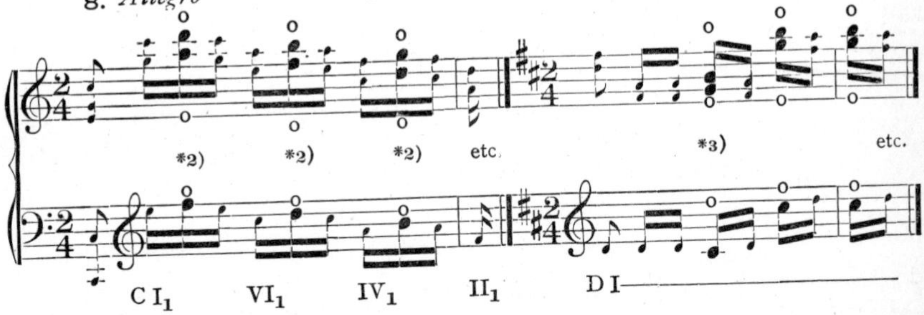
*2)
*2)
*2)
etc.
*3)
etc.
C I_1
VI_1
IV_1
II_1
D I

*1) Double Neighboring-note. — *2) *Neighboring-chords;* they are *too brief* to be essential. — *3) Accented Neighboring-chords. — *4) Here *a*♮ and *a*♭ appear together — *a*♭ as 7th of the dominant, in bass, and *a*♮ as lower Neighbor of *b*♭ (the root) in soprano. It would be impossible to define the multitude of combinations, or tone-clusters, that result from adding Neighboring-notes to the legitimate chord-forms. In his studies in Analysis the pupil will encounter many extraordinary tone-shapes, which are easily accounted for in this simple way. Glance at Ex. 211, No. 6, for instance.

LESSON 61.

1. Lesson 10, No. 4
SOPRANO

*1)

2. BASS (*See Appendix*)

*2)
A V D V
7
II
6
4

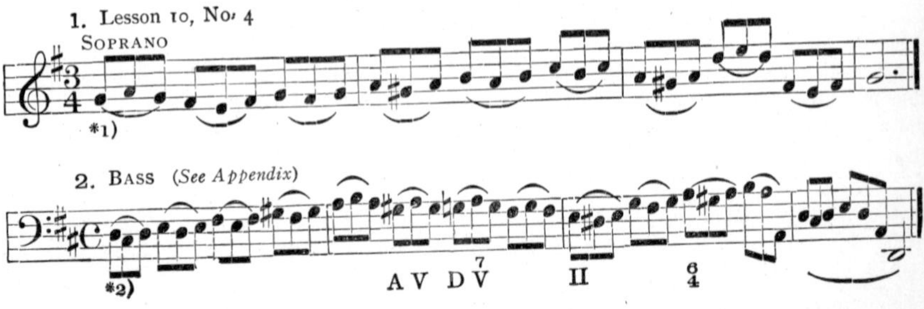

*1) This melody, in its original unembellished form, will be found in Lesson 10, No. 4. Add the three lower parts, in the usual manner. — *2) Add the three upper parts to this "running bass," together on the G-staff. *One melody-note (and chord) to each slur, strictly.* The Neighboring-notes are readily definable. — *3) Harmonize this embellished soprano in the usual manner, one chord to each slur. — *4) Add soprano, bass and tenor to this running alto. It will facilitate the task, to reduce the given part first to its original, unembellished form: etc. — *5) Here the alto pauses and the tenor takes up the embellishment. — *6) Add soprano, bass and alto to this running tenor; one chord (and soprano note) to each slur. First reduce it.

CHAPTER L.

THE PASSING-NOTE.

273. The Passing-note is an inharmonic tone which is touched in "passing" step wise *from one chord-tone to another.* Hence it serves to connect *two different* chord-tones. (Comp. par. 271, Rule I, for the distinction between the Neighboring-note and the Passing-note.)

274. *a.* This connection is almost always made **diatonically,** along the momentary scale; but occasionally it is also made *chromatically*, especially in ascending succession. *Descending chromatic Passing-notes* should, as a rule, be avoided.

b. Two, or even more, Passing-notes may occur in immediate succession if they follow each other *stepwise* in the *same direction.* This will depend upon the size of the harmonic interval to be filled out, and also upon the choice of diatonic or chromatic Passing-notes. For example:

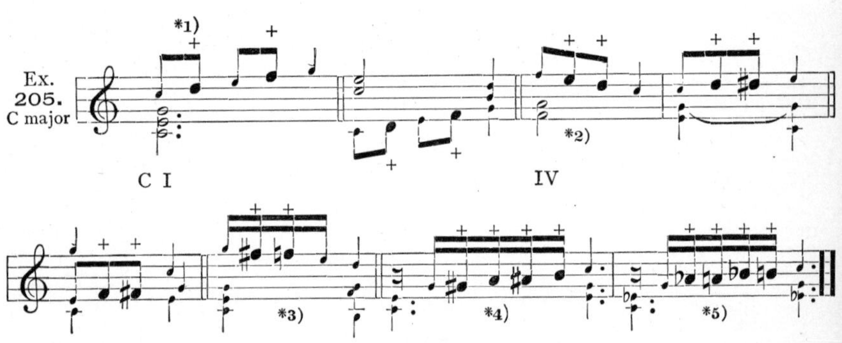

*1) The Passing-notes are indicated by +. — *2) Two Passing-notes in succession. — *3) Descending chromatic tones are generally written with flats, excepting the one immediately below the dominant of the momentary key, which is written, as here, as raised 4th step (in C, as f-sharp). — *4) Four chromatic Passing-notes in succession. — *5) C *minor;* the change of notation in the minor mode is significant. The notation of chromatic Passing-notes should conform to the *scale* of the momentary key, or to its *altered* steps.

275. In the above example, the Passing-notes are all **unaccented;** i.e., they stand between the beats, as light fractions. But they may also occur at the beginning of the beat, as **accented** Passing-notes, and are then usually more effective than the former, because more conspicuous. For illustration:

*1) The accented Passing-note is indicated by ×.— *2) These measures are all valid for *c minor* (with *e-flat* and *a-flat*), excepting this beat and the next, which would read *a-flat* and *b-flat*.

276. RULE I. Unaccented Passing-notes are admissible and effective in *any part*. Accented Passing-notes are best in soprano; in the inner voices, or in bass, they are apt to obscure the harmonic sense, and must therefore be carefully tested, by ear.

RULE II. Passing-notes usually necessitate the subdivision of their beat, and are therefore subject to the rule of rhythm given in par. 38, namely, the *light* beats must be broken first, so that the unbroken beats (if any remain unsubdivided) are the *heavier* ones of the measure.

RULE III. Successive perfect 5ths or 8ths, which may result from the insertion of Passing-notes, will be objectionable only in case the *second 5th or 8ve is perfect and harmonic*. For example:

A few of the very numerous forms of embellishment with Passing-notes, accented and unaccented, are exhibited in the following example:

3. Allegro
CHOPIN
8va
*1)
c♯ II♮
V
I
4. Lento
CHOPIN
5. Allegro
CHOPIN
*6)
*2)
C V
I
V
I
D♭ I
6. Allegro
CHOPIN
7. Allegro
J. S. BACH
*3)
*4)
E I
IV1—V V
I
e min. I
8. Allegro
CHOPIN
S
*5)
c♯ V
I
9. Allegro
CZERNY
8va
S.
S
*5)
or, simplified:
C I
IV
I2

*1) The lowered second step (*d*) of *c-sharp* minor. — *2) Double Passing-notes. — *3) *Passing-chords.* In such rapid tempo they are too brief to be essential. Comp. Ex. 204, note *2). — *4) The descending chromatic tones are *intercepted* Passing-notes, separated by the reiterated *e*. — *5) *Repeated* Passing-notes. — *6) Comp. Ex. 204, note *4).

LESSON 62.

Elaborate the following melodic sketches as Running soprano, in a *uniform rhythm* of first 2 notes, then 3 notes, 4 notes or 6 notes to *each* beat, as indicated; using Passing-notes, unaccented and occasionally accented, Neighboring-notes, and (when unavoidable) harmonic (chord) tones. The lower voices need not be added.

By means of *Neighboring-notes*, any single tone develops into a group of 3 or 5 (7, 9) tones, thus:

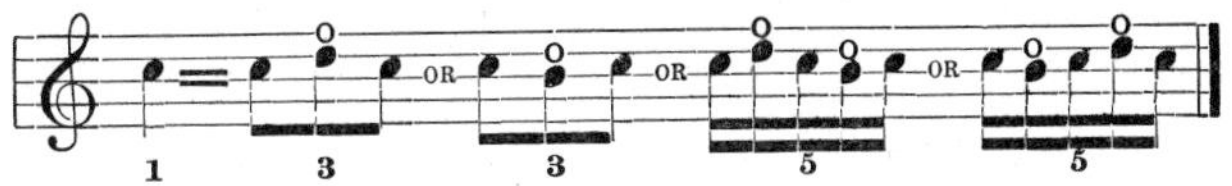

without involving the question of space (interval to the next essential tone) at all. These groups can then easily be extended to 4, 6 (and more) tones, by adding Passing-notes or harmonic (chord) tones:

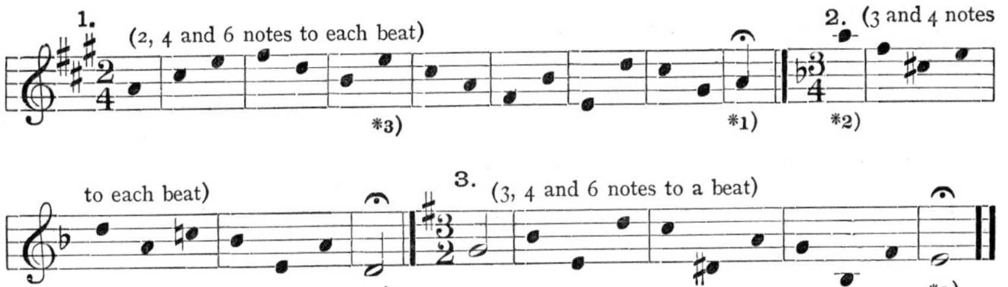

EXERCISES.

1. (2, 4 and 6 notes to each beat) *3) *1)

2. (3 and 4 notes to each beat) *2) *1)

3. (3, 4 and 6 notes to a beat) *1)

*1) The cadence-tone is not to be embellished. — *2) Review par. 271, Rules II and III.

*3) The given melody-tones should appear, as a rule, upon the first fraction of their respective beats — where they stand; *occasionally*, however, they may be shifted to the second fraction — not beyond.

Further experiments may be made with any melodies from the earlier Lessons.

CHAPTER LI.

THE APPOGGIATURA.

277. The Appoggiatura is an **unprepared neighboring-note,** which is simply *placed before its principal tone, without reference to what precedes,* i.e., without regard to the manner in which the Neighboring-note enters. Comp. par. 271, Rule I, for the distinction between the *regular* Neighboring-note and the Appoggiatura.

N.B. The distinction is purely theoretical, and has no practical value. As stated in par. 249, every inharmonic tone is a *Neighbor,* no matter what specific name it may assume. The student is therefore advised to adopt the generic term ""Neighboring-note" for the Appoggiatura — and also for the unprepared Suspension (comp. Ex. 198, note *1).

278. Either the *upper or lower* Neighboring-note may thus precede any chord-tone; it may be *long or short,* and although it usually stands upon the *accented fraction of its own beat,* it may also appear upon an unaccented fraction of the preceding beat. For illustration:

*1) These measures are all valid for *c minor* also (with *e-flat* and *a-flat*), excepting this *d-sharp.* — *2) It is usually possible, and *always effective,* to substitute a rest for the first (accented) tone of an embellishing group. — *3) When very short, and accented, the Neighboring-note is called an Acciaccatura. — *4) The choice between *upper and lower* Neighb.-notes may conform with par. 271, Rule II; or, as exception, the figures may *all run in the same form.* In the first case the groups will be *regular;* in the other case, *uniform and symmetrical,* though irregular.

DOUBLE APPOGGIATURA.

279. Upon the same principle, *both the upper and lower* Neighboring-notes may successively precede their *common* principal tone, as **double appoggiatura.** And here again, both the duration and the rhythmic location of the inharmonic tones are entirely optional. Thus:

Ex. 209, note *4)

280. The rules for the treatment of the Appoggiatura correspond largely to par. 271, Rules II and III, which review. But see Ex. 209, note *4). As to the Double-appoggiatura, note that one Neighbor leaps a third to the other, and the principal tone, *common to both*, follows as resolution.

This mode of embellishment in its manifold phases is illustrated in the following example:

Ex. 211.

1. *Vivace*

C I

BEETHOVEN. Op. 120

—V I C V I V

2. *Allegretto* BEETHOVEN

C I

3. *Presto* BEETHOVEN

C IV I V I F V I

4. *All^o^.* SCHUMANN

*1)

b I —IV I

5. Allegro
Chopin
6. Vivace
Chopin
*2)
F I
e I

7. Allegro
Beethoven
*3)
*4)
C II1

Beethoven
8. Allegro
*3)
B♭ I
V
I

9. Presto
Chopin
*3)
c♯ V
I
II1
I1
V
I

*1) This unprepared Neighboring-note (*g*) illustrates the resemblance which frequently exists between the Appoggiatura and the unprepared Suspension (see par. 265). — *2) The *f-sharp* is in reality an accented *Passing*-note, but its effect is precisely the same as that of the adjoining Appoggiaturas. Observe the effective chromatic Passing-notes in bass. — *3) Double appoggiatura. — *4) *B-natural*, and not *b-flat*, because the chord is distinctly *in C major* and not in *d minor*. — *5) A *Triple* appoggiatura. — *6) An extraordinary passage. Each Neighboring-note in soprano is *repeated* (comp. Ex. 208, note *5), and accompanied by an additional Appoggiatura in tenor. The second chord contains the raised 4th step (*d-sharp*).

LESSON 63.

Take the three melodic sketches given in Lesson 62, and elaborate each one as Running soprano, as before, in a rhythm of two notes, then three notes, and then four notes to every beat (excepting the cadence-tone), according to some of the embellishing figures shown in Exs. 209 and 210. Simple chord-accompaniment may be added, on the lower staff. Also experiment with some short melodies of the earlier Lessons.

CHAPTER LII.

EMBELLISHMENT IN ALTERNATE PARTS.

281. When these various classes of auxiliary tones are employed in alternating parts, with a view to the *embellishment of the entire harmonic structure*, the following rules must be observed:

RULE I. The adopted rhythm (of two, three, four or more notes to a beat, as the case may be) must be adhered to throughout. That is, *every* beat must be subdivided, in some voice or other, in similar rhythm; only excepting an occasional interruption at an **accented beat,** if desirable.

In **soprano,** on account of its prominence, the rhythm should be regular, as a rule, irrespective of the other parts; i.e., *only the lighter beats should be subdivided in the soprano.* This restriction is neither possible nor necessary in alto, tenor or bass.

RULE II. The embellishing rhythm must not continue in any one voice longer than one or two (or three) beats, after which some other voice must take it up. The choice of voice is optional, and will depend upon circumstances, and upon the taste or judgment of the pupil. Two (very rarely three) voices may occasionally embellish simultaneously; probably in the same rhythm, but not necessarily.

RULE III. Parallel and intercepted 5ths and 8ves must be avoided, according to par. 276, Rule III, which review.

RULE IV. **Ties** should be freely used, especially from a light beat over into an accented beat. They are most effective when they give rise to a Suspension. It is, however, usually awkward to tie any *short note* (less than a *half-beat* in duration) to the following tone.

A similar advantageous effect is produced by a **rest,** which, as stated in Ex. 209, note *2), may generally be substituted for the *first* note of an embellishing group. Observe the directions given in Lesson 62.

LESSON 64.

Embellish the following phrase *three times*, first in a rhythm of 2 notes, then 3 notes, and then 4 notes, to each beat. Employ Harmonic tones, Neighboring-notes, Passing-notes (especially *unaccented*), and *occasionally* Appoggiaturas — with reference to the above rules, and to the subjoined model (Ex. 212):

MODEL Ex. 212.

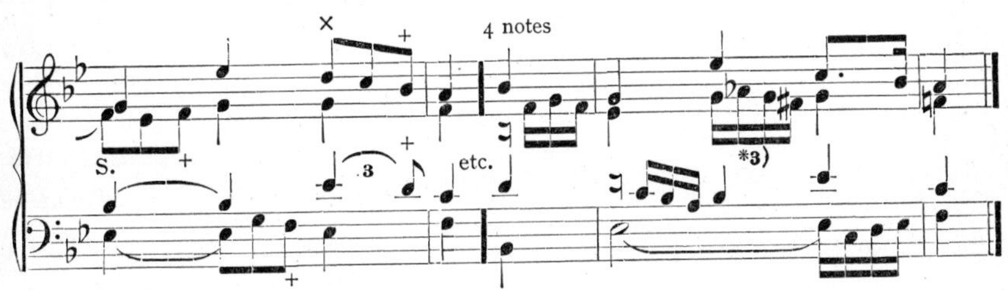

*1) Each of these fragments represents but one of a *very great number* of possible elaborations; they are to be imitated, but not copied literally. — *2) The *ties*, given in the original, may, as here, be removed by the embellishment. — *3) See par. 271, Rule III; here, the *prevailing scale* is momentarily that of *E♭*, therefore the upper neighbor of *g* must be *a-flat*. — *4) Continue the given rhythm during the first beat of the cadence-measure.

LESSON 65.

A. Elaborate the following phrase three times, as in Lesson 64, with first two, then three, and then four notes to each beat. Review par. 271, Rule III:

B. Elaborate, similarly, some of the completed (4-part) phrases of the earlier Lessons; or construct Original phrases, in embellished form.

CHAPTER LIII.

HARMONIZING OF EMBELLISHED MELODIES.

282. Before determining the chords for the harmonization of a florid melody, it is necessary *to reduce the melody to its original unembellished form*. Such notes as are obviously (or probably) only ornamental inharmonic tones will not be harmonized at all, and may therefore either be omitted or imagined absent, while choosing the harmonic basis.

283. Tones of *short* time-value, especially in diatonic or chromatic succession, and tones with *accidentals* (unless distinctly indicative of a modulation), will probably be **inharmonic,** and unessential. On the other hand, all comparatively *longer* tones, and all tones which progress *with a skip*, will generally prove to be **harmonic,** and essential. The indications of a Suspension or Anticipation have already been given. Aside from these very general principles, the pupil will be best guided by his judgment, experience and taste.

LESSON 66.

Harmonize the following florid melodies, with reference to the subjoined notes:

*1) One bass note (and chord) *to each slur;* or, the student may ignore the slurs, and use his own judgment. An inner part may move, at any time. — *2) During six measures, the rhythm of the accompanying lower parts will be | 𝄽 𝅘𝅥𝅮 𝄽 𝅘𝅥𝅮 |. — *3) The three lower parts together on the bass staff.

LESSON 67.

Continuation of Lesson 66:

1. *Andante*

*1)

S.

6
4

Ant.

2. *Allegro*

*1)

B I_2

G

semi-cad.

C

F

E

6
4

f♯

E

rall.

S.

$_oV^9$

I_2

cad.

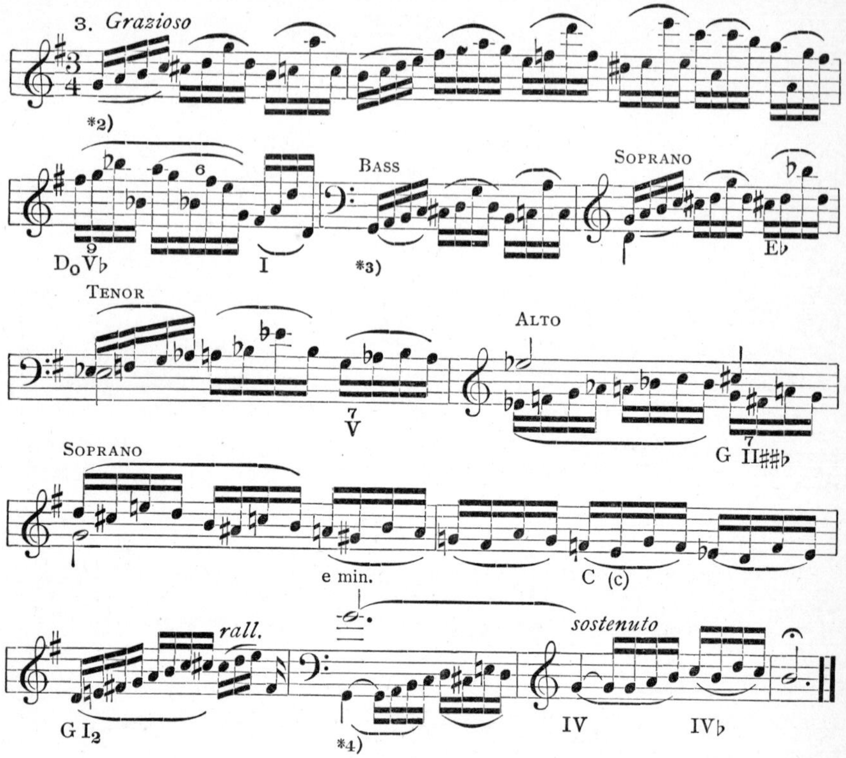

3. Grazioso
*2)
$D_0\overset{9}{V}\flat$
I
Bass
*3)
Soprano
E♭
Tenor
$\overset{7}{V}$
Alto
G $\overset{7}{II}$♯♯♭
Soprano
e min.
C (c)
rall.
sostenuto
G I_2
*4)
IV
IV♭

*1) One bass tone (and chord) to each slur. The three lower parts together on the bass staff. — *2) One chord to each slur. — *3) At each of the next 4 bar-lines the embellishment alternates, as indicated. — *4) Bass. In the next measure, soprano again. Plagal ending.

LESSON 68.

Harmonize the following embellished basses, with reference to par. 282, 283, and the subjoined notes:

1. *1) (See Appendix)
c
$\overset{7}{V}$
B♭

2 *1)
f♯

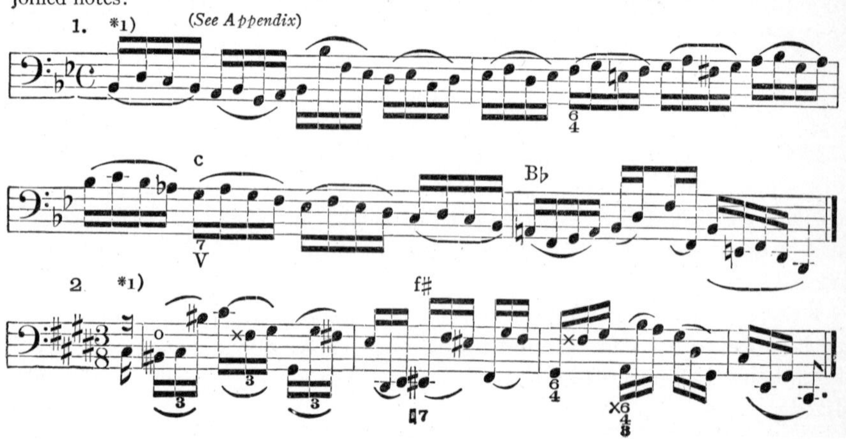

*1) The first care must be to obtain a *good, melodious soprano*, throughout, before adding the inner parts. Use one melody-note to each slur, and place the inner parts (the number of which may *occasionally* be more or less than three) together on the upper staff.

CHAPTER LIV.

ANALYSIS.

284. The following sentences are to be copied out and analyzed. The keys (modulations), chords, and inharmonic tones (Organ-points, Suspensions, Anticipations, Passing-notes, Neighboring-notes, Appoggiaturas) must be accurately indicated, in the manner shown in the foregoing examples, and given in parts of Lesson 70, No. 1.

RULE I. Place the **simplest construction** upon every chord; i.e., define it as **tonic** or **dominant** chord if possible; not overlooking the possibility of its being a **Second-class** (subdominant) chord, especially if Altered or Mixed.

RULE II. **Look forward.** The identity of a chord depends upon what it *does*, i.e., upon what follows.

RULE III. Take the **tempo** into consideration. What will produce the effect of an *essential* tone or chord in moderate tempo (or upon a full beat), will probably be an *unessential* embellishing tone or chord, in very rapid tempo (or upon a short fraction of a beat). Every note must be accounted for.

LESSON 69.

A. Mark every *inharmonic tone* in the following extracts, with the usual signs (Org.-pt., S., o, +, ×). The keys and chords are given:

*1) Intercepted Passing-notes. — *2) The upper Neighbor of the Neighboring-note — rare, but sometimes fully recognizable. — *3) The *d*♯, in each part, is an Anticipation.

B. Analyze **Mendelssohn,** "Song without Words," No. 12. — **Beethoven,** pfte. Sonata, op. 13, second movement (*Adagio cantabile*). — **Chopin,** Prelude, op. 28, No. 3.

LESSON 70.

Continuation of analysis; review par. 284:

J. S. BACH. St. Matthew Passion

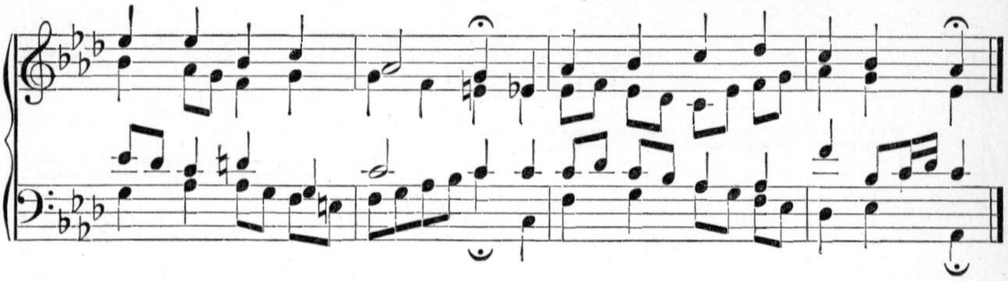

2. *Allegretto*

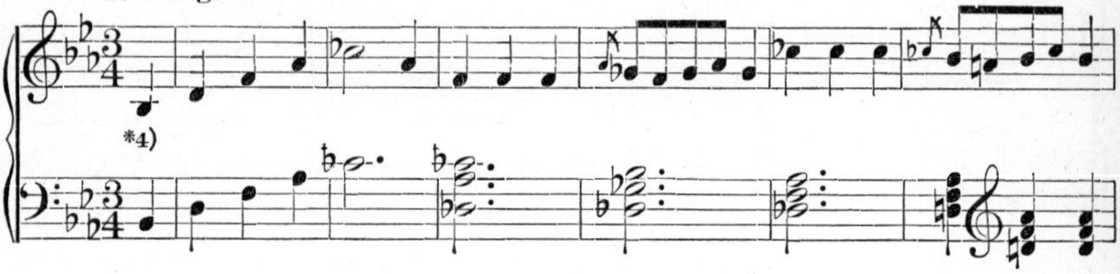

*4)

HAYDN. (Symph., E-flat)

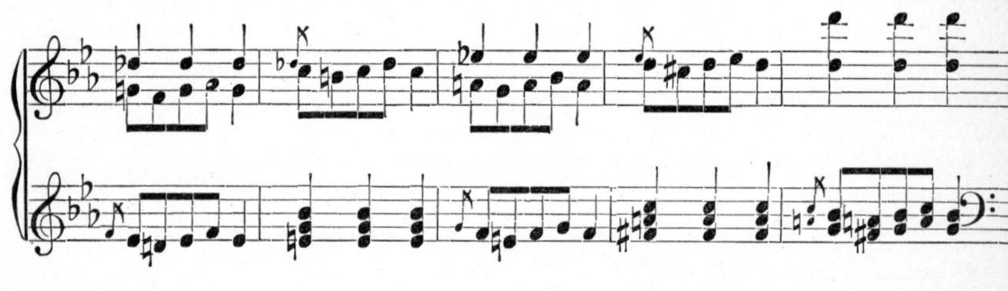

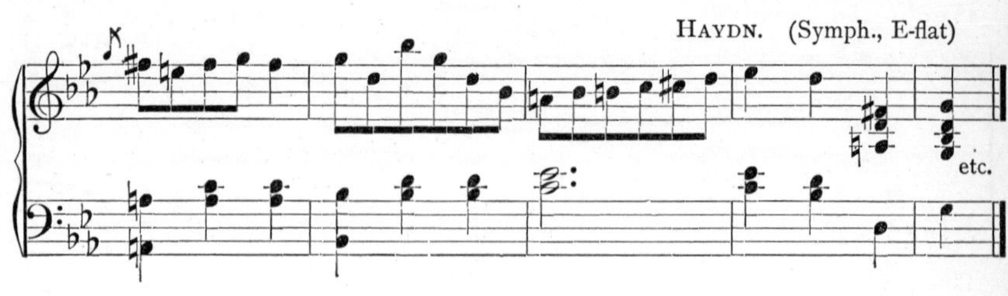

3. *Adagio molto*

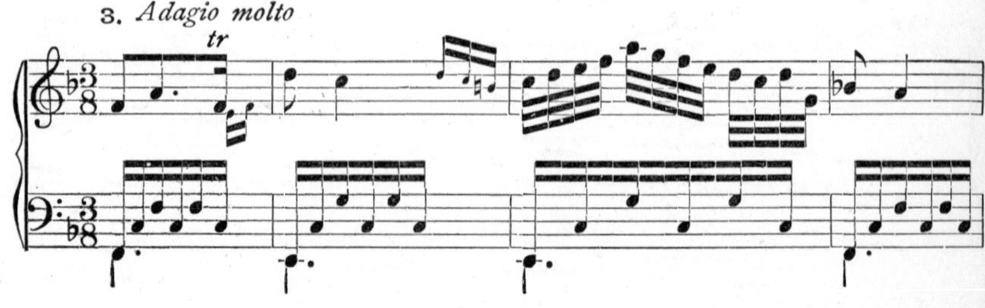

*1) The analysis of a few measures is given, as a guide. — *2) At this point the second Part of the chorale begins. The melody is an almost exact reproduction of the first Part; but note the remarkable changes in its harmonization. The latter is prompted throughout, as will be seen, by the *independent melodic progression* of the individual voices. — *3) A good example of cadence-modulation. — *4) E-flat major (or minor) V9.— *5) The modulation into C is effected at this place, through what proves to be the IV of the new key.

LESSON 71.

Continuation of analysis:

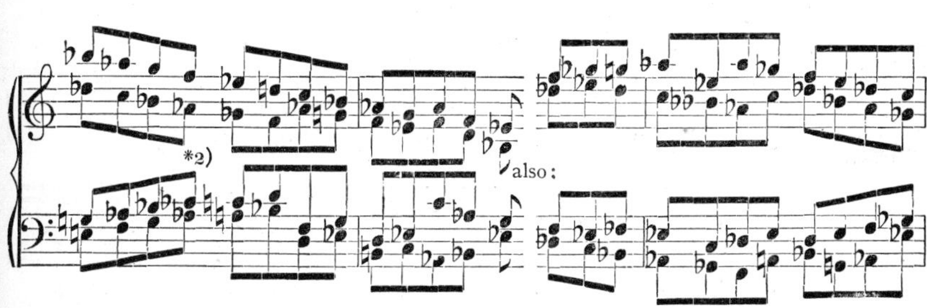

*1) The *g-flat* in tenor is a Passing-note, which might be written *f-sharp*. — *2) Like note *1). The chord is *f-minor* I, with *c-flat* (*b-natural*) as Passing-note.

LESSON 72.

Continuation of analysis:

*1) Such irregularities as this ascending 7th (*f* in tenor) are sometimes encountered in *pianoforte* music, even in **Beethoven,** and are due to the restrictions of the keyboard. — *2) B minor begins here. — *3) The *A* in bass is an Organ-point. — *4) C in bass, an Organ-point.

REFERENCE INDEX OF SUBJECTS

Except where otherwise indicated, figures refer to paragraph numbers

APPENDIX

Each of the following examples represents only one of many possible solutions—usually the simplest and most regular one, though in some cases (in the more advanced Lessons) a more ingenious and stimulating solution is given.

* High inner voices, in view of the high Soprano note in next measure

Lesson 22, No. 5
Lesson 23, No. 5
* 3rd and 5th omitted allowed at the beginning
Lesson 23, No. 8
Lesson 25, No. 4

Lesson 27, No. 4
*Third doubled
Lesson 28, No. 2
Lesson 30, No. 3
*Stationary dissonances
Lesson 31, No. 9
*Doubled leading-tone; justified by smoothness of progression

Lesson 35, No. 3
Lesson 36, No. 3
Lesson 38, No. 6
mod.
Lesson 40, No. 5
mod.
* mod.

*207, 1.

Lesson 42, No. 15

Lesson 43, No. 5

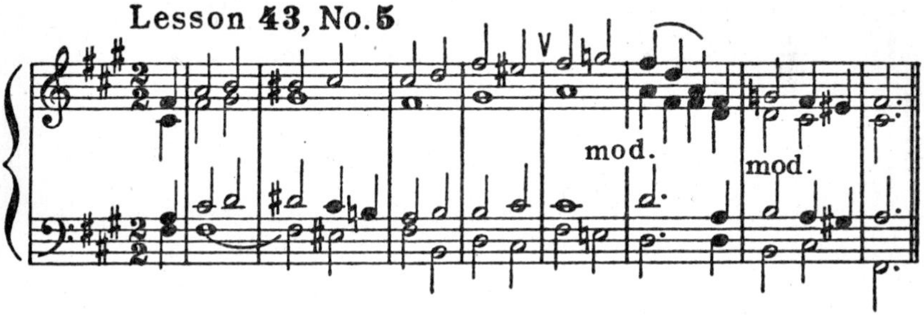

mod.

mod.

Lesson 43, No. 10

Lesson 44, No. 8

Lesson 48, No. 6
mod.
**
*
* b to F♯
** e to B
Lesson 49, No. 6
D-d
C-c
*
mod.
6 6 5 6 ♮ ♭3 2 ♮6 ♭6 ♮3 ♭7
4 3 ♭5 ♭5
♭3
* b♭ minor, instead
of the related B♭ major
Lesson 50, No. 3
*
*
*
* Sequence-modulations
*
*
*
Plagal ending

Lesson 52, No. 5

* Sequence-modulations

Lesson 53, No. 4

Lesson 54, No. 2

Lesson 57, No. 10

Lesson 58, No. 3
Lesson 59, No. 2
Lesson 60, No. 6
Lesson 61, No. 2

Lesson 66, No. 4
ritard.
Lesson 68, No. 1
or ♯